D1138317

Psychotherapy, Counselling and Primary Mental Health Care

Psychotherapy, Counselling and
Primary Mental Health Care
Assessment for brief or
longer-term treatment

Mary Burton

Clinical Psychologist and Psychotherapist
in Private Practice, London, UK

JOHN WILEY & SONS
Chichester • New York • Weinheim • Brisbane • Singapore • Toronto

Copyright © 1998 by John Wiley & Sons Ltd,
Baffins Lane, Chichester,
West Sussex PO19 1UD, England

National   01243 779777
International   +(44) 1243 779777
e-mail (for order and customer service enquiries):
cs-books@wiley.co.uk
Visit our Home Page on http://www.wiley.co.uk
or http://www.wiley.com

All Rights Reserved. No part of this book may be reproduced, stored in a retrieval system, or transmitted, in any form or by any means, electronic, mechanical, photocopying, recording, scanning or otherwise, except under the terms of the Copyright, Designs and Patents Act 1988 or under the terms of a licence issued by the Copyright Licensing Agency, 90 Tottenham Court Road, London, UK W1P 9HE, without the permission in writing of John Wiley & Sons Ltd, Baffins Lane, Chichester, West Sussex, UK PO19 1UD.

Other Wiley Editorial Offices

John Wiley & Sons, Inc., 605 Third Avenue,
New York, NY 10158-0012, USA

Weinheim · Brisbane · Singapore · Toronto

CCTA LIBRARIES LLYRGELLAU CCTA	
Morley Books	
616.8914	£17.99
Ro3o582	

British Library Cataloguing in Publication Data
A catalogue record for this book is available from the British Library

ISBN 0-471-97657-1 (cloth)
ISBN 0-471-98228-8 (paper)

Typeset in Linotype Palatino 10/12pt by Stephen Wright-Bouvier of the Rainwater Consultancy, Faringdon, Oxfordshire.
Printed and bound in Great Britain by Biddles Ltd, Guildford and King's Lynn.
This book is printed on acid-free paper responsibly manufactured from sustainable forestry, in which at least two trees are planted for each one used for paper production.

CONTENTS

About the Author vi

Foreword by Dr Graham Curtis Jenkins vii

Preface viii

1 Psychological therapies in primary care 1

2 Patients and their problems 19

3 Therapy models and professional disciplines 53

4 Assessment for short vs. longer-term treatment 95

5 Assessment II: early loss, comorbidity and
   treatment modality 137

6 Does it work? Service evaluation and audit
   in primary care 163

7 Organizational issues 193

Appendix 213

References 227

Index 253

ABOUT THE AUTHOR

Mary Burton is a Chartered Clinical Psychologist and UKCP Registered Psychoanalytic Psychotherapist with more than fifteen years' experience in the UK National Health Service and private practice. For four years she was Course Tutor for the Brief Psychotherapies Certificate Course in Coventry, now being offered in a tutorial version to general practitioners sponsored by the Division of General Practice of the Royal Society of Medicine. She is a research associate of the Counselling in Primary Care Trust and has studied the supervision needs of counsellors in primary care. She has supervised the work of clinical psychology trainees and counsellors in primary care for many years, and was extensively involved in evaluating the effectiveness of psychological therapies in the NHS. With Ronald Parker, a consultant surgeon in Coventry, she held a Cancer Research Campaign grant for research with breast cancer patients in the 1980s. She is co-author with Maggie Watson of *Counselling People with Cancer* (Wiley, 1998) and is the author of a number of scientific papers in counselling and psychotherapy.

FOREWORD

Since 1990 growth in the provision of counselling in primary health care in the United Kingdom has been explosive. More than half of all general practices now, in 1998, have counsellors working as part of the primary health care team. About a third are employed or managed by a National Health Service provider or other agency. The rest work either as salaried employees of the general practices in which they work or are self-employed. About 10 per cent are volunteers receiving no remuneration for the work they do.

The collision of cultures causes many tensions, the main one being the difficulties of language and understanding. Psychiatry and psychology can sometimes appear to be uneasy bedfellows with counselling and psychotherapy. With many years of experience as a therapist in the National Health Service, the author has successfully provided the vital bridge to aid shared understanding. The arguments for short- and long-term therapy, treatment modality and the role of assessment which is vital for safe, effective practice are covered in depth. The author provides a coherent and cogent account that is authoritative and amply documented with case vignettes and references.

We have waited a long time for this book and I am sure it will remain the standard text for many years to come. I unreservedly recommend it, not only to counsellors and psychotherapists who work in primary care but also to general practitioners and purchasers of services who will play an increasingly important role in ensuring the appropriate provision of the highest quality counselling services in primary health care.

Dr Graham Curtis Jenkins
Director, Counselling in Primary Care Trust

PREFACE

This book has grown out of many years' experience in the UK National Health Service and in private practice working with patients referred for psychological therapy by their general practitioners. The approach taken – with the emphasis on assessment – has been informed by clinical practice with patients, the teaching and supervision of other clinicians, and the evaluation of the effectiveness of psychological therapies in primary care. The book has also been informed by the UK Department of Health's recent strategic review of psychotherapy services in the NHS (Parry and Richardson, 1996) and recently published referral guidelines for GPs (Camden and Islington MAAG, 1996).

'Short-term counselling or in-depth psychotherapy?' is a frequently debated question in primary care today. How can practitioners best determine which service is most appropriate for a particular patient? What assessment procedures will help GPs, counsellors, psychologists and other mental health providers to arrive at a decision on the suitability of a particular treatment? Brief and ultra-brief therapies in primary care are not, as some have argued, a less expensive substitute for longer-term treatment. Although they may be suitable for some patients, short-term therapies are not a panacea for the range of psychological problems being presented in primary care. The costs of the 'six sessions for every-thing' model, inappropriately applied, are borne by patients.

In too many places, decisions on which therapy to offer are taken on an ad hoc basis: which clinician has a vacancy when the telephone rings, for example. A careful assessment should be the first step in determining the appropriateness of short- vs. longer-term intervention. The psycho-social history is the cornerstone of the assessment process, and the Inventory of Early Loss is a useful new assessment tool. On the whole, patients with many early loss experiences or a number of comorbid pre-senting problems including personality disorder will be better helped by longer-term treatment. Practical suggestions are made for assessing treatment outcomes, clinical supervision and multidisciplinary collaboration. The underlying theoretical framework of the book is psychodynamic, but the fundamentals of assessment are applicable to therapeutic work across theoretical orientations. The book provides:

- an up-to-date review of the major issues in counselling and psychotherapy in primary care;

- a wide-ranging survey of counselling models in primary care (psychodynamic, cognitive-behavioural, cognitive-analytic, humanistic, brief and ultra-brief therapies, group and couples therapies), all informed by research;

- a review of outcome studies in counselling and psychotherapy in primary care, together with recommended service evaluation measures;

- a 'how-to-do-it' approach for clinicians in primary care describing a range of clinical interventions, assessment techniques, service evaluation materials, and service delivery issues.

1. Are patients seen in primary care 'the worried well'?	Research is summarized demonstrating the severity of disorder in primary care.
2. How many patients with psychological problems find their way to help?	The numerous 'filters' through which patients must pass on the way to help are identified: perception of a problem, consulting the GP, GP recognition of a psychological problem, and referral for specialist help. Improving the access to care means addressing barriers at each of the filter levels.
3. How can we assess which patients need longer-term treatment?	Specific 'how-to-do-it' guidelines on the assessment of patients in primary care.
4. How can we assess the effectiveness of primary care treatments?	Specific 'how-to-do-it' advice on service evaluation, including instruments to use.
5. How do we decide which professionals are best suited to treating which patients?	An integrated counselling and psychotherapy service in primary care incorporating the contributions of a variety of professional groups.

The emphasis throughout is on the importance of a careful assessment at the primary care level. Recommendations are made on how to select patients who can benefit from brief and ultra-brief therapies. A critique is offered of the American experiment with managed care and the headlong, uncritical rush toward unresearched brief therapies in the NHS. It is argued that although they may be suitable for some patients, brief and ultra-brief therapies are not a panacea for the range of psychological problems being presented in primary care.

Clinicians seeking to improve their assessment and evaluation skills will want to read this book – including counsellors, psychologists and psychiatrists in primary care, general practitioners, psychotherapists, and community psychiatric nurses. Trainers in counselling, psychotherapy and general practice will appreciate the emphasis on assessment and evaluation skills. Managers and purchasers of mental health care will find much to challenge the current trend toward 'six sessions for everything' on both sides of the Atlantic.

1

PSYCHOLOGICAL THERAPIES IN PRIMARY CARE

Until a few decades ago, most patients who consulted their general practitioner with a psychological problem were either counselled briefly by the GP or referred to secondary mental health services based in a psychiatric hospital. In the new primary-care led National Health Service in the UK, expanded service provision at the primary care level has been a key development (Dept of Health, 1994). Services close to patients' homes have a number of advantages: a reduction in the use of expensive and potentially stigmatizing hospital-based services a bus ride away, earlier diagnosis and intervention, community-based primary prevention and health promotion clinics, shorter waiting lists, and high levels of patient satisfaction. In this new climate, GP surgery-based psychological therapies are growing and thriving.

Other recent changes in the National Health Service are also affecting patterns of care for psychological problems. These include increasing attention to cost containment, the search for proven benefit or 'health gain', heightened awareness of consumer satisfaction with services, the realization that hospitals are not the only places where 'hi-tech medicine' can be provided, and changes in the boundaries between primary and secondary levels of care.

Even in today's more open society, the stigma of attending a mental health clinic in a psychiatric hospital can be considerable. Faced with the possibility of a psychiatric referral, many patients prefer to discuss the problem with their own GP or a counsellor based in the GP surgery. Counselling in general practice is a growth industry. However, as with any development in health care, rigorous research of the effectiveness of an innovative service is vital. Along with enthusiasm for the new services have come calls for in-depth outcome evaluations (Chapter 6).

PSYCHOLOGICAL SERVICES IN PRIMARY CARE

Over the past two decades, most of the mental health professions have made forays into the primary care setting. Psychiatrists have offered primary-care based outpatient clinics (Mitchell, 1989; Williams and Balestrieri, 1989); health visitors have provided counselling to women with post-natal depression (Holden, Sagovsky and Cox, 1989); social workers and marriage guidance counsellors have offered sessions in GP surgeries (Corney, 1984, 1987, 1995); and community psychiatric nurses have adopted more of a counselling role (Paykel et al., 1982; Marks, 1985).

Clinical psychologists have offered sessions in GP surgeries or in community-based 'direct access services' (Brunning and Burd, 1993; Corney, 1996); counselling psychologists have worked alongside clinical psychologists in some parts of the country (Collins and Murray, 1995; Knight, 1995; Milton, 1995; Papadopoulos and Bor, 1995); primary care counsellors have started working in GP surgeries in increasing numbers (Corney and Jenkins, 1993; Sibbald et al., 1996a, b); and the potential of the GP-as-counsellor has been increasingly recognized (Cape, 1996; Rowland, Irving and Maynard, 1989; Salinsky, 1993; Stuart and Lieberman, 1993).

An annotated bibliography on the contributions of these professions to psychological problems in primary care was published six years ago (Burton, 1992a), and no attempt will be made here to review the historical development of all of these services over the past thirty years. Our focus in this chapter is on current activity and practice in primary care among the three professional groups who remain principally involved: psychiatrists and community psychiatric nurses, clinical psychologists, and practice counsellors. However, before turning to the contributions of each of these groups, we should consider the question of the GP-as-counsellor.

GPS AS COUNSELLORS IN PRIMARY CARE

The potency of 'the drug, doctor' and the potential of the GP-as-counsellor were pioneered in the UK by Michael Balint and his colleagues. In his now classic book *The Doctor, His Patient and The Illness* (1957) Balint proposed that the most frequently used drug in general practice was the doctor. Using psychoanalytic principles, he offered a seminar for GPs on psychological aspects of their work – what he came to call 'the pharmacology of the drug, doctor'. He noted that:

No guidance was provided to GPs as to the dosage in which the doctor should prescribe himself, in what form, how frequently, what his curative and his maintenace doses should be, and so on. Still more disquieting was the lack of any literature on the possible hazards of this kind of medication, on the various allergic conditions met in individual patients which ought to be watched carefully, or on the undesirable side-effects of the drug.

The Balint Society continues to promote 'Balint groups' for GPs, and the movement has made a considerable impact on general practice and GP training since its origins at the Tavistock Clinic in London in the 1950s (Stewart, Elder and Gosling, 1996). Balint's principles of 'patient centred medicine' (Hopkins, 1972) have increasingly been incorporated into GP vocational training.

GPs differ enormously in their interest in and sensitivity to the psychological aspects of their work. Those who are aware of the powerful interactions between physical and psychological processes are often concerned about an artificial separation between mind and body and dislike splitting psychological issues off to others in the health care team. They use counselling and psychotherapy skills in their work with patients, and refer only when their own efforts have failed. Others are only too happy to delegate this part of the work to others, most of the time. GPs who listen only for physical symptoms, ignoring the psychological overlay in the consultation, are at risk of missing significant emotional disorder. They may also manage in the process to miss a great deal of human suffering. Their patients may need to be unusually articulate about their problems and very assertive in requesting referral if they are to receive appropriate help. Other patients may be surprised to find their GPs responding not only to physical symptoms but to the hints they drop during the consultation about their feelings. Their GPs are alert to somatization and to psychological reactions to chronic illness, bereavement, stressful life events, and loss. These GPs are especially aware of the many serious illnesses in which physical and psychological processes powerfully interact. Occasionally unpsychologically minded patients dislike having their emotional issues detected. The sensitive GP knows when to notice emotional issues but not to comment on them. Today's informed consumer of medical services, however, often wants a psychologically sophisticated GP and often comes prepared to ask for counselling. Indeed some come demanding counselling for a wide range of problems.

Campkin (1995), a GP and psychotherapist with a Balint group background, has summarized the difficulties and advantages of GPs taking on a counselling role with patients. Difficulties include the ambiguity of boundaries when one person is both doctor and counsellor to a patient; dilemmas about confidentiality when the GP has been privy to confidences from a spouse or other family member; difficulties patients may have in accepting the different boundaries and ground rules in counselling vs. medical relationships; and the severe time constraints of a busy general practice. Advantages include the continuity of a long-established relationship and trust which has built up over many years, knowledge of the family over a long period of time, and the structure of general practice which allows appointments to be scheduled with greater flexibility than in many other settings. At the end of the first year of her 'dual existence' Campkin reviewed her patient contacts. Of 3,670 consultations, 486 were for psychological problems, nearly one-third of which involved 'long consultations' lasting 20–45 minutes. During the same year she conducted 59 fifty-minute psychotherapy sessions with eleven patients, ranging from 1 to 21 sessions each. She found weekly slots left open for assessments or brief therapy particularly valuable. In this model, both long consultations and more structured psychotherapy sessions played a role.

Salinsky (1993), another GP who has taken on a psychotherapeutic role with some of his patients, also cites difficulties with the GP-as-counsellor. First is the privacy required during sessions, difficult to achieve in general practice, even if patients attend at the end of an evening surgery for the last appointment of the day. Telephone calls and poor soundproofing are two practical problems. Second is the temptation to take on too many patients for this kind of work, because 'last appointments' result in the GP arriving home late two or three nights each week. Third is obtaining appropriate clinical supervision to address the transference and countertransference issues that emerge. The advantages, however, have outweighed the disadvantages in his experience. He has found his involvement to have been invaluable for a small number of patients for whom appropriate help had not been available on the NHS. He notes the long waiting lists for assessment and often a second wait for treatment, and therapy in secondary services is frequently provided by trainees who either leave the service after a six-month rotation or break off treatment before a complete enough result has been achieved.

A very different model, the 'fifteen-minute hour', has been described by Stuart and Lieberman (1993) in the USA. They suggest that five elements are optimally present in every general practice consultation, examples of which appear below:

Background: 'What is going on in your life?' *or* 'What has been happening since the last time I saw you?'

Affect (feeling state): 'How do you feel about that?'

Trouble: 'What is it about this situation that troubles you most?'

Handling: 'How are you handling that?'

Empathy: 'That must be very difficult for you.'

While 'handling' may be better translated as 'coping' in the UK, the focus is on the patient taking responsibility for behaviour. The model has the virtue of a clear focus and economy of expression, it is likely to foster the patient's trust in the doctor, and may help GPs better diagnose the issues underlying presenting symptoms, both physical and psychological. In the final minutes of the consultation the GP is encouraged to ask what is the best thing that has happened recently, an intervention that may help patients positively reframe the situation and focus on future coping efforts. The authors argue that 'small wins' and the sense of mastery derived from them are vital to the change process. GPs are encouraged to assign homework for the next meeting – writing out the problem in detail, listing options, or identifying sources of support. This approach is derived in part from the cognitive-behavioural model of psychological therapy, in part from humanistic 'active listening', and its origins are firmly rooted in Engel's biopsychosocial model of health and illness (1977, 1980).

Also in the USA, patients attending their GP for depression were prescribed cognitive-behavioural techniques at the same time as anti-depressant medication. GP interventions included advice on activities that improved their mood, planning pleasurable activities, problem solving, challenging depressive thoughts, and confidence-boosting activities. Patients who received the cognitive-behavioural interventions used those strategies following their visit and showed better adherence to psychotropic medication (Robinson et al., 1995).

Few GPs have the dedication of the pioneers we have described or the time during a busy surgery for longer consultations. Contrasts between the medical and biopsychosocial models also limit the number of GPs wishing to adopt the counselling approach (Small and Conlon, 1988). Recent changes in the NHS have also made it difficult for doctors to seek in-service training or supervision in specialties such as counselling. Many GPs will continue to depend on mental health professionals for the treatment of their patients' psychological problems. It is to these groups that we now turn.

PSYCHIATRISTS IN PRIMARY CARE

Much of the psychiatric literature on primary care has focused on the epidemiology of psychiatric disorder and GPs' diagnostic skills in detecting these problems (see Chapter 2). However, according to a survey conducted in 1984, psychiatrists have been offering outpatient clinics in GP surgeries since the 1970s, especially in rural communities (Strathdee, 1987). At the time of the survey, almost 20 per cent of adult psychiatrists had moved out of their hospital bases to work in GP surgeries for one or more sessions a week. Similar primary care liaison systems are developing in the USA (Nickels and McIntyre, 1996).

Such an arrangement has a number of advantages: GP–psychiatrist liaison is improved, background information on patients and their families is more readily available, referrals are made an at early stage before a crisis has developed, continuity of care over the course of an illness is facilitated, joint assessment and treatment are feasible, and some costly admissions to psychiatric hospital are prevented. Patients are seen closer to their homes, the stigma of a psychiatric referral is greatly reduced, and the psychiatrist's presence in the surgery helps patients perceive them as an integral part of the primary health care team. Similar arguments have been brought to bear in the introduction of clinical psychologists and counsellors to the GP surgery.

It is argued that the best practices in which to introduce a visiting psychiatrist are those with high psychiatric morbidity and heavy referral rates to hospital-based psychiatry (Ferguson et al., 1992; Strathdee and McDonald, 1992). Some psychiatrists have offered GPs more than a 'shifted outpatients' model. In 'liaison attachment', they arrange informal lunchtime meetings with GPs as well as more formal consultation focused on the management of difficult patients. In the 'joint assessment' model, GP and psychiatrist assess patients together and treatment is undertaken by the GP with continuing advice from the specialist. The liaison–consultation model has a number of advantages and may be more widely used in future (Gask, Sibbald and Creed, 1997).

Another approach is to base a multidisciplinary mental health team in GP surgeries (Jackson et al, 1993). Patients are seen either at a community health centre or in the GP surgery. The team consists of consultants and senior registrars in psychiatry, community psychiatric nurses, a social worker, an occupational therapist and a clinical psychologist. One of the functions of the team is to operate an emergency on call rota, so that urgent referrals can be seen for assessment the same day. This model of service delivery was piloted on a large council estate in South Manchester, with encouraging results. A marked increase was noted in the number of patients with psychiatric illness referred for treatment.

COMMUNITY PSYCHIATRIC NURSES IN PRIMARY CARE

Historically, community psychiatric nurses (CPNs) were based in psychiatric hospitals and received most of their referrals from psychiatrists. Most of the patients referred to them had psychotic disorders. When CPNs are based in GP surgeries, most of their referrals come from GPs, and more of their caseload is taken up with neurotic and adjustment disorders (East, 1995). Easy access to CPNs has also avoided the stigma of a psychiatric label or the need for a psychiatric referral in some cases (Forth, 1996). A particular benefit is the ease with which a home visit can usually be arranged. CPNs use mostly short-term interventions, although since they are likely to be called on at times of relapse, their contact with individual patients may span several years. Some community psychiatric nurses extended their work to include counselling and brief psychotherapy with selected patients. In most cases the theoretical model used has been cognitive-behavioural. Surgery-based CPNs have been popular with GPs, and some CPNs with special training have been appointed as practice counsellors in GP surgeries.

In the mid-1990s, however, supported by a study by Gournay and Brooking (1994), a Department of Health guideline suggested that CPNs be moved out of general practice settings and refocus their attention on people with serious mental health problems. The study randomly assigned non-psychotic patients to routine care by the GP or counselling by a CPN. No differences were found between experimental groups, and the results were used to suggest that CPNs should return to their more traditional role with the seriously mentally ill. In some areas, the removal of CPNs from GP surgeries has produced the need for more counselling services from clinical psychologists and counsellors in primary care.

CLINICAL PSYCHOLOGISTS IN PRIMARY CARE

'Direct access services' accepting referrals from GPs without a psychiatrist acting as intermediary have been offering psychological services to patients in primary care for many years in the UK. Some of these services continue to be based in psychiatric hospital settings. In the 1980s, increasing numbers of clinical psychologists began offering sessions in GP surgeries, while remaining part of a hospital-based psychology department. Most recently, clinical psychologists working in primary care have seen themselves as an integral part of the primary health care team based in GP surgeries and health centres (Day and Wren, 1994).

GP fundholding substantially increased the number of clinical psychologists working in general practice (Corney, 1996). So great is the interest among clinical psychologists in the primary care setting that a Primary Care Special Interest Group has been set up within the British Psychological Society. National and regional conferences are well attended, and a 1994 issue of *Clinical Psychology Forum* was devoted to the specialty. What began as an interest of a minority in the 1980s has become a fast-growing specialty attracting many recently qualified clinical psychologists. A variety of therapeutic models is used, including cognitive-behavioural therapy, brief psychodynamic therapy, cognitive-analytic therapy, and other integrative or eclectic approaches. Much of the work in primary care is short-term psychological therapy with individuals, but time-limited group, couples and family approaches are also offered by some services. There is wide local variation in the number and kind of approaches offered around the UK.

In the primary care setting, clinical psychologists have taken on a number of roles in addition to direct patient contact: consultation and liaison with GPs on the management of difficult patients; lunchtime meetings for case discussion; training days for the primary health care team; team-building exercises; health promotion programmes for the prevention of mental and physical illness; advice on service evaluation; clinical audit and primary care research; and supervising the work of practice counsellors. Some primary care psychologists also have expertise in promoting health-related behaviours such as compliance with medication, smoking cessation programmes, diet, and interventions tailored to the needs of patients with cancer, cardiovascular disease or diabetes. The broad range of skills offered by clinical psychology in primary care is frequently emphasized in marketing the service to GPs (Brunning et al., 1994).

The clinical psychologist's consultation role may involve working at a number of levels. One GP may ask for help with an individual patient, while another may wish to develop skills that will be useful with future patients as well as a current one. Help may be requested in setting up, running and evaluating a stress management or health promotion programme. A practice manager may request assistance with a time management study, and team-building exercises and organizational analysis are examples of consultation at the organizational level (Casey et al.,

1994). Similar developments in multimodal primary care consultation are occurring in the USA (e.g. McDaniel, 1995; Pace et al., 1995). Thus 'clinical psychology in primary care' now embraces issues considerably broader than face-to-face patient contact.

Clinical psychologists working in primary care cite all the benefits claimed by psychiatrists in primary care, such as reduced stigma, early intervention, joint work and liaison. Having a clinical psychologist as a member of the primary health care team can reduce the stresses and burdens placed on GPs by a small number of difficult patients (Brunning and Burd, 1993). Some clinical psychologists in primary care have also become involved in staff support for members of the primary health care team. Another benefit is that a psychological rather than a medical model offers patients strategies for managing their symptoms after treatment has ended. GPs are pleased to be able to refer patients to a clinician whom they know and trust, and in the surgery setting patients may give direct feedback to the doctor on the quality of care they have received.

Waiting lists for psychologists in primary care began to lengthen as soon as the potential for this service became apparent to GPs. A variety of approaches has addressed the waiting list problem. One department offered a six-session didactic stress management group to patients after an individual assessment appointment. At the end of the course, patients were offered a self-help support group with individual follow-up sessions at 2–3 month intervals until they felt they no longer needed help (Howells and Law, 1996). This approach may be helpful with patients at the milder end of the diagnostic continuum. Another approach is for GPs to give patients an information booklet about the clinical psychology service and a form to complete. It is then up to the patient to take responsibility for 'opting-in' to treatment (Seager, 1991). With this system in place, waiting times have dropped along with failures to attend the first assessment session. Strategies to reduce waiting lists will be discussed in more detail in Chapter 7.

PRACTICE COUNSELLORS IN PRIMARY CARE

In parallel with the growth of clinical psychology in primary care, the number of practice counsellors has greatly increased in recent years, and several universities in the UK now offer Diplomas in Counselling in General Practice for previously qualified counsellors. The British Association for Counselling (1993) has published guidelines for the employment of counsellors in general practice, and the BAC's Counselling in Medical Settings

(CMS) Division is active in promoting the work of counsellors in primary care. The Counselling in Primary Care Trust (1996) provides information and advice to GPs who wish to employ practice counsellors, sponsors annual conferences, maintains a computerized database and bibliography on primary care counselling, and supports a variety of educational and research projects in the field. Seven part-time postgraduate training courses sponsored by the Trust are in place around the country with starting dates between 1997 and 1999: Metanoia Institute, London; Bristol University; Stockton Psychotherapy Training Institute; University of Strathclyde; Bilston Community College, Wolverhampton; University of Keele; and University of Newcastle Upon Tyne.

Three books have appeared on counselling in primary care (Corney and Jenkins, 1993; East, 1995; and Keithley and Marsh, 1995), and the Leeds centre for MIND published a guide to good practice for counselling in primary care (Rain, 1996). The research literature in psychological and medical journals is growing. A special issue of *Clinical Psychology Forum* in 1997 focused on clinical psychologists and counsellors working together in primary care. Several large-scale research projects on the effectiveness of counselling in primary care are in progress (see Chapter 6). All the benefits of the primary care setting cited by psychiatrists and clinical psychologists are relevant to practice counsellors, with the additional benefit that counsellors who have been working in relative isolation in private practice experience the professional benefits of being part of the primary health care team. Also some patients, fearing a psychiatric label, will refuse to see a psychiatrist or clinical psychologist but agree to see a counsellor. Their acceptance of the counselling assessment may open the door to the help they need, because some of these patients need further intensive psychotherapeutic help.

One motivation of GPs in employing a practice counsellor has been an attempt to avoid the long waiting lists for clinical psychology, psychiatry and psychotherapy at the secondary level. However, experience has shown that in the primary care setting, waiting lists also begin to develop. Another motivation to employ counsellors has been cost containment, because practice counsellors' sessional fees tend to be lower than those of clinical psychologists or psychiatrists. As we intend to demonstrate, short-term interventions provided by counsellors and others should not be viewed as a panacea for the broad spectrum of psychological morbidity in primary care. Some patients need longer-term help which can be safely and competently provided only by secondary services.

Patterns of referral to practice counsellors vary widely across the UK in the absence of generally accepted referral guidelines (Parry and

Richardson, 1996), although this state of affairs is beginning to change. Camden and Islington Health Authority recently distributed referral guidelines to GPs setting out which patients are appropriately referred to counsellors and which are likely to require more specialized help (Camden and Islington MAAG, 1996). The profession of counselling in primary care is rapidly becoming more sophisticated, better trained and better informed and is gaining the respect of GPs around the country.

Practice counsellors work within a variety of therapeutic models, including humanistic (House, 1996), psychodynamic (Hoag, 1992; Hopkins, 1995; Jones et al., 1994), and family systems approaches (Bor, 1995; Lees, 1997). Some self-employed psychoanalysts and psychotherapists work sessionally in GP surgeries in addition to seeing private patients elsewhere. Some practice counsellors have begun to offer consultation to primary health care teams (Waskett, 1996). There is considerable variability across the UK in the training and theoretical orientation of practice counsellors (Curtis Jenkins and Einzig, 1996; Watts and Bor, 1995), which is one of the factors making it difficult to assess the impact of their work.

Several surveys of counselling in primary care have appeared in the past five years. Studies prior to 1992 were covered in an annotated bibliography published that year (Burton, 1992a), and outcome studies will be reviewed in Chapter 6. Webber, Davies and Pietroni (1994) reported the use of practice counselling in an inner city London practice; Speirs and Jewell (1995) described the work of a counsellor in two practices in Cambridgeshire; and Monach and Monro (1995) studied counsellors in Sheffield who were working in 14 per cent of GP practices in that city.

Kendrick et al. (1994) surveyed the number of mental health professionals working on site in English and Welsh general practices: 9 per cent of practices reported a psychiatrist working in the practice; 12 per cent a clinical psychologist; 34 per cent a community psychiatric nurse; 17 per cent a practice counsellor. Mental health professionals were unevenly distributed, tending to cluster in larger training practices. In related research, Sibbald et al. (1993) reported that three types of counsellor predominated in the practices surveyed: CPNs, practice counsellors and clinical psychologists. It is difficult to interpret some of this study's findings because of the heterogenicity of the professions surveyed. Some clinical psychologists in primary care would be reluctant, for example, to describe their work as counselling. Further findings from the Sibbald et al. study appeared as an Occasional Paper of the Royal College of General Practitioners (Sibbald et al., 1996a). The data presented were unfortunately several years out of date at the time of publication, and the improvements called for in minimum national standards for training and in researching the cost effectiveness of counselling are already occurring.

Burton, Henderson and Curtis Jenkins (1998) surveyed the working practices of 90 counsellors in primary care across the UK, approximately half of whom had completed the postgraduate Diploma in Counselling in Primary Care: 63 per cent of counsellors worked only in a GP surgery; 36 per cent worked both in a surgery and elsewhere. Given the low rates of pay in some primary care settings, some counsellors supplement their income with private practice or agency work in the private sector. The mean number of hours worked in the surgery per week was 10.5 (range 3–30), with many counsellors working part-time.

Eighty-five percent of counsellors had a waiting list. Mean waiting times for assessment were 5.6 weeks (range 0–26 weeks) and 7.1 weeks for counselling (range 0–26 weeks), which shows that long waiting lists can develop in primary care just as they do in secondary services. Most work was very short term – the mean number of counselling sessions per patient was 6.8 (range 3–20), and the mean maximum number of sessions per patient was 13 (range 4–100). The range of responses reflects the tremendous variability in length of treatment around the country. Monach and Monro (1995) found similar variation. Only 67 per cent of counsellors had a clear contract with each patient regarding the number of sessions planned; 95 per cent were able to extend the agreed length of treatment for some patients, and 95 per cent varied the frequency of sessions from weekly to fortnightly or monthly. The mean number of cases open at any one time was 14.5 (range 3–65).

At the time of writing, practice counsellors are working in more than half of fundholding practices in the UK and in just under 40 per cent of nonfundholding practices. There is wide regional variation.

COMPETITION FOR THE PRIMARY CARE MARKET

Given competition for primary care contracts in the NHS internal market, it is not surprising that some psychiatrists and clinical psychologists have viewed the arrival of counsellors on the scene with a degree of scepticism and inter-professional rivalry (Brunning et al., 1994; Wessely, 1996). Some clinical psychologists, perceiving the growth of primary care counsellors as a threat to their service contracts with GPs, have attempted to co-opt the fledgling profession into their own departments. Co-option of the perceived threat under the protective aegis of clinical psychology has been seen by some as a politically astute way of dealing with a tricky 'survival' problem.

Competition for the primary care market has become an important issue in the NHS, but some of the divisiveness which has resulted should be understood in terms of the social defences that come into play when clinicians are required to devote part of their time and energy to marketing their services to purchasers. As Hinshelwood (1996) has pointed out, two kinds of anxiety are operating in this situation. 'Clinical' anxiety results from long-term exposure to the anxieties that have overwhelmed patients. 'Market' anxiety is about the survival of jobs and professions in the internal market (for example, those of psychiatry, psychotherapy, clinical psychology, community psychiatric nursing and counselling). Whether this state of affairs will change if the NHS internal market is abolished by the Labour government remains to be seen. Undercutting the competition has become too important in some parts of the country, and a 'primitive survivalism' has resulted (D. Bell, 1996; Bruggen, 1997).

In this setting, something has had to be done with the double load of clinical and market anxiety. One way in which this anxiety has been discharged has been via its projection into colleagues who are seen as lower in the pecking order than the profession engaging in the projection. Hinshelwood (1996) describes how psychiatrists may unconsciously perceive psychotherapists as being at the bottom of the status pecking order. Psychotherapists may feel the same way about their psychiatric colleagues, but may simultaneously gain sustenance from perceiving themselves as a persecuted minority group. Similar patterns can be seen in the rivalries between clinical psychologists and psychiatrists, clinical psychologists and counsellors, clinical psychologists and CPNs, psychotherapists and counsellors, psychotherapists and CPNs, counsellors and CPNs, and psychiatrists and counsellors.

Whichever party perceives itself at the top of the pecking order at a given moment in time collects a feeling of moral superiority, while those at the bottom are accused of ignorance (Hinshelwood, 1996). In extreme cases, those at the bottom are accused of carrying out psychological therapies without qualifications. In the mental health field, it has sadly become commonplace to hear one profession attacking another as lacking the clinical skills to deal with the patients referred to them. As long as these rivalries are understood as the social defences they are, we do not fall into the trap of holding our colleagues in contempt. There is an enormous mental health workload in primary care (much of it still going undiagnosed) – more than enough work to ensure the survival of all the relevant professions.

Marmor (1953), in a now classic article that deserves to be read by all clinicians, set out the forces operating on psychotherapists that tend to create in them a feeling of superiority. Externally, therapists are in a real sense important to their patients, but the constant exercise of authority carries with it the occupational hazard of unrealistic feelings of superiority. Internally, feelings of grandiosity may be at least in part a defence against 'clinical anxiety'. Some therapists deliberately draw a cloak of mystery around themselves, which can intensify their idealization by patients. Others who are leaders in the field may prefer to surround themselves with disciples rather than independent thinkers. Supervising therapists are subject to the idealization not only of patients but also of supervisees. A related occupational hazard is the tendency to be destructively critical of colleagues.

Marmor argues that the emotional hazards and insecurity of the work, plus its seductive aspects and isolationism, tend to foster defensive arrogance. A case in point is the degree of separatism and mutual hostility that exists between adherents of different schools of counselling and psychotherapy. By becoming part of a group that lays claim to possessing the 'only true theory', therapists find security against the challenges of the complex realities of working with patients. Therapists may find they feel comfortable only with members of their own group. Marmor suggests the following safeguards against this kind of arrogance and isolationism: a good personal therapy, an adequate period of supervised work, learning from and acknowledging one's mistakes, arranging as many interdisciplinary contacts as possible, and nurturing relationships outside one's own professional field. Although written 45 years ago, Marmor's words were never more pertinent than at present when psychiatrists, psychologists, psychotherapists, counsellors and others pit themselves against their colleagues in pursuit of primary care contracts instead of building constructive collaborative links. The same observations can be made of the internecine warfare between proponents of cognitive-behavioural, psychoanalytic (Freudian, Kleinian and Independent), person-centred, cognitive-analytic, systemic and integrative psychotherapies, to name but a few.

The focus of this book is only tangentially on the differences between professions. We are principally concerned to describe the differences between what can be achieved in short- and long-term therapies, and the implications of those differences for the assessment process in primary care. The contributions of various mental health professions will enter the discussion, especially in Chapter 3, but only as they bear on the focus of this book, which is clinical assessment.

ASSESSING PATIENTS IN PRIMARY CARE: CHALLENGES AND DILEMMAS

We have seen that many professions are now active in the primary care setting. Because of the wide variety of problems being presented by patients to their GPs (many of which, as we shall see, are at the severe end of the clinical spectrum), the challenges to the assessing clinician can be considerable. Among the questions requiring careful consideration are the following:

- Is this patient suitable for outpatient psychological therapy in the primary care setting?

- Do I have the skills required to help this patient?

- If not, to whom could this patient be referred for more appropriate help?

- Does this patient need individual, group, couples or family therapy? A cognitive-behavioural, humanistic, psychodynamic or eclectic approach?

- Is this someone who could benefit from a short-term intervention or is longer term, more in-depth treatment needed?

- Do I have the skills to make that assessment?

- How will I know whether my intervention has had a positive outcome?

'Short-term counselling or in-depth psychotherapy' is a question often asked in today's NHS. How can practitioners best determine which service is most appropriate for a particular patient? What assessment procedures will help GPs, counsellors and psychotherapists arrive at a decision on the suitability of a particular treatment? Finally, what kind of outcome evaluation will help determine the treatment's effectiveness?

OVERVIEW OF THE BOOK

The UK Department of Health's strategic review of psychotherapy (Parry and Richardson, 1996) outlines at least five standards by which NHS psychotherapy services need to be judged – accessibility, equity, comprehensiveness, integration and effectiveness. Accessibility and equity are covered in Chapter 2, comprehensiveness in Chapters 3 and 7, effectiveness in Chapter 6, and integration in Chapter 7. Chapters 4 and 5 deal specifically with clinical assessment.

Chapter 2 describes the 'pathway to care' and the range of adult patients in primary care and their problems. How much of the GP's caseload is psychological – including physical illnesses where psychological processes play a significant part? What kinds of psychological problems do people bring to their GP? How deep-seated are the psychological problems being presented in primary care? Who are the frequent attenders in the surgery? What are the characteristics of so-called 'heartsink' patients? How adequately do GPs diagnose psychological problems? Where do they refer patients with different psychological problems and why (e.g. to psychiatrists, psychotherapists, clinical psychologists, community psychiatric nurses, or practice counsellors)? What patient characteristics affect the outcome of the therapy they receive: expectations of care including the effects of culture and gender, goals for treatment, motivation for change, psychological-mindedness, and the quality of existing relationships.

Chapter 3 describes the range of counselling and psychological therapies now available, and some of the professional disciplines that provide them. What is meant by counselling and how does it differ from psychotherapy? Which approaches are short-term and which longer term? Psychodynamic, cognitive-behavioural, cognitive-analytic and humanistic models are described, with some attention paid to brief and ultra-brief, group, couples and family therapies. This chapter sets the stage for the central question of the book: how are decisions best made about therapy modality, and short- as opposed to longer-term treatment? It is argued that short-term treatment is not a panacea. Both approaches are needed for the range of problems being presented in primary care.

Chapters 4 and 5 focus on assessment for short- vs. longer-term treatment. An adult patient has been referred for psychological help: what treatment modality is most appropriate – individual, couple, family, or group? If individual therapy, is this problem best suited to short- or longer-term treatment, within which theoretical model? Suggestions are made for structuring the assessment interview and the use of pre-assessment questionnaires to help answer this question. Why include a psychosocial history in the assessment interview? Is a history necessary for cognitive and humanistic approaches? Areas to cover in the assessment interview include the problem and its history as well as a psychosocial history. At the same time the assessor is developing a preliminary diagnostic impression, beginning to formulate the problem, building a therapeutic alliance, and weighing up the best form of treatment. Attention is also given to cases where no treatment may be recommended, and to issues of referral to psychiatric or inpatient services.

The Inventory of Early Loss (Burton and Topham, 1997) is one assessment tool to help the assessor decide whether short- or longer-term treatment is appropriate. On the whole, patients with many adverse early experiences will be better helped by longer-term as opposed to short-term therapy. Another issue is 'comorbidity': is this anxious or depressed patient, for example, also suffering from a personality disorder? In terms of the fourth edition of the Diagnostic and Statistical Manual (DSM-IV; American Psychiatric Association, 1994), is there a diagnosis on Axis II (personality disorder) as well as on Axis I (symptomatology)? The answer to this question helps inform a decision on the suitability of short- or longer-term therapy.

Chapter 6 focuses on outcome evaluation in the psychological therapies. A variety of outcome measures presently in use in the USA and the UK are described. Recent studies of outcome in the primary care setting are reviewed, and several research studies in progress are outlined. Evaluation of the effectiveness of interventions is an integral part of psychological therapy services in primary care. A number of predictor and outcome variables are described together with suggestions for their measurement: demographic information, problem type, personality structure, risk factors, type and length of treatment offered, goals of treatment, motivation for change, psychological-mindedness, quality of existing relationships, therapist-rated outcome, and standardized pre- and post-therapy measures of change. Practical guidelines are suggested for service evaluation and clinical audit, along with strategies for gaining staff support for outcome studies.

Chapter 7 describes an integrated counselling and psychological therapy service. In one example of good practice, referrals are centrally received, allocated for specialist assessment at a clinical meeting, seen by a member of staff in one or two assessment interviews, and assigned for treatment to a counsellor or clinical psychologist. In another model, each locality is served by a brief intervention team including a clinical psychologist, counselling psychologist, counsellor, and nurse therapist. Each sector also has its own community mental health team responsible for assessing and treating people with serious and enduring mental illness. Models such as these point to an interdisciplinary future in which case mix and skill mix are carefully balanced so that patients have the best chance of receiving the treatment they require. In each locality, a range of treatments should be available including group, couples and family therapies, and short- and longer-term individual psychotherapy. Attention needs to be given to maintaining good links with secondary services, team building, confidentiality issues, and waiting list management.

Clinical supervision should be provided for staff at all levels of expertise as an integral part of the day-to-day work of the service. The chapter closes with future directions in primary care counselling and psychotherapy, and the need for further research.

All clinical illustrations in the book have been disguised and fictionalized to preserve confidentiality, while retaining a thematic resemblance to actual cases.

2

PATIENTS AND THEIR PROBLEMS

THE PATHWAY TO HELP

The pathway to help for psychological problems in primary care has been described in terms of five 'filters':

- being 'at risk' for psychological problems,

- experiencing symptoms,

- seeking help from a general practitioner (GP),

- GP identification of a psychological problem, and

- GP referral for specialist help

(Kat, 1997a, b)

Risk factors

Stressful life events may or may not lead to psychological problems. Vulnerability factors predict those at greater risk, and protective factors identify those who may not need psychological help. Selected stressful life events, vulnerability and protective factors are included in Kat's (1997b) *At Risk Checklist*. Whatever the presenting problem, people who have experienced these events, particularly in the recent past, may need psychological health care:

- *Events*

— death of spouse, close family member, or stillbirth or perinatal death

— loss of spouse or long-term partner through divorce or separation

— retirement or enforced unemployment

— serious personal assault, injury, accident or unwanted pregnancy

— enforced house move as a result of financial or other problems

- *Vulnerability factors*

— loss of one or more parents before the age of 11

— physical or sexual abuse as a child

— needed help with emotional problems in the past

— long-term problems associated with maladaptive coping strategies

— a history of unsatisfactory or broken personal relationships

- *Protective factors*

— a spouse, partner, close family member or friend with whom they can discuss their problems

— the security of a stable and reliable income, adequate to their needs.

(Kat, 1997b, p.7)

If such a checklist were placed on the front of each patient's medical record, the detection of psychological problems by GPs might be greatly enhanced. Those at risk for psychological problems are identified by a life-time history of exposure to known risk factors, current exposure to stressful life events, and current maladaptive coping strategies. Many of those at risk never seek help. Those who do seek help from their GP for psychological problems are more likely to have limited and difficult relationships, low job satisfaction and poor social support networks (Mann, 1993).

Another list of risk factors has been proposed by Stuart and Lieberman:

- loss, either personal such as bereavement or divorce, or the loss of something valued, such as a home, job, or object

- conflict: interpersonal or intrapersonal, having to do with conflicting internal demands

- change, triggered either by life events or a geographical move

- maladjustment: longstanding interpersonal problems, failure to adjust to demands at home or at work

- other stresses, whether chronic or acute

- social isolation

- failure or frustrated expectations

- any anniversary of a significant loss or traumatic event.

(Stuart and Lieberman, 1993, p. 112)

One GP has identified nine groups of patients whom he has found to be at increased risk for hidden depression: children, adolescents, post-partum mothers, the 'trapped' young housewife and mother, middle-aged women with role identity problems, the executive alcoholic, the bereaved, the lonely and the elderly, and those experiencing occupational stress including unemployment and redundancy (Beaumont, 1983). To this list should be added any patient with a recently diagnosed chronic physical illness, or who has undergone surgery. Those who have suffered recent traumatic stress are also at risk, including rape victims, and those who were physically, sexually or emotionally abused as children. Harris (1996) identifies four severe events which may act as provoking agents in depression: humiliating rejections or separations, major revelations in the family (e.g. son is disclosed as a paedophile), the death of someone close, and entrapment events (e.g. nothing more can be done for the patient's chronic disease). Vulnerability factors among women include lack of an intimate confidante, three or more children at home under the age of 15, lack of outside employment providing an alternative role identity, and loss of mother before the age of 11.

Parkes (1971) described the key role of psychosocial transitions in triggering psychological distress. Life change may lead to better adjustment or may act as a trigger for illness (Higgs, 1984). Not all life changes are negative, but even positive life changes may involve an element of loss, in that a previous way of life has been permanently altered. Some people are prone to 'success depressions' (experiencing low mood around the time of a major success), the underlying causes of which vary depending on the precipitating event and the patient's psychosocial history.

Bereavement is a particularly important risk factor because it leads to increased mortality, psychosomatic disorders, aggravation of pre-existing medical conditions, psychiatric disorders such as reactive depression and pathological grief, and more frequent visits to the GP (Parkes, 1996). The risk increases when the death occurred in traumatic circumstances, or when the bereaved is vulnerable in a number of identifiable ways: insecure attachment to parents in childhood, low self-esteem, low trust in others, ambivalent attachment to the deceased person, dependent or interdependent attachment to the deceased, previous psychiatric disorder, previous suicidal gestures or attempts, and an absent or unhelpful family (Parkes, 1996).

Symptoms

During periods of stress or distress, if bodily changes are interpreted by the patient as symptoms, the further step of consulting a GP may be taken. Usually, however, an appointment with the doctor follows initial attempts at coping and self-management and conversations with lay helpers and advisers. Often ten or more lay consultations precedes each consultation with the GP. Many months may elapse between the onset of the problem and consultation with the doctor.

Most people have a reportable symptom of one kind or another about once a week, but the rate of consulting for such symptoms is low. Possibly as many as 25 per cent of the population have severe symptoms warranting a visit to the doctor, but they avoid consulting. It has been estimated that only 1 in 29 cases of abdominal pains is presented to the GP, 1 in 14 chest pains, 1 in 456 cases of fatigue, and 1 in 46 of those experiencing psychological symptoms (Banks et al., 1975). In general, if symptoms are present two days in a row and interfere significantly with some aspect of daily life, a consultation with the GP is arranged. The rate at which people consult their doctors is affected by:

- demographic factors (women, children, and the elderly consult more often)
- ethnicity (certain minority groups consult more often)
- socioeconomic status (patients from social classes 4 and 5 consult more frequently)
- employment status (unemployed people consult more frequently)
- housing (those in rented accommodation consult more often)

- family and social networks (patients with poorly developed social networks consult more frequently)
- perceived vulnerability to illness
- perceived worsening severity of the symptom
- perceived benefits from seeking medical care
- knowledge about illness and information-seeking behaviour
- belief in the ineffectiveness of self-care
- stressful life events
- distance from the GP surgery
- barriers to consultation such as appointment systems at the surgery (frequent attenders are more likely to attend without an appointment).

(Campbell and Roland, 1996, pp. 76–79)

GP consultation is also dependent on people's expectations of the outcome of consulting the doctor. If the potential benefits of consultation exceed the potential costs and hassles, an appointment with the doctor is arranged (Kat, 1997, a, b).

Seeing the doctor

At the consultation, differential diagnoses are considered by the GP and an interpretation is made of the patient's presentation. The GP decides to focus partly or wholly on the psychological dimension of the presenting problem, or the psychological dimension may be missed altogether. The doctor's task begins with imaginative listening and putting the symptom in the context of the patient's life situation (Higgs, 1984). GP detection of psychological problems is enhanced by adopting the patient- and problem-centred biopsychosocial model rather than the traditional biomedical model which is disease and physician centred (Engel, 1977, 1980; Zimmermann and Tansella, 1996).

Referral for specialist help

Should the GP recognize the potential benefits of referral for psychological help and expect the outcome of the service to be beneficial, should a suitable service be available where waiting times are not excessive and the cost to the patient and the practice are acceptable, a referral is made (Kat, 1997, a, b).

It is evident that there are many stages at which a referral for specialist help may founder. Many of those at risk do not seek help. Some attempt to ignore changes in their bodily state, while others perceive them but do not identify them as symptoms. Some consider the risks and hassles inherent in consulting their doctor to outweigh the potential benefits. All of these individuals are sometimes called *non-consulters*. Some biomedically oriented GPs are minimally interested in the psychological dimension of their patients' problems, and many of them fail to detect psychological morbidity when it is present. Still others have little faith in the available NHS services to respond adequately or quickly enough to be of benefit to their patients. A small number counsel their patients themselves.

If a patient has passed through all five filters, a referral is made for psychological help. The potential need is enormous, but if all of those in need are to receive help, attention should be focused at the barriers of each of the filter levels. Having described the five filters through which the primary care patient must pass in order to be referred for specialist help and keeping in mind the focus on assessment throughout this book, we need to consider in more detail the process by which a diagnosis of the problem is reached by the GP.

PROPORTION OF PRIMARY CARE PATIENTS PRESENTING WITH PSYCHOLOGICAL PROBLEMS

How much of the GP's caseload is psychological – including physical illnesses where psychological processes play a significant part? The presence of a clearly identifiable psychological problem has been estimated to occur in as many as 33 per cent of GP attenders, only about one-half of whom are detected as having a psychological problem by the GP (Goldberg and Huxley, 1980). Of these, a much smaller number are ultimately referred for help. In the USA, one study found that primary care physicians failed to recognize almost two-thirds of their patients with a current mental disorder, judged against the findings of a structured psychiatric interview (Borus et al., 1988). Given that about one-third of primary care patients exhibit significant psychological distress, 15–25 per cent warrant a diagnosis of depression or anxiety (Stoudemire, 1996). Worldwide, the most common psychological disorders in primary care

are depression (10 per cent), generalized anxiety (8 per cent), and alcohol use disorders (6 per cent). Of these patients 95 per cent presented to their doctors with physical rather than psychological symptoms (Goldberg, 1995). In the USA, the frequency of childhood physical or sexual abuse may be as high as 22 per cent of women who consult a primary care physician (McCauley et al., 1997). Such women often show numerous physical as well as psychological symptoms (Lechner et al., 1993).

Many primary care patients visit their GP in connection with a chronic illness such as arthritis, diabetes, hypertension, or pulmonary disease. An increased prevalence of psychiatric disorder has been found in these conditions. Among fatigued patients, 20–40 per cent may be depressed and 33–66 per cent of those with insomnia may be suffering from a psychiatric disorder. Depression following a heart attack is estimated to occur in 20–50 per cent of patients; in Parkinson's disease, 33 per cent; in stroke patients, 25–50 per cent; and in cancer patients, 20 per cent (Stoudemire, 1996). Other medical illnesses with commonly associated depression include endocrine disorders, autoimmune disorders, multiple sclerosis, metabolic disorders, chronic infectious diseases, HIV/AIDS, and patients who are terminally ill. Many of these depressions are not diagnosed because the GP considers the patient 'has a good reason to be depressed – who wouldn't be depressed with such an illness?' (Boswell and Stoudemire, 1996). Post-partum depression also commonly occurs after delivery, and depression can complicate grief reactions. Depression can occur as a result of substance abuse, as a side effect of medication, as a complication of bereavement, or in association with other psychiatric illnesses (see Chapter 5 for a discussion of comorbidity). Thus the differential diagnosis of psychological problems including depression is a complex and demanding part of every GP's caseload.

In this era of cost containment in health care, the cost of failing to diagnose depression has come into focus. The monetary cost of depression in the UK has been estimated at £240 million annually but the cost in terms of human misery is probably incalculable (Wright, 1995). American studies have shown that those with mental and addictive disorders are at increased risk for concurrent medical problems, and psychiatric patients with comorbid medical conditions have longer hospital stays, an increased number of procedures, and higher total health care costs (Pincus et al., 1995). Societal costs include lost productivity, increased incapacity benefit claims, and increased mortality. One recent review listed these among the consequences of untreated depression:

- increased risk of suicide and parasuicide

- marital breakdown

- increased absence from work due to illness, labour turnover, problems with colleagues, and poor performance

- accidents

- increased vulnerability to emotional impairment among children of depressed parents

- chronic depression and persistent unresolved grief reactions may act as a trigger for alcohol and drug abuse, excessive utilization of medical services, and a loss of economic productivity.

(Jenkins, 1992, p. 238)

GP DETECTION OF PSYCHOLOGICAL PROBLEMS

A number of studies have confirmed that GPs miss depression approximately 50 per cent of the time. At present, treatment is almost entirely pharmacological, with little referral for psychotherapy. One in six patients is prescribed minor tranquillizers for associated anxiety symptoms, many patients stop taking their tablets, and often there is poor monitoring of repeat prescriptions (Kendrick, 1994). Because of the potentially life-threatening nature of depression, its serious impact on health, social relations and productivity, and because it goes too often undiagnosed and untreated, the Royal College of Psychiatrists and the Royal College of General Practitioners set up the Defeat Depression Campaign in 1992. The campaign was designed to reduce the stigma of depression by improving both public awareness and health professionals' knowledge. As part of the campaign launch, a MORI poll of the general public was conducted late in 1991:

- although 73 per cent believed that depression was a medical condition like any other illness, only 46 per cent viewed antidepressants as effective, and 78 per cent (against all the evidence) regarded them as addictive; 85 per cent viewed counselling to be effective

- 60 per cent said they would consult their GP if they suffered from depression, however 60 per cent also considered that people feel embarrassed to consult their GP with this problem for fear of being regarded as unbalanced or neurotic

- 75 per cent were not sure their GP was trained sufficiently to deal with depression and 57 per cent believed that GPs tended only to prescribe pills.

(Sims, 1993, p.31)

Depression can in the long term be a sign that something important is being left unattended, and a positive opportunity for growth. Crisp (1996) said of the campaign, 'I gather it was not totally successful. . . Depression may not always be sinister: it can, properly handled, sometimes be a gateway to greater self-awareness and maturity' (p. 16). But it cannot become that gateway to self-awareness until patients bring the problem to the doctor, the GP makes an accurate diagnosis, and then arranges for appropriate treatment.

We have seen that one barrier to the treatment of depression is the attitude of the general public toward consulting their GP about the problem. Another barrier to treatment is the low detection rate among GPs. A number of studies have attempted to identify doctor variables and patient variables predicting better detection. Those GPs who are better at identification show more interest and concern in the patient as a person, are sensitive to cues from the patient, make more empathic comments, ask about feelings, have better interviewing skills, use appropriate psychiatric questions and probes, are particular personality types themselves (less conservative and more sensitive to their own needs), and are better qualified generally. They avoid an either/or approach to diagnosis, for example, either physical or psychological, recognizing that the two frequently coexist. They make early eye contact with the patient, clarify the presenting complaint, and show less urgency and hurry – doctors interrupt patients, on average, 18 seconds after the patient has started talking. They pick up verbal and non-verbal cues, are patient-centred and patient-led, make supportive comments, are able to deal with interruptions and talkative patients, do not bury themselves in the medical notes, and ask more questions about psychosocial issues. Research suggests that these skills are teachable (Boardman, 1991).

Poorer GP recognition of depression is associated with patients who present only with somatic symptoms, or psychological problems coexisting with somatic symptoms. Poor detection also occurs with patients who fail to disclose distress because they believe that doctors do not deal with psychological problems, do not have the time or inclination to help, do not need to know, or will reject or dismiss these problems (Boardman,

1991). Other studies have shown better GP detection of psychological problems among patients who are Caucasian, female, in the middle of the age range, separated or bereaved, unemployed, presenting with psychological as opposed to somatic symptoms, and who look depressed. When there is a past history of a mental health problem, and when the patient has an ongoing relationship with the examining GP, detection is improved (Howe, 1996).

Poorer detection is likely if the patient is physically ill, is unwilling to consider a psychological cause to physical problems, and when cues to depression are presented late in the interview or not at all. Depression causes feelings of unworthiness and guilt, and patients will often volunteer physical symptoms rather than say they feel miserable (Wright, 1995). Some patients fear their GP will regard them as mentally ill, and even when it is offered some patients will refuse treatment for anxiety or depression. Others may want the doctor simply to exclude a serious physical cause for their symptoms. A personal list system in practices – where patients see only their own GP – is associated with improved continuity of care and increased patient satisfaction and may improve the detection of psychological problems (Wright, 1996).

The detection problem is not limited to hidden depression. As one recent article put it, 'Why is it so difficult for general practitioners to discuss alcohol with patients?' (Arborelius and Thakker, 1995). Among the reasons cited were lack of time, fear of spoiling their relationship with the patient, having more work to do if more patients were detected, the view that patients have given priority to other problems and how much they drink is their own business, and the belief that doctors cannot affect their patients' drinking habits. A ten-item, self-report questionnaire (Piccinelli et al., 1997) and a two-item screening test (Brown et al., 1997) have recently been published. The Health of the Nation Outcome Scales (HoNOS) require assessment of the patient's use of drugs or alcohol, which is not commonly carried out at present (Wing, Curtis, and Beevor, 1996). The importance of dual diagnosis in primary care – detecting and treating both addictions and emotional problems – has been highlighted by Ziedonis and Brady (1997). Often both the substance abuse and the psychological problem are hidden from the GP; therefore any patient presenting with either a psychological or a substance abuse problem should be evaluated for both. Family members and significant others can be important sources of information, but patients' acceptance that there is a problem and their willingness to engage in treatment are key predictors of outcome.

This brings us to the question of how GP detection of psychological problems might be improved, remembering that the GP spends on average only seven minutes with each patient. The Defeat Depression Campaign has produced educational packages for GPs, whose efficacy needs to be evaluated. Studies also need to be conducted on whether detection fluctuates with length of the consultation, overall duration of the surgery, and numbers of patients seen. An excellent set of clinical guidelines for GPs was published in the *British Medical Journal* (Craig and Boardman, 1997). Problems suggesting an underlying mental health problem include seemingly inappropriate requests for urgent attention, an increased frequency of consultation, unexpected emotional outbursts in the consulting room, excessive anxiety about another family member, a 'fat file', unstable relationships, and distressing or deteriorating social circumstances. Factors that should prompt questions about suicide include the following, especially if the patient is male, single, older, isolated, or shows several factors simultaneously:

- previous suicidal thoughts or behaviour

- marked depressive symptoms

- misuse of alcohol or illicit drugs

- longstanding mental illness, including schizophrenia

- painful or disabling physical illness

- recent psychiatric treatment as an inpatient

- self-discharge against medical advice

- previous impulsive behaviour, including self-harm

- legal or criminal proceedings pending, including divorce

- family, personal or social disruption such as bereavement, marital breakdown, redundancy, or eviction.

(Craig and Boardman, 1997, p. 1610)

Several screening questionnaires have been used in general practice in recent years, the best known of which are the General Health Questionnaire and the Hospital Anxiety and Depression Scale (Wright, 1994). It has been suggested that the Geriatric Depression Scale (GDS) be incorporated into the over-75 health check (Tylee and Katona, 1996). The PROQSY, a computerized self-assessment questionnaire for psychological problems has also been developed for use in primary care (Lewis et al., 1995). Primary care versions of the International Classification of Diseases-10 Primary Health Care (ICD-10-PHC) and the Diagnostic and Statistical Manual of Mental Disorders, Fourth Edition for Primary Care (DSM-IV-PC) have recently received field trials. The ICD-10-PHC makes use of 24 cards, the front of which considers diagnosis while the back is devoted to management strategies (Goldberg, Sharp and Nanayakkara, 1995). The manual for the American DSM-IV-PC contains algorithms for the diagnosis of the nine most frequently encountered psychiatric conditions in primary care (Pincus et al., 1995).

Both schemes were developed with the aim of improving the diagnosis of psychological problems in primary care. In the USA, the PRIME-MD system employs a 1-page patient questionnaire completed in the waiting room followed by a 12–page structured interview form used by the primary care physician to follow up any positive signs on the questionnaire (Spitzer et al., 1994). Similarly, the SDDS-PC uses a 16-item patient questionnaire and six 5-minute, physician-administered diagnostic interview modules based on DSM-III-R criteria allowing the diagnosis of six common psychological problems in primary care (Olfson et al., 1995). However, time-intensive screening devices such as these are unlikely to be taken up in the near future by GPs in the UK.

Underserved populations

Although the emphasis of this book is on adults, the psychological needs of children and the elderly are going unmet in many areas. Approximately 14–18 per cent of children have significant mental health needs, and the rates can be double in deprived inner cities. A recent needs assessment found that over 33 per cent of children in part of South London had three or more mental health problems. Only a minority of these children received help, and most of the helpers had long waiting lists (Day, 1997).

When adult members of a family are in treatment, some of their children may also be in need of mental health care. Danger signs of which primary care counsellors should be aware when working with adults include the following, which is by no means an exhaustive list:

• Parents who physically or sexually abuse children, who abuse drugs or alcohol or who are involved in illegal activities that place their children in danger.

• Parents who are excessively critical, overprotective, overly intrusive or neglectful of their children.

- Parents who take their children into bed with them when their spouses or partners depart, especially when this behaviour carries sexual overtones.

- Parents who use their children as confidantes, sharing their marital and sexual problems with them, turning them into 'little adults' and preventing them from remaining children.

- Children who have a parent or close relative who is terminally ill or has recently died.

- Children who are performing poorly at school as a result of parental conflicts at home, sexual or physical abuse, violence in the home, or sudden losses including unwelcome house moves.

- Hyperactivity, intractable temper tantrums, antisocial behaviour such as stealing, shoplifting, aggression toward other children, or cheating at school.

- Physical problems such as asthma and eczema exacerbated by family conflict.

- Sleep disorders, repeating nightmares and persistent bed-wetting.

- Post-traumatic stress disorder following a major incident.

- The gamut of psychiatric symptomatology ranging from obsessive-compulsive disorder, phobias, anxiety, clinical depression and suicidal gestures, to social withdrawal, the failure to make or keep friends, and pre-schizophrenic symptoms.

Childrens' drawings brought to the counsellor by worried parents can also sometimes provide clues to the nature of their problems and their need for mental health treatment.

Among the elderly, depression is the most common mental health problem, 10–20 per cent according to various surveys. Depression in the elderly is especially likely to go undetected and therefore not treated. It may still go untreated even though it has been detected, either because it is seen as a low priority by referring GPs, or due to ageist processes in the system. However, depression in the elderly is strongly linked with increased mortality, and deserves far greater attention than it is presently receiving (Roper-Hall, 1997). Some localities have excellent psychogeriatric services with specialist clinical psychologists on their teams; other areas have few services for this neglected group.

FREQUENT ATTENDERS AND 'HEARTSINK' PATIENTS

The sight of certain patients' names on the morning list can elicit a dispirited groan from the GP in anticipation of the consultation. Among these are so-called 'heartsink' patients and frequent attenders at the surgery (Jewell, 1988). They are disproportionately high utilizers of all medical services and psychological problems are very common in both groups. They are also likely to be dissatisfied with their medical care (Hahn et al., 1996). An extreme example of the repeat attender was 'Annie' who, suffering from severe and chronic abdominal pain, was convinced she had an undetected cancer. She cost the NHS more than £50,000 in unnecessary hospital consultations and investigations – excluding the cost of her general practice, community and psychiatric care (Cohen, 1992).

It is important to bear in mind that the patient whom one GP finds very trying may pose no problems for another doctor. 'Heartsink' occurs in the GP, and what frustrates or angers one GP may be patiently tolerated by a colleague. Balint groups have often helped GPs to discover which type of patient 'turns them off' and aided in the development of creative management strategies. Nevertheless, classification systems for 'difficult patients' abound. Groves (1978) described four types: dependent clingers, manipulative help-rejecters, entitled demanders, and self-destructive deniers. Doctors find these patients very trying; many of them are suffering from personality disorders. Hypochondriacs suffer from anxiety and depression but focus their attention on physical symptoms and on the inability of the GP to cure them, while chronic complainers have multiple complaints, rarely improve and never seem to appreciate their doctors' efforts (Stuart and Lieberman, 1993).

Gerrard and Riddell (1988) found that their respective 25 most difficult patients shared 10 key characteristics:

- 'black holes': they demand help persistently but are expert at adopting an oppositional stance to whatever approach is made by the doctor

- family complexity: it is impossible to disentangle these patients' problems from those of the family, and often the patient who presents is its least ill member

- punitive behaviour: they make the doctor pay for real or imagined grievances, hoping to prove the doctor wrong

- personal links to the doctor's character: the doctor shares the patient's hopes and fears and may foster a dependent

relationship, obscuring decisions that have to be taken and
deskilling the doctor

- differences in culture and belief: there is no shared language and both can feel antagonistic toward the other

- poverty and deprivation: the doctor can act only through
  changing social and environmental factors

- medical complexity: doctors may feel deskilled by a patient
  who suffers from one or more complicated or obscure illnesses – and sometimes the patient knows more about
  these than the doctor

- medical connections: nurses, doctors and their families as
  patients make the GP want to provide special care while
  being fearful of making mistakes

- wicked, manipulative, and playing games: often the sweet-
  est and most flattering patients play games that turn colleagues against each other and cause disruption

- secrets: a missing link is always avoided in consultation – the secret which is the core of the patient's life and
  problems.

(Gerrard and Riddell, 1988, pp. 530–531)

Those displaying punitive behaviour, the game-players and those who
cling to secrets may be suffering from an underlying personality disorder. Another more recent classification of difficult patients is as follows:

- psychosomatic patients can generate anxiety about missing
  real physical disease

- patients who present problems of such enormity and
  urgency can create pressure to do something immediately

- severely depressed patients can engender feelings of hopelessness

- self-destructive patients, including those with addictions,
  can be very disturbing

- highly dependent and vulnerable patients may increase
  anxiety

- when patients' problems are too close to home for GPs (for example, a recent bereavement of their own), it can be difficult for the doctor to respond

- patients who are out of touch with their feelings can leave the doctor feeling helpless

- a very likeable patient may provoke the doctor to 'act out' in an attempt to make everything quickly better, and

- there are patients whom the doctor does not like or does not want to help.

(Dammers and Wiener, 1995, p. 43)

'Somatizers' are in actuality anxious and depressed but suffer from a variety of physical symptoms. They tend to present with minor physical symptoms for which no organic cause has been found, they are demanding in asking for referrals elsewhere or other forms of treatment, and are regarded by their doctors as chronically anxious or depressed. Family and marital difficulties are common in those living in family groups, and social isolation in those living alone. Their lack of insight into the psychological cause or component of their symptoms increases the GP's frustration (Corney et al., 1988).

GPs attending a study day on difficult patients were asked to relate the occurrence of physical illness to known psychosocial stressors, from information already in the patient's medical notes. Patients were asked to compile a life-event chart, keep a daily diary, and fill in simple questionnaires. The results could be very informative:

medical problems	social events	psychological problems
asthma	father died	felt low
	failed 'A' levels	on valium
duodenal ulcer	divorce	panic attacks

(Corney et al., 1988, p. 351)

GPs were asked to review their consultation behaviour and the feelings which the patient generated in the doctor. Most of the difficult patients discussed on the study day were repeat attenders, 'fat file' patients whose cases could profit from stock-taking and review, sometimes in one or two extended consultations. 'Heartsink' patients exasperate, defeat, and overwhelm their doctors (O'Dowd, 1988), evoking a sense of angry helplessness or plain dislike. A workshop on 'heartsink survival' suggested five tasks for the doctor: taking a full history, attending to emotional cues, exploring social and family factors and health beliefs, and a brief focused physical examination. Patients are given feedback from the physical examination, and an acknowledgement that the symptoms are real despite the lack of a clear physical cause. They can often then begin to make sense of their symptoms in the light of recent life events (Mathers and Gask, 1995).

Frequent attendance is more likely with increasing age, female gender, marital disharmony or separation, and lower socioeconomic status or unemployment. Past and present physical health, perceived health, psychological health and somatization are also associated with frequent attendance. Personality, family factors and life events also affect attendance rates (Neal et al., 1996). 'Fat file' patients are more likely to have suffered recent stress, to be more anxious and vulnerable and less self-reliant, to have weak social networks, to be on psychotropic medication, and to change doctors more frequently than those who consult less frequently (Kat, 1992).

Gill (1996) studied repeat attenders over five years in an Oxfordshire practice. While the practice list remained relatively stable, there was a large and progressive increase in all consultations, as well as among repeat attenders. The increase in workload accounted for by frequent attenders was 28 per cent. The surgery was located in an area of relatively low socioeconomic status, which may partly account for the findings. Repeat attenders presented with medically unexplained symptoms with or without associated physical disease, severe physical disease with significant distress, and severe disease requiring frequent medical attention. More than 50 per cent of repeat attenders had evidence of some form of psychological disorder, either emotional distress associated with physical illness or medically unexplained symptoms. Some of these patients may be helped by a counsellor or clinical psychologist in primary care. Indeed, repeat attendance with somatic complaints for which no organic cause can be found is a frequent reason for specialist referral.

SEVERITY OF PSYCHOLOGICAL PROBLEMS IN PRIMARY CARE

How deep-seated are the psychological problems being presented in primary care? Are these patients the 'worried well' who would recover spontaneously without the need for specialist help? One argument that is heard in opposition to counselling in primary care is that treating patients at the 'easy end of the market' diverts help from the severely mentally ill toward the so-called 'worried well' (Sage, 1997). The emerging evidence is to the contrary. A considerable proportion of psychological problems treated in general practice are of a severe nature. Only 5 per cent are referred to psychiatrists, and many severe conditions are treated at the general practice level (Fallowfield, 1993).

It is well known that many people who successfully commit suicide have consulted their GP in the previous week, suggesting both that a number of severely depressed patients are treated at the primary care level and that severe depression may go undiagnosed. Almost half the neurotic patients treated in two GP practices in Warwickshire had a chronic course over 11 years. They had high psychiatric morbidity, an increased consultation rate with their GP, and increased mortality from all causes. While the increased mortality in psychiatric patients has been attributed to suicide, accidental death, or even misdiagnosis of underlying physical conditions, all the patients in this study died from common physical disorders such as cardiovascular disease, respiratory illnesses or malignancies. Severity of disturbance at diagnosis was the best predictor of long-term outcome and GP consultation rate (Lloyd, Jenkins and Mann, 1996).

We have already noted the significant association between physical illness, depression and anxiety in primary care in the context of low detection rates of psychological morbidity by GPs. Evidence is accumulating that lack of social support or chronic stress is associated with depressed immune function, which could have a substantial impact on rates of physical illness. The death rate among psychiatric outpatients with neurotic disorders is raised by a factor of 1.5 to 2.0, and the findings of the Lloyd, Jenkins and Mann study are consistent with this excess risk. The patients described in their study cannot be described as the 'worried well'.

A recent paper addressed the question of whether patients waiting for outpatient psychotherapy were the 'worried well'. The implication of the term is that 'psychotherapy departments see patients who are not "really ill" psychiatrically but who enjoy chatting about themselves . . . and psychotherapists are happy to indulge them in this' (Amies, 1996, p. 153). Forty-five percent of those on the waiting list in this study had been referred by GPs, with the remainder referred by psychiatrists. These patients showed high levels of morbidity on standardized psychological tests, and a high frequency of personality disorder. More than one suicide attempt had been made by 25 per cent of the sample.

The level of morbidity in Amies' group is not dissimilar to that of many patients being treated at the primary care level. Because of long waiting lists in many areas, patients with similar profiles are not being referred to secondary services but are being seen by GPs, practice counsellors and clinical psychologists in primary care. Tata, Eagle and Green (1996) have provided further evidence of high levels of morbidity in primary care by examining whether the provision of more accessible primary care psychology services had lowered the clinical threshold for referrals. The study found equivalent levels of psychopathology in specialist and primary care clinics.

ADULT PATIENTS' PROBLEMS IN PRIMARY CARE

Adult patients bring an enormous range of psychological problems to their GP: stress/generalized anxiety, phobias, panic attacks, depression, obsessive-compulsive disorder, habit disorders (including alcohol and drug misuse), psychosexual problems, marital/relationship problems, anger/aggression, psychosomatic (physical reactions to psychological problems), somatopsychic (psychological reactions to physical illness), post-traumatic stress, eating disorder, psychotic state, borderline personality disorder, other personality disorder, atypical grief reaction and other problems (including adjustment reactions to stressful life events).

As we shall see when we consider comorbidity in Chapter 5, many patients bring more than one problem. Anxiety and depression so commonly occur together that a controversial new diagnostic entity has been proposed, mixed anxiety-depression, with the unfortunate acronym of MAD. Both mixed anxiety-depression (MAD) and generalized anxiety disorder (GAD) are prevalent in primary care settings and are associated with significant social and occupational disability. GAD is often associated with medically unexplained somatic complaints such as chest pain, irritable bowel syndrome and hyperventilation (Roy and Peter, 1996). Many patients presenting with symptoms are basically psychologically healthy with good ego strength, but others bring symptoms in addition to an underlying personality disorder. Treatment for the presenting symptom is likely to take much longer in the presence of a personality disorder. If assessment at the primary care level is accurate, multiple referrals until the appropriate source of help is found can be avoided. The importance of accurate assessment for the patient is that if they are repeatedly referred from one clinician to another, it will be confirmed to them that their problem is indeed unmanageable, as they had perhaps always feared.

The wide range of problems presented is reflected in this sample of patients referred for psychological help at the primary care level:

- *Relatively mild problems*
  - panic attacks of recent onset
  - examination anxiety
  - atypical grief reaction
  - agoraphobia
  - mild depression
  - anorgasmia and sexual inhibition
  - premature ejaculation in the absence of other marital problems
  - monosymptomatic phobia (heights, spiders, dark, snakes, etc.)
  - stress and anxiety following a house move
  - migraine headaches, stress-related
  - witnessed a violent incident at work (post-traumatic stress)
  - irritable bowel syndrome as a response to stress and anxiety
  - adjustment reaction following divorce

- *Problems of moderate severity*
  - stress at work leading to depression, alcohol misuse and problems with the police
  - anxiety, depression, insomnia, mid-life crisis, atypical grief reaction following father's death
  - decompensation after gynaecological operation for cancer
  - impotence and lack of libido since wife's hysterectomy
  - compulsive picking of eyebrows and eyelashes
  - single parent with two jobs and two young children, depressed, mother died recently, youngest son in trouble with police
  - anxiety, somatic symptoms, apprehensive about unspecified disasters, depression, marital problems, irritable bowel syndrome
  - divorcing, husband sexually abused their children, one child in psychotherapy
  - anxiety, depression, somatic symptoms, termination of pregnancy with congenitally malformed baby

— atypical grief reaction following toddler's accidental death

— longstanding dependency on tranquillizers, lost mother at an early age, sister schizophrenic

— unconsummated marriage, marital problems, deprived childhood

— anxiety, hyperventilation, severe headaches, claustrophobia since air raid shelter in World War II, traumatic nightmares

— systemic lupus erythematosis, relationship problems with husband and daughter

— gross obesity, relationship problems

— AIDS phobia, compulsive handwashing, panic attacks

- *Severe psychological problems*

  — panic attacks, suicidal depression, obsessive-compulsive disorder, alcohol misuse, longstanding relationship problems, unable to work, borderline personality disorder

  — suicidally depressed, unable to continue studies, eating disorder, physically and emotionally abused as a child, borderline personality disorder

  — early retirement due to depression, unable to form intimate relationships with women, schizoid personality disorder

  — sexual perversion, alcohol misuse, sexual abuse of children

  — inability to adjust to colostomy, lack of intimate relationships, frequent attender at surgery, high utilizer of hospital services, obsessive-compulsive personality disorder

  — aggression, banned from previous GP surgery, prison sentence, violent with partner and baby, antisocial personality disorder

  — physically abused by both parents, sexually abused by father who made her pregnant, father imprisoned, single parent, both husbands violent, relationship problems, eating disorder, borderline personality disorder

  — depression, anorexia nervosa, alcohol misuse, distressed by sadomasochistic relationship with husband, mother died recently, recently lost her job, personality disorder, several psychiatric admissions, referred for psychosexual problems

— sexually abused by previous counsellor, childhood history of sexual and emotional abuse, longstanding relationship problems, homicidal and suicidal risk, borderline personality disorder

— divorced, pathological jealousy with new girlfriend, sexual perversions, anger/aggression, narcissistic personality disorder.

All these patients were referred for psychological treatment by their GP. Some can profit from a short-term intervention while those with complex problems will almost certainly need longer-term work, assuming they are able to engage in psychotherapy (Claxton and Turner, 1997; Parker, Leyland and Paxton, 1997). Some of the most disturbed may be poor risks for psychotherapy and may be more effectively managed within a community mental health team when psychiatric emergencies occur.

GP REFERRAL PATTERNS
FOR PSYCHOLOGICAL PROBLEMS

Where do GPs refer patients with different psychological problems? Depending on their level of specialist training, some GPs prefer to counsel certain patients themselves. If they refer on, their options may include practice counsellors, community psychiatric nurses, clinical psychologists in primary and secondary care, psychiatrists, and consultant psychotherapists. Some counselling psychologists are beginning to work in primary care in the UK, but they are few in number at present.

An inconsistent pattern of GP referral for psychological problems has been found in a series of recent studies. Sibbald et al. (1993) found similar rates of referral for anxiety, depression and stress-related illness to practice counsellors, community psychiatric nurses (CPNs) and clinical psychologists. Clinical psychologists saw more patients with psychosexual problems, eating disorders, phobias, and obsessive-compulsive disorder, while practice counsellors saw more people with bereavement reactions and marital problems. Not surprisingly, CPNs saw more patients with psychotic illness and drug and alcohol dependency. Both clinical psychologists and CPNs saw more patients with personality disorder than did counsellors.

Burton, Sadgrove and Selwyn (1995) audited the work of a practice counsellor and a clinical psychology direct access service in Coventry. They found that counsellors in general practice saw significantly more patients with anxiety, depression, marital problems, child management and physical illness than did clinical psychologists, who treated more patients with relationship problems and personality disorders. Clinical psychologists saw more patients with serious emotional problems such as those with past psychiatric problems and histories of childhood sexual abuse. Clark, Hook and Stein (1997) similarly found that specialist services saw more complex cases than counsellors. The principal diagnoses seen by counsellors in their study were relationship problems, depression, anxiety and bereavement reactions.

Cheston (1995) compared patients being seen by clinical psychologists in primary and secondary care, and found they did not differ in terms of 'caseness' on a standardized psychological test. However, the overall number of symptoms and symptom intensity was higher among patients seen in the secondary care setting. Gordon (1995) found that patients seen by practice counsellors tended to present with psychosocial problems rather than formal psychiatric diagnoses. Their symptom level was comparable to people referred to secondary mental health services, however they less often had a history of past psychiatric disorder.

O'Neill-Byrne and Browning (1996) compared GP referrals to psychiatrists, clinical psychologists and CPNs in two practices where all three professions offered in-house sessions in the surgery – an arrangement which is atypical in the UK as a whole. In this setting, most patients with depression or personality disorder were referred to psychiatrists, while anxiety and panic disorders were the largest single category referred to CPNs and clinical psychologists. A large proportion of the psychologists' referrals fell into the catch-all 'other' category which included relationship difficulties, lack of confidence and low self-esteem. When there is no in-surgery psychiatrist, referral patterns can be very different to those described.

In a pilot study of ten GPs in four practices in Surrey, considerable overlap was found between referrals to practice counsellors and CPNs who were members of a community mental health team (Ward and Loewenthal, 1997). As expected, CPNs saw more patients with schizophrenia, manic-depression, and long-term problems. However, eight diagnoses were referred either to CPNs or counsellors: short-term problems, anxiety/panic attacks, marital problems, neurotic disorders, bereavement, anorexia, other eating disorders, and sexual abuse. Criteria used by GPs in deciding where to refer patients included patient variables and GP variables:

1. Patient preference, age, diagnosis, financial standing, involvement with other professionals, insight, and need for home visits.

2. GP knowledge of the patient, personal interest in counselling, links with other counselling services, past experience of counselling, time

available to consider options, geographical location of the service, and length of the practice counsellor's waiting list (CPNs had no waiting lists in their community mental health teams).

Burton and Ramsden (1994) compared GP referrals to outpatient psychiatry, clinical psychology, CPNs and practice counsellors in Hertfordshire. Patients with psychotic problems including major depression were referred to outpatient psychiatry and CPNs, reactive depression mainly to counsellors and psychiatrists, and most of the eating disorder referrals were made to psychiatrists and psychologists. Psychologists received the majority of referrals for habit disorders, psychosomatic problems, anxiety, panic attacks, phobias, and obsessive-compulsive disorder, while counsellors received most of the marital problems, adjustment reactions to physical illness, bereavement reactions and stress and lifestyle problems. Counsellors received more sexual problem referrals than any other group. Somewhat worryingly, 67 per cent of GPs said they referred cases of childhood abuse to counsellors. Nearly all GPs said they would refer relationship problems to counsellors, whose skills may or may not be adequate to the task when there is an underlying personality disorder. The picture with personality disorder was mixed, with half referring to psychologists and half to the psychiatric unit. A referral rate of 24 per cent of these patients to counsellors gave some cause for concern, as some of them may not have trainings equipping them to deal with these difficult patients.

In a recent study of GP referral patterns in surgeries with in-house counsellors, 80 per cent of GPs referred to practice counsellors when one was available. Among GPs who did not have access to a counsellor, the referral rate to clinical psychologists was almost four times that of GPs who had a counsellor in the surgery (Heywood, 1997). This suggests that some of the patients who might previously have been referred to secondary clinical psychology services are now being seen by counsellors based in GP practices.

Parry and Richardson (1996) observed that in the absence of guidelines on which patients are most appropriately seen by a counsellor or other psychological therapist in primary care, patterns of referral to different services vary widely across the country. GPs tend to develop their own custom and practices concerning which patient is referred where, with the unfortunate result that some patients are seen and assessed by a number of different services before receiving treatment by one of them. The Camden and Islington MAAG (1996) has published a set of guidelines on the appropriate referral of patients with different kinds of psychological problems. Three psychological treatments readily available locally were considered: counselling, cognitive-behaviour therapy (usually offered by clinical psychologists), and psychodynamic psychotherapy.

> *Counselling* is considered most suitable for adjustment to life events, illnesses and losses (including bereavement), situational anxiety and stress, low mood and subclinical depression, interpersonal problems (assertion, self-confidence, problems of intimacy) and marital and relationship problems. While psychodynamic or cognitive-behavioural therapy may also be appropriate treatments, cost considerations suggest that counselling be tried in the first instance.
>
> *Cognitive-behavioural therapy* is the treatment of choice for panic attacks, phobias, generalized anxiety disorder, obsessions and compulsions, and behaviour problems such as impulse control, sleep problems and habit disorders. CBT may also be appropriate in major depression, eating disorders, and post-traumatic stress disorder.
>
> *Psychodyamic psychotherapy* is most appropriate for personality disorders, more severe interpersonal and social difficulties, and may also be appropriate for major depression, eating disorders, and post-traumatic stress disorder. Drug and alcohol problems, and psychosexual problems are best referred to specialist resources in the locality.
>
> *Severity, chronicity and complexity* of the problem should also contribute to referral decisions. Less severe problems involve only minor impairment of the activities of daily living. Chronic problems have been present for a year or more. Complex problems are those which are marked by other comorbid disorders, a previous history of unsuccessful treatment, and the involvement of a number of agencies with the patient. By and large, less severe, less complex problems of recent onset are most suitable for counselling.

(Camden and Islington MAAG, 1996, pp. 9–13)

The Leeds MIND referral guidelines for counselling in primary care (Rain, 1996) are similar to those of Camden and Islington MAAG with some important additions: response to a life crisis, relationship problems, anxiety and stress, breakdown in coping, depression, psychogenic physical problems and somatization, high utilizers of medical services, and pain management.

PATIENT CHARACTERISTICS THAT PREDICT THERAPEUTIC OUTCOME

Before considering therapy models in Chapter 3, we need to ask at the referral stage which patient characteristics will affect the outcome of psychological therapy. Patients' expectations of care, the effects of culture and gender, patients' goals for treatment, motivation for change, psychological-mindedness, and the quality of their existing relationships will all affect the success of treatment. In its advice to GPs, the Camden and Islington MAAG (1996) highlights three patient variables which are of particular importance in the referral process:

> *Patient preference* refers to the wish to receive one form of treatment in preference to another. Preference may be for length (brief vs. long-term) or for type of therapy (cognitive-behavioural therapy vs. psychodynamic psychotherapy). Matching patients to their preferred treatment tends to result in fewer dropouts and better outcomes. Those patients who prefer a short-term approach may be most suitable for counselling; those who prefer a structured treatment focused on symptom resolution may be most suitable for cognitive-behavioural work; those who prefer a longer, more exploratory approach are most likely to benefit from psychodynamic psychotherapy.

> *Interest in self-exploration* is the extent to which the patient is able to relate symptoms to other aspects of their life experience, along with an interest in exploring these links more fully. Interest in self-exploration is important for psychodynamic psychotherapy, and helpful for counselling and cognitive-behaviour therapy. When patients are interested principally in symp-

tom relief, cognitive-behaviour therapy is the best choice.

Capacity to tolerate frustration and psychic pain means the ability to tolerate emotional frustration and distressing states of mind without acting on them, for example by dropping out of treatment. Poor impulse control is a poor prognostic sign for all psychological treatments, but it is a particularly difficult problem in psychodynamic psychotherapy. When the patient shows relatively poor tolerance of frustration and psychic pain, cognitive-behaviour therapy or counselling may be more effective.

(Camden and Islington MAAG, pp. 6–8)

Motivation for change is another important predictor of outcome. A six-stage model of motivation for change has emerged from American research into recovery from addictions, but is applicable to many types of change in psychotherapy:

Pre-contemplation: the person either has or has not considered changing, but is not really interested in changing

Contemplation: aware that there would be benefits from changing and that current behaviour is harmful, however has not yet made the decision to change

Determination: poised on the brink of change and ready for suggestions as to how to go about it

Action: active efforts at getting help, finding alternatives, and changing other related habits

Maintenance: can be a struggle for years before a person feels the problem is no longer lurking in the wings

Relapse: most people who change an addictive behaviour have at least one relapse.

(Prochaska and DiClemente, 1986)

The relevance to referral decisions in psychotherapy is that people at the pre-contemplation stage are not interested in changing, and efforts to refer them will go unheeded. Many people with personality disorders are at the pre-contemplation stage: other people have difficulty living with them, but they do not perceive themselves as having a problem. Those at the contemplation stage may be willing to accept referral, but only at the determination stage are they truly ready to receive help.

Another model for dealing with stressful situations has been described by Stuart and Lieberman (1993, p. 135): *leave it, change it, accept it as it is* (getting support elsewhere), or *reframe it* (interpret the situation differently). If we take the example of an intolerable relationship with a partner, those who decide to leave may need help in weighing up the best and worst possible outcomes and the costs and benefits, and making plans for adequate support at the time of separation. Those who want to change the relationship may need in-depth individual or couples therapy in order to understand their contribution to the problem. Those who decide they must accept it as it is because the costs of leaving are too great may need psychotherapeutic support to come to that decision. Those who decide to interpret their situation differently may also need guidance from a therapist. Each of these strategies may be understood as a motivation for a particular kind of change, and that kind of change may suggest a particular form of psychological therapy.

Psychological-mindedness is an important predictor of therapeutic outcome, closely related to interest in self-exploration, already described. Although it has long been considered an important prerequisite for psychodynamic therapy, psychological-mindedness may best predict outcome in short-term group therapy. McCallum and Piper (1996) point out that the term has been used interchangeably with insight, introspection, self-awareness, self-reflection, and capacity for self-observation. When used in the context of psychotherapy, psychological-mindedness usually implies an habitual attendance to one's thoughts, motives and feelings – reading between the lines of behaviour, an interest in one's own and others' unconscious processes, and an ability to work in the transference. These attributes are important in assessing a patient's suitability for psychodynamic psychotherapy.

The *quality of patients' existing relationships* is a predictor of some importance in psychodynamic psychotherapy, as it provides useful information on the likelihood of a patient engaging with the therapist at an emotional level. Patients with few or no friends, especially if this is a lifelong pattern as in schizoid or paranoid personality disorder, are difficult to engage in treatment and the outlook for many of them psychotherapeutically is poor. One element of existing relationships is the *social support* available:

- *Excellent*: partner, family, friends, colleagues

- *Good*: partner, family, some friends

- *Fair*: unsupportive partner, some family support

- *Poor*: no partner, unsupportive family, few friends

- *None*: isolated, without family or friends.

Another element is the *quality of the patient's intimate relationships*. This 5-point rating scale is adapted from Howard, Lueger and O'Mahoney's *Global Assessment Scale* (1991):

1. Steady relationship with mutual affection, warmth, support, and effective communication; satisfactory sexual relations; conflicts are minor and rapidly resolved.

2. Steady relationship generally provides affection and support; good communication; occasional conflicts but these are readily resolved; sexual relationship is generally satisfactory to both partners.

3. Relationship sometimes lacks affection, warmth, and support; sexual relations are less than satisfactory or are somewhat lacking in intimacy.

4. Lack of support; only rare, occasional expressions of warmth; sexual interest diminished or excessive without regard to mate's feelings, pleasure, etc.

5. Warmth lacking throughout; no sexual initiative or advances are grossly inappropriate and inconsiderate; risk of physical or sexual violence.

— No information; romantic relationship does not exist due to lifestyle choice (e.g. celibacy) or to other factors (e.g. death of a spouse); or no current relationship and not seeking a relationship.

Where the patient's intimate relationships are abusive, primitive or absent, engagement in a therapeutic relationship may be difficult. Some patients who are functioning at a low level interpersonally can still be helped at a symptomatic level by brief counselling or cognitive-behaviour therapy.

The effects of demographic variables such as *gender, socio-economic status* and *culture* on psychotherapy are complex. Women are over-represented among those who seek psychological therapy, and the gender of the therapist may be important for those with histories of childhood sexual abuse. Many such women prefer a woman therapist, although this is not always the case. Most studies of outcome as a function of patient gender have produced negative results, but the match between patient and therapist on gender and personality variables is a more salient issue. Early termination of therapy is often significantly related to lower socio-economic status, a factor to be borne in mind at the time of referral. Educational level also needs to be considered when assessing suitability for insight-oriented psychotherapies.

Most of the research on psychotherapy with *culturally diverse populations* has been done in the USA, but studies are beginning to appear in the UK. All ethnic groups are heterogenous, despite prevailing stereotypes, and each patient needs to be met as an individual. At another level, however, some generalizations can be made about ethnic group characteristics to maximize the likelihood that interventions will be effective. Sue, Zane and Young (1994) reviewed the American research and concluded that certain conditions may be related to therapeutic effectiveness: ethnic similarity for patients and therapists in some minority groups; the use of culturally responsive forms of treatment; and the training of therapists to work with members of culturally diverse groups.

Some Asian patients tends not to make a distinction between emotional and physical problems and attribute both to bodily imbalances. Asians may also be more likely to believe that mental health is enhanced by the avoidance of negative thinking and by self-discipline. There is a tendency for some Asian patients, particularly those suffering from depression, to present with more somatic complaints than other patients. Mahtani and Marks (1994) describe the development of a primary care service that is racially and culturally appropriate in Tower Hamlets, East London. Their team consists of 8 Caucasian and 3 Asian members (two Bengali-speaking and one Hindi-speaking). Although this balance is not representative of the community, the shortfall in clinical psychologists from ethnic backgrounds makes it virtually impossible to match staff with the local population. An Asian psychology assistant speaks to patients in their native language having explained that she will occasionally be having a brief discussion with her English-speaking colleague. In this way the patient has immediate access to one psychologist who speaks Bengali and another psychologist with more clinical experience. Sometimes a relative of the patient can act as interpreter, but the provision of psychological help with interpreters has not always proved to be a smooth way of working. Use of an interpreter is advised only when there is no other option. One problem has arisen in translating the concept of *anxiety* for

Bangladeshi patients, as there is no equivalent for this word in Bengali.

There is a low referral rate of ethnic minority patients to many primary care psychology teams. One recent study in inner city Birmingham demonstrated that white patients who were cases on the General Health Questionnaire were significantly more likely to be identified by GPs than black or Asian people (Odell et al., 1996). In some general practices, patients from other cultures are more likely to be offered medication than psychological therapy. Other issues which affect the rate at which patients from ethnic minorities consult is the degree to which there is a cultural belief that psychological problems should be solved within the family. Issues of shame and honour may prevent those in need from seeking the help of a mental health professional. In particular, there is a deep stigma attached to seeing a psychiatrist among Muslims.

In related research, Kelleher and Islam (1994) described the difficulties that diabetic Bangladeshis may experience in following Western food restrictions that come into conflict with Muslim dietary rules, or as one patient put it, 'God is in front; doctor is behind.' Counsellor sensitivity to cultural beliefs and practices is important, including dietary rules, fasts, prayer rituals, and dress; first, second and third generation issues; post-traumatic stress disorder among refugees; the role of women in the family, attitudes toward contraception, abortion, homosexuality, and psychosexual problems; faith healing and belief in the role of malign spiritual forces in illness; arranged marriages, mixed marriages, communication patterns, the extended family, and rituals at times of birth and death. Qureshi (1989) and McAvoy and Donaldson (1990) provide a comprehensive discussion of these and other issues. Cross-cultural psychosexual counselling may founder because of a lack of understanding of cultural beliefs about sexuality. For example, many Indians believe that semen that is not ejaculated travels up the spinal column to the brain and makes the man more powerful (Kakar, 1989).

Suicides in women aged 16–24 in England and Wales are nearly four times as common among Asian as opposed to British women. Dosanjh, Marshall and Yazdani (1977) surveyed the mental health needs of young Asian women in Newham, in London. Themes most commonly mentioned in focus groups were sacrifice, honour, and coping. To be seen suffering brings shame to the family, including previous generations. Highly valued among Asian communities are women who are 'copers', sacrificing their own needs to protect the family's honour. Seeking help for emotional problems is viewed negatively; therefore many Asian women who find their way to help are in crisis situations. Unable to speak their distress, some resort to the language of the body – physical symptoms. Women may be seen either as copers or 'mad' ('pagal'), with few concepts for problems that fall in between. Women in the focus groups described experiences of racism and bullying. They reported high parental expectations to practise their religion and to succeed in education, career and marriage. Marital and relationship issues, periods of transition into the husband's family after marriage, and domestic violence were common themes. Few women had an understanding of the usefulness of counselling or psychotherapy, and many assumed that GPs, especially Asian GPs, viewed help-seeking for emotional problems as negative.

Prevention of mental illness among ethnic minority patients was reviewed by Patel (1996), who provides a detailed bibliography. Somatization of psychological problems is common in all ethnic groups, whereas 'psychologization' is more common among the white middle classes. Most research has concentrated on black or Asian immigrants, with a relative lack of attention given to white immigrants from Ireland or Poland. Patel suggests that the emphasis in the literature on psychosis in African-Caribbeans and parasuicide in young Asian women may reflect popular stereotypes of West Indians as out of control and Asians as too controlled. Such stereotypes may interfere with an accurate diagnosis. Common difficulties in detecting psychological distress in patients of ethnic minorities include a greater tendency to present with physical symptoms, varying expressions of distress, greater likelihood of concurrent physical illness, inhibition of cues of depression from the patient, difficulties in judging the patient's demeanour, ascribing abnormal behaviour to cultural factors, and misinterpreting culturally appropriate behaviour. Unfortunately in Britain patients from ethnic minorities are rarely referred for psychotherapy. Racially sensitive therapy does not necessarily have to be from a therapist of the same ethnic background, but from one aware of racial and cultural factors in the therapeutic process.

SUMMARY AND RECOMMENDATIONS

If access to psychological help in primary care is to be improved, barriers at each of the five 'filter' levels need to be removed. In practical terms this means helping GPs become better diagnosticians of psychological problems and improving their ability to make appropriate referrals for psychological help. Mental health promotion projects may improve patients' ability to recognize and cope with psychological problems before they become severe, but this issue remains outside the scope of this book. An At Risk Checklist on the front of each patient's medical record would increase the likelihood of psychological problems being detected by GPs.

The doctor's task begins with imaginative listening and putting the symptom in the context of the patient's life situation. The presence of a clearly identifiable psychological problem has been estimated to occur in as many as 33 per cent of GP attenders, only about one-half of whom are detected as having a psychological problem by the GP. Worldwide, the most common psychological disorders in primary care are depression, generalized anxiety, and alcohol use disorders. Depression in the context of chronic physical illness is often missed on the grounds that the patient 'has good reasons to be depressed'. Comorbid psychological problems and substance abuse occur frequently. When the diagnosis of one is clear, the presence of the other should be assessed.

Since GPs miss depression approximately 50 per cent of the time, attention needs to be given to continuing education for experienced GPs as well as to training schemes for young doctors. Screening questionnaires may have a role in the improvement of GPs' ability to detect psychological problems. Equity in the provision of psychological services needs to be ensured, especially for the elderly, children, 'heartsink' patients, and those whose first language is not English. 'Heartsink' occurs in the GP: what frustrates or angers one GP may be patiently tolerated by a colleague. Balint groups may help GPs to discover which type of patient 'turns them off' and aid in the development of creative management strategies.

Somatizers and repeat attenders may profit from psychological intervention. The high levels of psychological morbidity in primary care fail to confirm the impression in some quarters that these patients are the 'worried well'. Adult patients bring an enormous range of psychological problems to their GP, many of which are at the severe end of the psychopathological spectrum. All mental health workers at the primary care level need to be capable of recognizing the presence of severe mental illness and making an appropriate referral to secondary psychiatric services.

An inconsistent pattern of GP referral for psychological problems has been found in a series of studies. In the absence of guidelines on which patients are most appropriately seen by a counsellor or other psychological therapist in primary care, patterns of referral to different services vary widely across localities. Some patients are seen and assessed by a number of services before receiving treatment by one of them. Each time a patient is rejected for treatment, potential harm is done. The Camden and Islington MAAG (1996) has published a set of useful guidelines on the appropriate referral of patients with different kinds of psychological problems.

Patients' expectations of care, including the effects of culture and gender, their goals for treatment, motivation for change, psychological-mind-edness, and the quality of their existing relationships will all affect the success of treatment. Three patient variables which are of particular importance in the referral process are patient preference for treatment, interest in self-exploration, and capacity to tolerate frustration and psychic pain. A six-stage model of motivation for change may be helpful in assessing readiness for psychological therapy: is this patient at the pre-contemplation, contemplation, determination, or action stage? Patients at the pre-contemplation and contemplation stages may have poor motivation to seek therapy. Patients from ethnic minorities have special needs which are poorly met in many areas.

3

THERAPY MOD ELS AND PROFESSIONAL DISCIPLINES

SHORT- AND LONGER-TERM TREATMENTS

'How much counselling or psychotherapy is enough for this patient?' This is a pressing question in the present cost-containment climate in health care. The answer depends not only on the patient's problem, motivation, preferences for treatment and personality profile, but also on what kind of change is needed in a particular case. For some patients the principal concern is symptom remission – 'I want to be rid of my panic attacks' – but the resolution of anxiety symptoms is very different from altering long-term relationship difficulties. Anxiety symptoms in a patient without a comorbid personality disorder may be treated in six to twelve sessions; relationship problems in a borderline personality with a collection of associated symptoms may take a great deal longer.

We will address this issue in another context in Chapter 6, but *outcome measures* need to be selected carefully when answers to our question are attempted. In the managed care environment, the overriding concern has been reduction in medical utilization rates: if a treatment results in a drop in medical utilization rates, it has been successful – it has saved the insurance company money. But patients may see their GP less frequently for a variety of reasons. A distressed patient may have been so poorly treated as a result of a GP referral to a mental health professional that they do not wish to consult their doctor ever again. Such a case could hardly be called a treatment success, but the medical utilization rate has dropped to zero.

As we shall see in Chapter 6, some outcome measures tap a reduction in overall distress or an improvement in overall quality of life. Other measures provide fine-grained analysis of changes in symptomatology. But symptom remission in and of itself may not be an adequate outcome measure, because of the problem of comorbidity – there may be more than one problem, including an underlying personality disorder which is not picked up on a symptom inventory. Psychodynamic therapists argue that changes in object relations from more primitive to more mature, greater ego strength, improved impulse control and an increase in insight are important outcome measures. Despite our relative lack of knowledge in this area, the issue of optimal length of treatment is being hotly debated on both sides of the Atlantic.

THE MANAGED CARE CONTROVERSY

Since the advent of health maintenance organizations (HMOs) in the USA, managed care has transformed patterns of psychotherapy provision. In the UK, 'performance indicators' in the NHS have placed the emphasis on throughput (the number of patient contacts in a given month) with the implication of 'Why wasn't it more?' Clinical psychologists among others have felt the need to put the case to NHS managers that quantity in mental health care is not the same as quality. The 'Körner' data required of most NHS departments has amounted to a crude head count rather than meaningful outcome measures reflecting clinically significant change.

UK practitioners have much to learn from the American experiment with managed care. Few issues in recent years have stimulated more heated debate in the professional literature. A survey of some recent titles will serve to illustrate the tone:

Managed Care, Brief Therapy, and Therapeutic Integrity (Stern, 1993).

Unconscious Fiscal Convenience (Cummings, 1995).

Provision of Psychotherapy under Managed Health Care: A Growing Crisis and National Nightmare (Karon, 1995).

Managed Care: Is it the Corpse in the Living Room? An Exposé (Pipal, 1995).

How to Get Along with Big Brother: Surviving Managed Mental Healthcare in the 21st Century (Tuckfelt et al., 1997).

The Survival of Psychoanalytic Psychotherapy in Managed Care: 'Reports of My Death are Greatly Exaggerated' (Pollack, 1996).

Managed Care and the Borderline Patient: Where treatment Was, There Management Will Be (Lerner, 1996).

The Blind Oppressing the Recalcitrant: Psychoanalysis, Managed Care, and Family Systems (Stechler, 1996).

Is Long-term Therapy Unethical: Toward a Social Ethic in an Era of Managed Care (Austad, 1996).

Breaking Free of Managed Care: A Step-by-step Guide to Regaining Control of

Your Practice (Ackley, 1997).
The Private Practice of Subversion (Brown, 1997).

Cummings (1995) argues that managed care was introduced because as long as insurance companies were paying the bill, an increasing number of patients were willing to undergo 'unnecessarily protracted therapies' while their therapists rationalized these as leading to self-actualization. When insurance companies were paying for these unnecessarily long-term therapies, the therapist was allowed to develop a double standard, where overcharging the patient was unthinkable but overcharging an insurance company was appropriate. This phenomenon he termed 'unconscious fiscal convenience'. Austad (1996) has argued that long-term therapy may even be unethical. Managed care, in order to contain medical costs, has restricted almost all reimbursable psychotherapy to short-term (1–25 session) and very short-term (1–6 session) models.

Stern (1993) argues that managed care is effectively a form of externally mandated brief therapy achieved by limiting the number of sessions, placing dollar caps on annual psychotherapy benefits, or adopting utilization review (case management) mechanisms. He suggests that externally mandated brief therapy violates the integrity of the therapeutic relationship, which he defines as the establishment and maintenance by a competent therapist of the conditions necessary for successful therapeutic work. Achieving structural personality change or an emotional attachment to the therapist may be necessary means toward problem-solving for some patients. Much emphasis has been placed in managed care on avoiding 'unhealthy dependency on the therapist'. For those personality disordered and abused patients who are incapable of intimacy, however, the capacity to trust and become safely dependent on the therapist are crucial outcomes that will not be achieved in 1–6 sessions (see Tait, 1997, for a practical discussion and helpful review).

Because many insurance companies are unwilling to fund treatment of personality disorders (Axis II of the DSM-IV), their representative may tell the treating clinician: 'We don't like Axis II diagnoses, they take too long to treat. Give this patient an Axis I diagnosis and treat that.' Many clinicians have felt forced into providing incomplete or inaccurate diagnoses in order to continue to earn a living and remain on the company's panel of preferred providers. Accurate, detailed assessment is the hallmark of good clinical practice. When third-party reimbursement requires clinicians either to fabricate a reimbursable diagnosis or actively hide severe pathology, serious ethical questions must be asked.

Similarly, when longstanding hard-to-treat traumatic issues are shelved in favour of an immediate problem in problem-focused therapy, the result can be traumatic for the patient. Lambert (1997) describes how a problem-focused therapist who offers 1–8 sessions to all of his patients deals with childhood sexual abuse: 'Let's not talk about that, you'll only feel worse if we do. Let's pick an immediate issue in your life right now, and make progress with that.' If anything like this goes on in clinicians' work with abused patients, what is likely to result is re-traumatization. In cases of childhood sexual abuse where the father was the abuser, the patient may have been told something similarly disconfirming by her mother: 'Let's not talk about that.' If longer-term problems are being handled this way in some sectors of managed care, ethical questions must be asked. As Karon (1995) put it: 'Therapists who do not want to permit their patients to tell them about their real psychological problems can survive well in such a system, but ethical psychotherapists are demoralized' (p. 6).

Stern argues that 'making the therapist obsolete as quickly as possible' (Cummings and Sayama, 1995) or 'hitting the ground running' with early formulation and intervention (Budman and Gurman, 1988) can disturb and pervert the fragile process through which patient and therapist establish their unique mode of working together. Premature closure on the patient's problem or mode of intervention may lead to loss of the patient, either literally or affectively. Another crucial dimension of the therapeutic situation is safety, which is often violated in the utilization review process. Clinicians have repeatedly to justify their treatment plans to a third party and if continuing treatment is refused the patient may feel abandoned. Stern argues that such intrusions make meaningful treatment almost impossible and reinforce more disturbed patients' pathology, along the lines that they always suspected their problem was unmanageable. Caps on the number of sessions permitted are already occurring now in parts of the NHS.

Stern (1993) argues, and I agree, that the decision to terminate therapy should ideally be up to the patient. Especially for those in whom early loss is a prominent feature, when patients are able to make the ending their own positive step, rather than having to accept an abrupt ending imposed on them by others (which re-enacts the original trauma), therapy is truly finished. Stern favours a revised system in the USA in which a percentage of the fee, perhaps 50 per cent, is covered for one session of psychotherapy per week, so that those needing long-term therapy can obtain it. As he puts it: 'Physicians don't remove a cast when a broken bone is half-healed or stop radiation treatment when the cancer is half-controlled. Likewise, we shouldn't stop psychotherapy when a patient's problem is half-solved' (p. 172). He argues that the model of brief intermittent psychotherapy throughout the life cycle may be suitable for those patients who use therapy in this way, but the proponents of this model (Cummings and Sayama, 1995) imply that the model should also be made to work with patients whose problems are chronic, severe and disabling. Short- and very short-term therapy is not a panacea to be applied across the spectrum of pathology. When managed care companies refuse to pay for treatment deemed outside their responsibility, the cost is passed on to hospitals, schools, clinicians, social and governmental agencies – and most importantly, the patient (Lazarus, 1996b).

Shapiro (1995) argues that managed mental health care violates patients' rights to privacy, penalizes practitioners who refuse to break confidentiality by banning them from provider panels, exacerbates patients' anxiety by adding the worry about when therapy will end, creates a sense of mistrust between patient and practitioner through utilization reviews, and may restrict choice by requiring a change from a known and trusted therapist. It disrupts therapeutic timing and may create an atmosphere that judges and shames the patient by requiring periodic treatment review. Medication is sometimes coercively employed as a condition of treatment, and in order to shorten therapy. Those with drug and alcohol problems may be required to attend a 12-step programme regardless of whether it is suitable for that patient, and it may be stipulated that no psychotherapy will be underwritten by the insurance company until that 12-step programme has been successfully completed. If this begins to sound totalitarian, Karon (1995) points out that some HMOs require their employees, including psychologists, to sign a contract in which they agree never to criticize publically any of the practices of the HMO. Such 'gag clauses' have recently been declared illegal in some states.

A crucial difference between psychotherapy in the private sector and managed care has been raised by Pipal (1995): 'Managed care makes no effort to hide the fact that its sole goal is to bring people back to their premorbid levels of functioning. Absent is any reference to living fuller, more satisfactory lives . . . [But] no one can convince me that lasting repair of a spirit broken by years of emotional abuse can occur in six sessions or less' (pp. 325, 329). What is the level of premorbid functioning? In cases of personality disorder, this may be a very low level indeed. Emphasis in managed care is on 'medical necessity', although this remains a controversial entity in psychotherapy. In what does medical necessity consist in cases of comorbidity, for example? Is the therapist to treat only the life-threatening suicidal depression and ignore an obsessive-compulsive disorder that merely causes 'distress'? In cases of borderline personality disorder with multiple symptomatology, which of six different Axis I symptoms is it 'medically necessary' to treat?

Brown (1997) observes that while patients' benefit booklets may say they are covered for 20, 30 or even 50 sessions per year of psychotherapy, this statement is profoundly deceptive because, at the end of the day, only 'medically necessary' services are covered. 'Covered lives' may find that the therapist whom they have previously come to know and trust is not on the provider panel. Or their therapist may be removed from the panel in mid-treatment, with no consideration being given to the need to work through the traumatic ending. Therapists are 'like snap-on tools – anyone will do' (p. 454). Or, they may find their problem is not on the managed care list of treatable problems – for example, post-traumatic stress disorder, dissociative identity disorder, or borderline personality disorder, to name a few. Therapists may turn a blind eye to the severe diagnoses that are not covered and find instead a covered diagnosis, so they do not get dropped from the provider panel. Brown reminds us that, as Maslow suggested, therapist needs for survival may come before concerns about social justice.

In psychiatry, the risks of handing patients over to any psychiatrist in managed care were assessed by Westermeyer (1991). Seven cases were reviewed in which patients at major psychiatric risk received less than adequate care. Primary care physicians and bachelors' level case managers managed several of these cases without seeking appropriate psychiatric consultation. The deaths of five patients demonstrated the failure of a model which claims that any psychiatrist can substitute for any other, irrespective of pre-existing doctor–patient relationships.

A reality-based solution to the health care crisis would have to take into account the fact that research has yet to show that it is possible in psychotherapy radically to reduce cost and at the same time maintain quality (Welch, 1994). Managed care is, at its root, the economic incentive not to provide care. Some have suggested it be renamed managed cost (Howard and Mahoney, 1996). Welch argues that there is a powerful pressure which will ultimately undo managed care systems: reality. That reality is that 1–6 session contracts will not suffice for patients at the severe end of the spectrum. It takes considerable time for most patients to unlearn old patterns of behaviour and learn new ones (Alperin, 1997). Furthermore, the managed care system has led to inevitable self-serving abuses on the part of providers such as lying to patients, breaking confidentiality, and misrepresenting clinical truths to insurance companies in order to remain on provider panels. Other writers have observed that managed care fosters the violation of informed consent, abandonment of the patient when 'time is up', adversarial relationships within the triangle of patient, therapist, and insurer, scapegoating, and general mistrust.

Most of what is being funded in managed care at the moment is ultra-brief therapy, but as Miller (1996a) points out, there are no controlled studies of 2–6 session treatment. While mainstream psychotherapy has been shown to be effective in randomized controlled trials, evidence of efficacy is lacking in the ultra-brief therapies, especially regarding relapse or recurrence after treatment (Strupp, 1997). Rapid responders may not need as much treatment as longer-term patients, but research has shown that long-term patients have severer pathology and greater needs. Moreover, the quality of managed care outcome measures is poor, with most companies collecting only patient satisfaction data (91 per cent) and a dearth of companies gathering goal-attainment data (13 per cent). It is impossible to argue that quality care is being provided if outcome measures are grossly inadequate (Chapter 6).

Proponents of managed care argue that time-limited brief therapy is research supported and as effective as traditional therapy for most patients. However, Miller (1996b) points out that, correctly interpreted, the research shows that time-limited treatment is inferior to psychotherapy in which length of treatment is clinically determined. One of the most frequently cited studies has been the 'dose-response curve' of Howard et al. (1986). This study suggested that about half of patients undergoing psychotherapy showed significant improvement by the eighth session; optimal results were achieved for most patients within 26 sessions (six months, once a week); and more difficult cases could be significantly helped within a year. However, outcome scores reported in that paper were not necessarily drawn from the same patients over time, and some patients dropped out of therapy early. When outcomes of the same patients are obtained repeatedly at different points in their treatment, the 'curve' becomes a straight line: improvement continues linearly with time in treatment (Berman, 1996). Berman's study supports clinically determined termination: optimal results are obtained when the patient – not the managed care company – decides it is time to stop.

Psychodynamic therapies have come under particular fire in managed care, but continue to survive within it in their briefer forms, and in longer-term versions in the private sector. Alperin (1994) has written a trenchant critique of managed care from the perspective of psychoanalytic psychotherapy. He argues that managed care interferes with the provision of a secure and steady frame because when cases are reviewed every 5–10 sessions there is a constant threat that therapy will be terminated. It interferes with privacy and confidentiality by requiring frequent and detailed reporting by therapists, and it prevents the establishment of a secure therapeutic contract by frequent case reviews.

Alperin notes a disturbing feature which we have already observed about managed care, that therapists are advised to omit any reference to DSM-IV Axis II diagnoses (personality disorders) in correspondence with managed care companies. The reason behind this is that cover for these disorders will almost certainly be refused. The emphasis is on the relief of 'symptoms which result in identifiable impairment in functioning'. The fallacy in this argument is that personality disorders do result in identifiable and severe impairment in functioning, borderline and narcissistic personality disorders being the most obvious cases in point. However, managed care companies have adopted the language of psychopharmacology and behaviour therapy, an exclusive focus on symptoms and their alleviation. Psychodynamic psychotherapy, by contrast, is a comprehensive approach to the treatment of symptoms since it focuses on the resolution of conflicts within the underlying character structure.

Those psychodynamic therapists offering brief dynamic therapy will exclude from this treatment many patients with preoedipal conditions (that is, whose origin is in the first years of life, before the oedipal period), but preoedipal conditions comprise the bulk of most psychodynamic psychotherapists' practices. Will these patients obtain appropriate treatment in managed care? The short answer is that they will not.

A book has recently appeared devoted to the impact of managed care on psychodynamic treatment (Barron and Sands, 1996). In one of the chapters, Pollack (1996) argues that reports of the death of psychoanalytic psychotherapy have been greatly exaggerated. To the charge that intensive psychotherapy is not sufficiently cost effective, Pollack replies that appropriately prescribed psychodynamic outpatient psychotherapy is one of the most cost-efficient treatments today, when we consider that 70–80 per cent of the cost of all psychological and psychiatric care is for inpatient treatment. Hospital admission can be avoided in many cases by appropriate intensive outpatient psychotherapy. The 10–20 per cent of all patients who need more than six months of outpatient therapy require intensive psychodynamic treatment – not because short-term techniques or medications have not been tried, not because therapists are resistant to change, and not because of misdiagnosis or excessive 'dependency' – but because intensive psychotherapy is the treatment of choice for their condition.

A 'second generation' book on managed care is organized around areas of conflict and controversy (Lazarus, 1996a). Each chapter is framed as a question, among them, 'Is managed care ethical care?' and 'Who decides what is medically necessary?' These are serious and pressing issues. As might be expected, there has been a reactive swing back to private prac tice in some parts of the USA. Karon (1995) predicted that patients will learn 'that six sessions for everything is not psychotherapy; that therapists who are willing to pretend that six sessions for everything is reasonable do not even do those six sessions well; and that if they want help, they must escape managed care' (p. 8). Ackley (1997) explains why patients will choose to pay out-of-pocket for traditional services, and offers suggestions to practitioners on the local marketing of traditional services. The lessons for UK practitioners and managers in all of this are profound: six-session treatments are not a panacea for patients at the severe end of the continuum, many of whom present for treatment in primary care.

Offering six sessions to very needy patients with damaged backgrounds gives them a brief sample of what they need and discharges them to an uncertain future. There are at least four potential negative outcomes of 'six sessions for everything':

- Borderline patients who become attached to their therapist at the first or second session may make a serious suicide attempt when discharged after six weeks because they perceive the perceive the terrmination as an abandonment. In these cases, six sessions have not only not helped, they have been damaging to the patient.

- Other patients are not helped by six sessions and are passed from one clinician to another, each of whom offers brief or ultra-brief therapy while the underlying issues are left unaddressed. Frequently in these cases, no one has carried out an in-depth assessment of the patient. Not infrequently there is an underlying personality disorder and/or comorbidity.

- At the end of six sessions the patient may feel 'a little better, but counselling didn't change anything'. These patients often relapse or develop new symptoms.

- In other cases, the clinician offering the six-session package has not been trained to manage the patient's deep-seated problems, and specialist intervention is needed. Occasionally these cases have tragic outcomes.

On the positive side, six sessions can be used with carefully selected patients to motivate them for longer-term therapy and onward referral. Of course, some patients find they need only one or two sessions to air their problem and ventilate their feelings, and are happy to be discharged at that time. However, it should be their choice to stop treatment at that point, not the managed care company.

State legislation is beginning to curb some of the worst abuses of managed care. Missouri now bars managed care organizations from including 'gag clauses' in their contracts with providers. Such clauses often prohibit therapists from telling patients about all treatment options, particularly those not covered by the managed care company. Managed care companies must now give providers 60-day notice of their removal from provider panels and specify the reasons for their removal. Utilization reviewers must be trained and licensed at the same level as the therapist whose work they are reviewing. Grievance procedures are now guaranteed in Missouri for patients, allowing them to appeal denials of coverage to an impartial third party (Sleek, 1997a).

More seriously, managed care companies are seen by a growing number of psychotherapy researchers as 'cherrypicking' treatment research, basing their treatment guidelines on narrow, controlled outcome studies that make brief therapy appear to be the treatment of choice. This practice ignores indications that those treatments may be far less effective in real clinical settings, and it ignores or misinterprets data demonstrating the superior benefits of long-term therapy for certain disorders (Sleek, 1997b). As we shall demonstrate in our literature review in Chapter 6, efficacy in randomized controlled trials is not the same as effectiveness in clinical settings.

The 'six sessions for everything' ethos has already arrived in the UK in the form of Employee Assistance Programmes (EAPs). When an employer buys an EAP, it has not 'cost' the employee anything for the six free sessions that are on offer, but after six sessions treatment is terminated. Actually, it may have cost patients emotionally because some of them have experienced what it is they need, but they cannot receive enough of it to be of benefit. These emotional costs are borne by the patient. The Keele EAP Evaluation Scale is being used to study patient satisfaction with two local authority EAPs, and the only area of dissatisfaction found was length of treatment (McLeod and Worrell, 1997). As is true of primary care, people with serious mental illness and histories of sustained trauma telephone EAP helplines. Many of them are not screened out at the assessment stage and referred for specialist help, but receive six sessions from a counsellor as do those with mild or moderate problems. The damaging potential of six sessions for severe lifelong difficulties needs urgently to be researched.

In the NHS, 42 per cent of clinical psychologists recently surveyed said they were under external pressure to increase their caseloads, 34 per cent felt external pressure to increase weekly face-to-face contact with patients, 32 per cent felt under pressure to reduce the number of sessions they offered each patient, and 49 per cent felt under pressure to increase throughput generally (Skinner and Baul, 1997). Some psychologists undertook group work in order to be seen to be treating more patients. Others were told to do assessments that did not always lead to therapy. One respondent said, 'Client disposal is the new mission statement.' Another commented, 'Contracts are with GPs who are obsessed with the number of patients seen in a session or per year, and reluctant to see consultation meetings as part of the process to be included in contracts.' About half of respondents felt under pressure to offer sub-optimal treatment in order to increase the number of clients seen. Ethical questions need to be raised about such practices.

Gordon (1998) suggests that primary care counsellors may need help from their supervisors to 'avoid uncovering material which could not be dealt with in brief therapy and could potentially leave the client feeling worse rather than better'. In the long term this is an unsatisfactory answer to the problem because it is akin to turning a blind eye to the full extent of the patient's problems. Gordon admits that there is a significant minority of patients referred to counsellors in primary care who are unsuitable candidates for seven sessions of treatment.

We turn next to the three mainstream models of psychological therapy in primary care – psychodynamic, cognitive-behavioural and humanistic. Cognitive-analytic therapy, single-session therapy, 2+1 and other brief therapies will also be considered, and the role of group, couples and family therapies in primary care will be explored briefly. It is not possible in a book of this kind to describe all the psychological therapies presently in use, or to detail the range of treatments suitable for specific problems. A survey of the principal models in use will give a flavour of the kind of work that can be done. Much primary care work makes use of more than one model in an eclectic or integrative model. We consider one of the integrative therapies in detail – cognitive-analytic therapy.

PSYCHODYNAMIC PSYCHOTHERAPY

Psychodynamic therapists make genetic links between early childhood experiences and the patient's current character structure and symptomatology. The patient's emotional response to the therapist (transference) and the therapist's emotional response to the patient (countertransference) are also sources of learning. Key patterns of feeling and behaving from early childhood are repeated or 'transferred' onto people in the patient's adult life, including the therapist.

In Malan's model (1976, 1979), the triangle of insight (parent, therapist and current significant other) is interpreted to the patient each time it emerges in the material. For example, 'Given the pattern of physical and emotional abuse in your family, you came to expect that this was how you would be treated, so it was not surprising that you chose as a partner a man who would physically and emotionally abuse you. Now in therapy you expect that I will abuse you.' There are as many variants of this interpretation of the triangle as there are focal interpersonal issues brought by patients. The *current conflict* is a precipitating factor which has brought the patient for treatment, and the *nuclear conflict* is inferred from previous precipitating events, early traumatic experiences, or repetitive interactional patterns. Together, the current conflict and the nuclear conflict comprise the *focal issue* in brief psychodynamic psychotherapy. Elucidating the connection between the presenting problem and the nuclear conflict is part of making unconscious processes conscious, another hallmark of the psychodynamic approach. Dreams are very informative in this regard. Although described as 'brief', Malan's model consists of 20 sessions in the hands of an experienced therapist and 30 sessions when the therapist is inexperienced – three to five times as long as the six sessions currently in fashion.

More generally, self-defeating patterns from childhood are often unconsciously re-enacted in adult life. Once this pattern has been made conscious, the patient has the potential to achieve greater control over feelings and behaviour and avoid some of the repetitious negative outcomes of the past. Defence mechanisms are often a focus of interpretation in the psychodynamic model. A healthy respect on the part of the therapist for patients' needs to defend against painful or unwelcome material is important. Optimally, over time, defences become less rigid and more mature, but this may be a long-term process if the presenting pathology is in the narcissistic or borderline spectrum.

Another feature of psychodynamic therapy is the establishment of a secure holding environment (Winnicott, 1965), one aspect of which is the provision of reliable boundaries. Sessions are conducted each week in the same place at the same time, and the therapist's punctuality, reliability, abstinence and confidentiality are integral parts of the therapeutic space. Molnos (1995) describes this 'special place in which the past can reappear in the here-and-now, a space in which past emotional conflicts are re-lived and understood with clarity, and in which new solutions to old problems are found' (p. 26).

A major development in psychodynamic theory has been a shift away from Freud's emphasis on drives, drive derivatives and defence mechanisms erected against them, toward an interpersonal or object relations base. (Paradoxically, objects in this context mean people. The original use of the term was that people in the patient's external world could become objects of the drives, eros and aggression.) Object relations therapy, Kohut's self-psychology, and Harry Stack Sullivan's interpersonal model are all variants of interpersonally based psychodynamic therapy. Ways of relating are also crucial to the diagnostic and treatment process in the therapeutic models of Malan, Luborsky, Strupp and Binder.

Psychodynamic psychotherapy may be conducted short or long term. Brief psychodynamic therapies have proliferated in recent years. A recent meta-analysis of 26 studies has shown them to be comparable in effectiveness to other treatments including cognitive-behavioural therapy, and most effective when therapists are specifically trained in short-term models (Anderson and Lambert, 1995). However, not all patients suitable for psychodynamic therapy are suitable for brief psychodynamic therapy. One charge commonly levelled against psychodynamic therapists is that they foster unhealthy dependency in their patients. What is missed by those who promote this view is that for some patients, developing the capacity to trust and to become securely attached to another person is a central task of treatment. Patients whose early development was marked by separations, deaths, trauma, physical, sexual or emotional abuse not infrequently present with an aggressively independent 'false self' organization (Winnicott, 1960), underlying which is an inability to trust or become dependent on another person. Other patients with these histories become inappropriately dependent as adults on people who are unable to meet their needs – and one of those people may be a counsellor offering only six sessions.

Some patients with these traumatic early histories can profit from long-term psychodynamic psychotherapy, in which one of the goals may be to redo some of the developmental tasks of the first few years of life. Balint referred to this process as 'regression to dependence' (1968). Regression to dependence has a place in therapeutic practice for some of the personality disordered patients we see, but only in the hands of a skilled psychodynamic psychotherapist. If a counsellor or other primary care mental health worker has not diagnosed the severe personality disorder underlying what otherwise looks like an ordinary case of anxiety and depression, for example, they may have considerable difficulty in dealing with the intense, dependent transference that is evident by session two. If six sessions are offered to such a patient, the result can be a serious suicidal gesture or other acting out. Negative outcomes of this kind can often be prevented by accurate assessment and referral at the outset.

Each model of brief psychodynamic therapy has its set of *inclusion criteria*. The following are typical:

1. Must be suitable for long-term psychotherapy:

  - can respond to an interpretive approach

  - is able to work in the transference

  - has sufficient ego strength – no risk of ego diffusion or disintegration

  - no history of gross acting out such as repeated suicide attempts or life-endangering behaviour

  - not currently heavily dependent on drugs or alcohol

  - no active psychosis or past psychotic episodes

  - no severe borderline personality disorders without psychiatric backup

2. A psychodynamic focus can be found

3. Circumscribed pathology

4. Must be actively involved in object relations – no social isolates.

These criteria will tend to exclude patients with psychotic, chemically dependent, schizoid, psychopathic, narcissistic or borderline psychopathology, in other words, many of those with a severe personality disorder on Axis II of the DSM-IV. Also screened out will be those patients who, when asked to describe the problem, are unable to find a focus and reply, 'It's everything' (the problem of comorbidity). Such a patient may present with a collection of difficulties: marital and sexual problems, an eating disorder, chronic interpersonal conflicts, child management problems, a history of depression and suicide attempts, and the recent disclosure of sexual abuse in the family. The GP may hear only about the last of these and conclude, 'Might be a suitable case for short-term counselling: looks like an adjustment reaction to a recent trauma' – but the rest of the history and diagnosis are missing and a detailed assessment needs to be done. Such patients should not be offered brief or ultra-brief therapies, and need longer-term work.

There are a number of brief psychodynamic psychotherapies in use at the moment, and this survey will necessarily be selective. Crits-Christoph and Barber (1991), Groves (1996) and Messer and Warren (1995) give helpful overviews. Luborsky's brief supportive-expressive psychotherapy (1984; Book, 1998), with its emphasis on the core conflictual relationship theme (CCRT), developed from an inspection of relationship episodes – the stories people tell about their interactions with other people. The CCRT is expressed as a sentence with two components: (a) a statement of the patient's wish, need or intention; (b) a statement of the consequences of trying to get one's wish from another person. The CCRT is enacted in the triad of relationship spheres: (a) the therapeutic relationship; (b) current relationships outside therapy – family, co-workers, etc.; (c) past relationships, especially with parents. These three domains of object relations are familiar from Malan's triangle of insight.

The focus of brief therapy is on a facet of the CCRT and the symptoms related to it. Luborsky represents the CCRT diagrammatically with three overlapping circles. In the centre, where the three circles overlap, is the CCRT. For example, the patient's wish is to receive love and affection but the repeated result of attempts to secure these is rejection. This pattern first appeared with parents (who could not respond emotionally to their child), then with a spouse or partner (who could not tolerate the patient's clinging dependency), and now with the therapist (who cannot grant the patient the out-of-hours contact which has been requested). As in Malan's model, the basic pattern of the CCRT is made conscious and worked through in all three domains: parent, significant other, and transference.

Strupp and Binder's time-limited dynamic psychotherapy (TLDP, 1984) is an interpersonally focused treatment of 25–30 sessions or less. Early patterns of interpersonal relatedness which originally served a self-protective function are now seen to be anachronistic and self-defeating. These patterns recur in the therapeutic relationship which serves as a laboratory for studying *in vivo* the patient's difficulties in living. The essence of the model is that patients suffer from the ill effects of previous interpersonal relationships and the therapist can provide a new experience, seeking to effect changes in the faulty learning the patient has carried forward from the past. A central issue or dynamic focus must be identifiable, and the patient must be able to form a collaborative relationship with the therapist because transference analysis is a major area of the work.

In this model, *internal object relationships* come into focus: self-images, images of the other, and a set of transactions taking place between them. Enduring internal object relationships associated with strong emotions press for enactment in current interpersonal relationships, including the therapeutic relationship, where they can be observed and discussed. The patient unconsciously seeks to draw from the therapist behaviours that re-enact the role assigned to the other in the patient's enduring scenario. The interpersonal relationship between therapist and patient oscillates between the valid adult–adult relationship of the present and the anachronistic child–parent relationship of the past. The patient's problem in living is an unwitting tendency to enact unrealistic scenarios with contemporaries. For example, the self is seen as unlovable and unable to give love, and so relationships are structured so as to bring about what is both wished for and feared. This pattern is repeated in the therapist–patient relationship, where it can be examined.

The *dynamic focus* in TLDP is the central interpersonal story of the patient's life. In TLDP the patient and therapist are engaged in a joint narration and renarration of the patient's central interpersonal dilemmas. Through this activity patient and therapist collaboratively author a new story with more flexible outcomes. The recognition of alternative stories and outcomes signals the beginning of therapeutic change. Practitioners of transactional analysis will find in TLDP echoes of Eric Berne's *life script* (1972).

Psychodynamic therapy is not about blaming parents. It is about understanding both what parents were like *and how the child responded*. There are many possible maladaptive coping mechanisms or 'survival kits' in response to a single parental attitude. Consider children who are told they were unwanted. Coping strategies among such children may range from a search for a 'good enough' parent elsewhere (including inappropriately in romantic relationships), becoming delinquent ('If the world won't give me what I need, I'll take it'), becoming withdrawn and socially isolated, or developing a theatrical style of behaviour in which others are compelled to notice them. This list is by no means exhaustive. There are as many different survival kits in response to parental behaviour as there are patients. No dictionaries exist in which we can look up the predictable child's response to a particular parental behaviour. It is commonly believed, for example, that children who were sexually abused as children go on to sexually abuse their own children, when many other possible outcomes occur. 'Cookbook' approaches to this question are as flawed as similar approaches to dream interpretation. There is no substitute for listening to each story afresh. When the patient's story resembles the therapist's own personal history, special attentiveness is needed because the therapist may tend to assume similarity where there is marked difference. Once the story has been told and the survival kit has been identified, the patient is freer to choose other courses of action in the future.

A *12-session contract model* was devised by Mann (1973), who observed that all short forms of psychotherapy revive the horror of time, and therapists as well as patients have a will to deny this. The recurring life crisis of separation–individuation is the theoretical base upon which this treatment rests. All human beings are susceptible to re-experiencing the anxiety of the separation–individuation crisis at times of loss, and mastery of separation anxiety becomes a focus in this model. The patient is offered a statement about the nature of the central difficulty, which is both a formulation of the problem and a goal for treatment. Choosing the central genetically and adaptively important issue requires a clear understanding of psychoanalytic concepts, especially regarding object relationships.

The central issue is couched in terms of feelings and/or maladaptive function, is derived from childhood experience, and continues into the patient's present efforts at adaptation. Hence it is an issue which will be recurrent over time. Another ingredient of the central issue addresses the patient's *present and chronically endured pain*, and often begins with the phrase, *'All your life, you . . .'* Usually this statement does not meet with denial, indeed it often provokes tears of recognition:

> 'Because there have been several sudden and very painful losses in your life, things always seem uncertain for you. *All your life* you have been expecting the next catastrophe to strike.'

In Mann's model, a central unconscious statement about the self is formulated and remains fixed in the patient for a lifetime. This statement is an assessment of how much others are needed in order to exist. In the least satisfactory state, the patient is unable to exist without the constant and continuing presence of a sustaining other person. In the most satisfactory state one needs others and prefers to engage with others, but if deprived of them can give them up and build new relationships. The beginning of therapy restores to the patient the golden glow of unity with mother, pre-separation in endless time. The end of therapy brings the unavoidable reality that what was found must be given up.

As this is a time-limited model, patients are kept to the central issue and are offered the correct amount of distance so that optimal autonomy is preserved. For many patients, termination begins at the sixth session, halfway through. The last three meetings are reserved for dealing with termination issues, and an intense termination often results from a telescoping of dynamic events within a brief period. Mann's model is suitable for patients presenting with loss issues. However, those with very traumatic early histories and borderline pathology are poor candidates for this kind of brief work, and can suffer psychological damage as a result. Indications for this type of therapy are a specific complaint, at least one meaningful relationship with another person during the patient's lifetime, and the ability to interact with the therapist at a feeling level.

Exclusion criteria include patients so severely depressed as to be unable to negotiate a treatment agreement, and patients whose desperation centres exclusively around the need for and the incapacity to tolerate object relations (otherwise known as borderline).

Gustafson (1995a, b) offers suggestions on how to identify patients who will benefit from short- versus long-term psychotherapy. Some patients get worse the more treatment they are given, while others demonstrate the ability to change for the better. Those who will get worse the more they are given include those with a 'malignant basic fault' – patients who develop a malignant regression (Balint, 1968) in therapy, with escalating demands. Malignant regressions are to be expected with most schizophrenics, addicted patients, borderline personalities, paranoid and manic patients, false selves (Winnicott, 1960), antisocial personalities, and people seeking medical legitimization for 'ailments' (Main, 1957). Gustafson does not offer these patients psychotherapy, but remains available for psychiatric emergencies and suggests they may be best helped by a team of clinicians – in the UK, a Community Mental Health Team (CMHT). By contrast, those who are similarly wounded and deprived but have a 'benign basic fault' have received just enough parenting to believe the world has the capacity to be good to them:

> A benign basic fault is a perpetual vulnerability to abandonment and intrusion, which responds with calming to an understanding of the particular incident (injury). The tendency to fall back into the abyss remains like a scar that comes apart. The outer surface of such patients can be anything . . . The shadow side is this abyss, which yawns open when the patient is hurt again.

> (Gustafson, 1995a, p. 25)

In therapy these patients undergo what Balint (1968) calls a benign regression. Many of them will profit from long-term psychotherapy. Gustafson has found that others can use one session a month, or twelve sessions a year over several years ('long brief therapy'). As a group they are very sensitive to changes in schedule and plunge very fast when abandoned, yet they recover quickly if attended to promptly. The need for responsiveness is heightened when there is a history of early trauma.

Gustafson suggests that brief therapy will be successful when it does not shrink from focusing on the patient's 'collisions with the social world': the same things keep on happening and the patient is continually 'amazed, unprepared and injured' at the repetition. This repetitive cycle is the focus for treatment. After listening empathically to the story the therapist may ask, 'What is *your* part in this happening over and over again?' The gap in the patient's story, the bit that is not being told, is often the most informative. The patient's predicament is formulated as the horns of a dilemma: one horn is conscious, but the other one is the unconscious process driving the repetition. Those who bring 'impossible projects' are not taken on for therapy. For example, Gustafson does not shrink from telling some patients that however unhappy they are on their own, they are likely to be 'far worse off with company'.

Brief psychodynamic therapy is not without its problems. It requires a high degree of skill, knowledge and experience. Short treatment does not imply easy treatment, even for an experienced therapist. The best preparation for doing brief therapy is a thorough knowledge of psychoanalytic theory and many years experience doing longer-term psychodynamic psychotherapy. One potential area of frustration exists for those trained in longer-term work because in brief therapy there may be insufficient time for working through. Another problem is finding suitable patients. Coren (1996) has voiced a concern widely felt among traditional psychodynamic therapists. After applying the exclusion criteria:

> What we are left with is a patient who is relatively healthy, well-functioning, with a well-defined and circumscribed area of difficulty, who is intelligent, psychologically minded and well-motivated for change. Where are they? Essentially, as therapists we are all looking for the same patient who is proving to be continuously elusive. These criteria would gladden the heart of any therapist, long or short term.
>
> (Coren, 1966, p. 26)

Whether patients are presenting with more preoedipal problems and severe personality disorders or whether our ability to diagnose these is improving is as yet an unanswered question. However, our ability accurately to diagnose and assess those who are suitable for psychodynamic work is a pressing problem and one of the reasons this book has been written.

COGNITIVE-BEHAVIOURAL THERAPY

Until very recently, cognitive-behavioural therapy (CBT) has focused almost exclusively on the relief of symptoms, especially of anxiety, phobias, depression, obsessions or compulsions. Patients who are looking for rapid symptom relief and who do not have much interest in exploring the underlying intrapsychic or historical causes of their problems are likely to be offered either pharmacological therapy or CBT.

Behavioural assessment for CBT focuses on the target *behaviour* in terms of its *antecedents* and *consequences* (the A-B-C model): what triggers the problem behaviour, and what are its consequences. Negative automatic thoughts can be important in initiating and maintaining problem behaviours. A checklist for behavioural assessment would include a detailed description of the presenting problem; other problem areas; the patient's skills, pleasures and positive characteristics; the development of the problem; previous coping attempts; expectations of treatment, and the likely effect of change on the patient and significant others. A *functional analysis* of the problem is carried out with attention given both to behaviour and cognitions: antecedents producing increase or decrease in symptoms; background factors producing increase or decrease; consequences of the behaviour both positive and negative on the patient and significant others; and thoughts, images and behaviours which are incompatible with the problem behaviour (France and Robson, 1997, pp. 26–27).

The patient is engaged at an early stage in data collection – keeping a diary of symptoms and the contexts in which they occur, relaxation exercises completed, or automatic negative thoughts and positive answers to them. Many CBT therapists use handouts which include blank diary pages on which data can be entered and blank forms on which mini-goals can be recorded. Complex goals are broken down into numerous mini-goals which are more manageable. Many CBT sessions begin with a review of these homework assignments.

Behavioural interventions include reinforcement, modelling, shaping, response cost (the loss of positive reinforcement for certain behaviours), time-out, differential reinforcement of other behaviour, stimulus control, exposure, systematic desensitization, contingency contracts, and assertion and social skills training.

The principle of reinforcement undergirds much behavioural therapy – reinforcing adaptive behaviours and ignoring or extinguishing maladaptive behaviours. Attention is a powerful reward. If a parent withdraws attention by ignoring certain behaviours, those behaviours will cease to be rewarding for a child. Control of the environment is another important behavioural principle: if there are certain environmental cues that prompt problematic behaviours, rearrangement of the environment can be extremely effective. For example, not purchasing high calorie foods while dieting, and removing tempting but dangerous objects from play areas.

Whether taught in individual or group settings, relaxation techniques are an important component of anxiety management programmes in CBT. They are also useful in the treatment of psychosomatic ailments and pain relief. In the treatment of phobias, the patient may be gradually exposed to the anxiety-arousing stimulus in fantasy (systematic desensitization) or *in vivo* (graded exposure). In both cases, the relaxation response is paired with the frightening stimulus, so that gradually the patient responds without fear to the anxiety-arousing stimulus. A *desensitization hierarchy* consists of a graduated series of images, starting with relatively non-threatening images and moving up to the most threatening ones. The hierarchy is developed in collaboration with the patient, because what is most frightening to one patient may not be at all frightening to the next patient.

Systematic desensitization begins with relaxation training. Then, starting with the easiest scene in the hierarchy, patients imagine themselves in that situation, while relaxed. If anxiety occurs, they are advised to move back a step and repeat the relaxation. The process is repeated for the next level of the hierarchy, and so on, each session beginning with the last successfully completed stage of the hierarchy – further sessions may be assigned as homework. Treatment may progress to graded *exposure in vivo* when the patient feels ready. Family or friends can sometimes be enlisted as co-therapists, accompanying the patient into feared environments. This procedure is especially helpful for patients suffering from social anxiety and agoraphobia.

Written materials and homework assignments are very helpful in CBT. One useful handout for anxiety problems covers bodily changes in anxiety states, thoughts patients experience when anxious, fear of fear, coping with panic, setting goals (long and short term), a list of mini-goals to be filled in by the patient, using rewards for self-change, stress inoculation training, an anxiety diary to be completed, relaxation exercises, notes on improving concentration, and a relaxation diary to be completed by the patient. Relaxation tapes are also frequently used. France and Robson (1997) provide an up-to-date review of the use of CBT for a wide range of disorders in primary care, with separate chapters on anxiety, depression, sexual problems, habit disorders, childhood behaviour problems, specific medical disorders, and problems of later life.

Perhaps the most widely practised form of CBT in primary care today is Beck et al.'s (1979) cognitive therapy for depression. Well-known changes in thoughts, feelings and behaviours occur when people are depressed. Many *thoughts* are of the negative automatic variety, concerning self, world and future. The *feelings* of depression include loss of pleasure in usual activities and feeling miserable, exhausted, guilty, and lacking in energy. *Behaviours* are largely avoidance of usual activities and pursuits. It can be helpful to draw the thoughts, feelings and behaviour triangle for depressed patients, explaining how they are interrelated. Some patients are already on antidepressant medication, which alters depressed feelings biochemically. Cognitive-behavioural methods can address negative automatic thoughts and avoidant behaviours, and these changes in turn will positively affect depressed feelings. Keeping a diary of negative thoughts, answering these with more positive thoughts, and designing a weekly activity schedule are commonly prescribed homework activities for depressed patients.

The cognitive model of depression acknowledges the importance of early experiences of loss, criticism or rejection from parents, leading to the formation of dysfunctional assumptions, for example, 'unless I'm loved, I'm worthless' or 'anything good that happens to me is taken away'. Some critical incident or incidents (e.g. the death of a partner) activates the dysfunctional assumptions, which lead to the development of negative automatic thoughts (e.g. 'I can't live without him', 'I can't bear it', or 'I shall never find anyone else like that'). The symptoms of depression follow:

- Feelings: sadness, guilt, shame, anxiety, anger.

- Behaviour: lowered activity levels, slowness, withdrawal from positive activities, impaired coping with practical problems, social skills deficits.

- Motivation: apathy, inertia, avoidance, loss of self-reliance, ordinary tasks feel overwhelming.

- Cognitive: indecisiveness, poor memory and concentration, ruminations.

- Physical: sleep disturbance, loss of appetite, loss of libido.

Handouts on depression from a CBT perspective may include advice on looking for rational answers: 'What evidence do I have to support my thoughts? What alternative views are there? What is the effect of thinking the way I do? What thinking error am I making? What can I do to change my situation?' Typical thinking errors in depression are:

- all or nothing thinking ('If I don't do it perfectly, there's no point in doing it at all')

- overgeneralization ('I never get anything right')

- mental filter ('I didn't have a moment's pleasure today')

- discounting the positive ('OK, so I got my work done today. So what, it's only what's expected of me')

- jumping to conclusions ('I'm depressed again, everyone is fed up with me, and I'll never get over it')

- catastrophizing ('The worst will happen, and there's nothing I can do about it')

- emotional reasoning ('I feel guilty, therefore I must have done something wrong')

- 'shoulds' ('I should be able to pull myself together')

- global judgements ('Another argument – I'm a rotten person')

- predicting from the past ('I've never, ever achieved anything')

- personalization ('Why does it always rain the day I arrange to go to Wimbledon?')

(Beck et al., 1979)

Patients are asked to keep a daily record of their negative automatic thoughts. Many depressed patients, asked to divide a sheet of paper in half with the negative thoughts on the lefthand side and the positive answers on the right, will say either that they cannot find any positive answers, or if they do, they do not believe them. Truth resides in the lefthand column and falsehood on the right. This is a common state of affairs at the beginning of treatment for depression. Another handout used in this model may cover the problem of thought blocks to becoming more active. A number of negative automatic thoughts are listed, along with their rational answers. For example:

- It's too difficult ('It only seems difficult because I'm depressed').

- There's too much to do – I can't cope ('Believing that is all part of depression').

- I won't enjoy it ('How do you know? Try it and see').

The handout suggests that activity takes the mind off painful feelings, reduces fatigue, improves motivation and thinking ability, and provokes praise from loved ones. Patients are asked to record what they do hour by hour for a few days. Each activity is rated at the time (not retrospectively) between 1 and 10 for pleasure (P) and mastery or sense of achievement (M).

The next step is to plan each day in advance, including activities which provide a sense of enjoyment and mastery. A particular time of day is set aside to record what was done during that day and to plan for the next day. Patients are advised to be aware of self-defeating thoughts, to place limits on distractions such as television, to avoid retreating to bed, and to reward themselves for what they have done each day. A weekly activity schedule is filled in and brought to the next therapy session.

In an application of the CBT model, White (1997) devised a computerized three-session anxiety management programme installed in GP surgeries to be used by patients with mild disorders, eliminating the need for a therapist. Session one is a computerized assessment and teaching session, with written handouts to take home. Sessions two and three cover relaxation, controlling stressful thoughts, facing up to stress, coping with panic attacks, getting a good night's sleep, and coping with the future. Patients complete pre- and post-treatment questionnaires, their scores are displayed on screen, and can be printed out. Such programmes could be extended to cover depression, anger control, and alcohol misuse.

Beck has more recently turned his attention to CBT for personality disorders (Beck and Freeman et al., 1990). This model resembles some of the brief psychodynamic therapies in that maladaptive interpersonal patterns and the cognitions that accompany them are addressed. Therapist and patient identify incidents that illuminate the personality problems and focus on the cognitive underpinnings of these incidents. First steps attempt to recover *automatic thoughts*, for example, 'They don't like me.' A chain of cognitions will often lead to the *core schema*:

> T: What thought went through your mind at lunch?
>
> P: Linda is ignoring me. (selective focus, personalization)
>
> T: What did that mean?
>
> P: I can't get along with people. (self-attribution, overgeneralization)
>
> T: What does that mean?
>
> P: I will never have any friends. (absolute prediction)
>
> T: What does it mean 'not to have friends'?
>
> P: I am all alone. (core schema)
>
> T: What does it mean to be all alone?

P: That I will always be unhappy. (core schema, starts to cry)

(Beck and Freeman et al., 1990, p. 82)

There may be more than one core schema. The therapist helps the patient to identify the dysfunctional cognitions that are dominating life, and works with the patient to make the alterations necessary. Schemas are traced to their childhood roots. Reliving childhood experiences opens up windows for understanding the origins of maladaptive patterns. A variety of techniques may be used to generate new schemas. Sometimes building entirely new schemas is not possible for a given patient. In such cases schematic modification may be all that is possible. Comprehensive tables for each of the DSM-III personality disorders have been compiled showing the view of self, the view of others, main beliefs, main interpersonal strategy, and core schemas (Beck and Freeman et al., 1990). For example:

- Obsessive-compulsive personality disorder

  View of self: responsible, accountable, fastidious, competent.

  View of others: irresponsible, incompetent, self-indulgent.

  Main beliefs: 'I know what's best', 'Details are crucial', 'People should do better and try harder'.

  Main strategies: apply rules, perfectionism, evaluate and control, use 'shoulds', criticize and punish others.

  Core schemas: 'I have to do this myself or it won't be done correctly. To make a mistake is to have failed, and failure is intolerable. I must be perfectly in control of my environment as well as myself. Loss of control is dangerous.'

Schema-focused cognitive therapy is becoming more widely taught in the UK (Kennerley, 1997). Schemata are stable and enduring themes developed during childhood that become templates for the processing of later experience. Early maladaptive schemata derive from dysfunctional experiences in the first few years of life, a concept very similar to the psychodynamic emphasis on the child's early experience with caretakers, and the Inventory of Early Loss described in Chapter 5. Power and Brewin (1997) provide several examples of early maladaptive schemata economical in their simplicity and clarity: self as powerless, self as inferior, self as non-existent (identity diffusion), self as futureless, other as abandoning, other as betraying, and other as hostile.

Persons and Tompkins (1997) describe cognitive-behavioural case formulation in terms of seven components:

- *Problem list*, an exhaustive list of the patient's difficulties in simple, descriptive terms; a typical problem list for outpatients has 5–8 items.

- *Core beliefs*, the patient's views of self, world and others that cause or maintain the patient's problems; a *Thought Record Sheet* may be helpful in identifying a series of thoughts that contribute to core beliefs.

- *Precipitants and activating situations*, external events that activate core beliefs to produce symptoms and problems.

- *Working hypothesis* that ties together the problem list, core beliefs and activating events.

- *Origins* of the core beliefs in the past, incidents or circumstances of the patient's early history, especially with parents, that explain how the patient learned the core beliefs.

- *Treatment plan* based directly on the working hypothesis.

- *Predicted obstacles to treatment*, potential difficulties that could disturb the course of therapy.

Sessions tend to focus on recent situations and their associated thought patterns and core beliefs. CBT is an educative model, helping patients to alter their cognitions and actively problem-solve their way through difficulties. Although it is the most frequently used brief therapy in clinical psychology departments in the NHS, it is not suitable for everyone (March, 1997). Hughes (1997) offers several arguments against cognitive therapy for depression. Some patients complain that although they believe what their therapists are saying to them, they don't *feel* it is right. Others resent what they see as an attempt to make them 'think correctly'. A few perceive it as a totalitarian form of thought control. Others with poor literacy skills, limited family support and low socio-economic status may be poor candidates for CBT but are referred because they are opposed to psychotropic medication. Still other patients, having read something about the technique in advance, announce at the assessment session that they will not cooperate with any therapy promoting 'positive thinking'. Such patients often have an intuitive sense of what will help them, and they know that CBT is not what they need. These preferences should be respected.

COGNITIVE-ANALYTIC THERAPY

One of the fastest growing integrative therapies in primary care is Ryle's (1990, 1995) cognitive-analytic therapy (CAT) which draws from cognitive-behavioural and psychodynamic brief therapy. Mann's central issue describing the patient's chronically endured pain is an important part of the model: *'All your life you . . . and therefore . . . and so . . .'* For example:

> *'All your life you* have felt abandoned and rejected because of your mother's early abandonment of you, *and therefore* you have been looking for someone to become the perfect parent for you, *and so* you have in every relationship experienced a profound disappointment.'

CAT relates acts to outcomes, thoughts to feelings, beliefs to acts, provides an accurate description of sequences repeated in the patient's life, and uses the therapist as a good teacher of accurate self-reflection. CAT uses the here-and-now interaction with the therapist as one source of understanding, using the psychodynamic concept of transference. A diagrammatic description of the core problem is shared with the patient early in the therapy, usually after the fourth session. *Sequential diagrammatic reformulation* is the focus and scaffolding of therapy. This diagram depicts the patient's repetitively used, ineffective, hitherto unrevised and usually unrecognized set of 'procedures'. Reformulation is a joint task between patient and therapist. A final agreed description is written down. *Target problems* (TPs) and *target problem procedures* (TPPs) are identified and diagrammed in a way that is meaningful to the patient. *Traps, dilemmas and snags* are examples of target problem procedures. Maladaptive *reciprocal role relationships* are also diagrammed.

Prior to beginning CAT, patients have had an outpatient psychiatric assessment including a full developmental history. Four CAT sessions are used to make the reformulation. At the end of session three the therapist says to the patient, 'I'll bring a draft next time, and you bring one too.' It is not uncommon for patients to burst into tears when presented with a clear model of their problem, since the diagram addresses their chronically endured pain. The therapy lasts 8 or 16 sessions. CAT is promoted as a safe first therapy for most patients, including more disturbed patients such as borderlines, because the structured setting does not foster the development of intense transferences which would take a long time to resolve (Ryle, 1995).

The sequential diagrammatic reformulation includes core state(s), coping modes, interpersonal procedures and symptomatic procedures. Arrows between boxes illustrate sequences. Very complex diagrams may be constructed, with multiple core states in borderline personalities. As an example, the patient's core state is deprived, generating daydreams of ideal care. The survival mode of total compliance leads the patient to feel misunderstood and abused which causes her to fly into a rage. She fantasizes murder or suicide and develops fears of madness which in turn lead to feelings of depersonalization and anxious dependency. In this mode of anxious dependency she returns to her survival mode of total compliance. The vicious circles are shown by arrows in the diagram.

There are similarities between Beck's schema and Ryle's core state (Bamber, 1997). Schemata, like core states, are not easily changed and are the product of early developmental history. Proponents of both models claim they are of benefit to people with longstanding personality disorders. CAT has recently been reviewed in the treatment of survivors of childhood sexual abuse (Llewelyn, 1997), eating disorders (Bell, 1996), and borderline personality disorder (Dunn and Parry, 1997; Ryle, 1995; Ryle, Leighton and Pollock, 1997). It is one of the more systematically researched brief integrative therapies and is growing steadily in popularity. With any of the short-term therapies, however, accurate assessment is essential because treatment may expose the chaos underneath the surface and then discharge the patient to cope alone. Premature termination has the potential to confirm the patient's worst fear: 'My problems are unmanageable. My therapist couldn't manage it any better than my parents could. Both of them got rid of me.' Most but not all recipients of CAT terminate therapy at 16 sessions. Some patients require further therapy.

HUMANISTIC THERAPIES

The founder of the humanistic therapy movement was Carl Rogers who coined the term 'client-centered therapy' (Rogers, 1951). Rogers' three basic conditions have been confirmed by research as key factors in the success of psychotherapies of all theoretical orientations: empathy, unconditional positive regard, and genuineness or openness to feelings. Empathy is the therapist's ability to sense the other person's world of felt meanings as if they were their own, but without ever losing the 'as if' quality. Unconditional positive regard is a positive, warm, accepting response to others, regardless of how difficult their behaviour may be at the moment. Genuineness is the therapist's ability to interact honestly with the patient at a feeling level, and is closely related to another key attribute, openness to feelings. The therapist wants to communicate that any feeling can be talked about. Some feelings are painful and there may be a wish to avoid them. However, the therapist will make an effort not to avoid them with the other person if possible.

An adaptation of the client-centred approach for helping parents interact more effectively with their children (Gordon, 1970) will make some of the fundamentals of this model clear. Most of the time, people interact using the 'typical twelve': commanding, warning, moralizing, giving solutions, lecturing, judging, praising, ridiculing, interpreting, reassuring, questioning and distracting. There is an alternative to the typical twelve, in reflecting back the feeling that the other person is expressing. For example, 'It sounds like this has been very upsetting for you.' Receptivity to others' feelings includes the use of silence, a non-verbal attending attitude, good eye contact, an open body posture, and encouraging noises like 'Um hm' and 'Uh huh'. Door-openers include 'It sounds like you have very strong feelings about that', 'It sounds like this must be very hard for you', and 'Would you like to say a bit more about that?' Once the other person has had an opportunity to speak about the problem in detail, the therapist uses a reflection such as, 'It sounds like you're very unhappy about that.' The therapist refrains from interpretation and as many of the other typical twelve responses as possible (Burton, 1991).

Gendlin (1962) explains how the reflection of feelings response works therapeutically. Counsellors can tell when they have accurately reflected a feeling because the patient says, 'that's right, and another thing is. . .' Experiencing is always a felt complexity of feeling. There is always more than one feeling about a situation, and the therapeutic task is to explore as many of these as possible, on the assumption that decision-making and coping are facilitated by awareness of the full range of feelings.

Gendlin argues that when a person expresses accurately in words for the first time how they are feeling, just then they are no longer that way. In the act of sharing the feeling with another, the feeling has already changed. Also, only certain words will exactly fit the way a person feels at one time. When the right word is found, it is accompanied by the feeling, 'that's exactly right'. When the feeling is unclear, the therapist can still point to it as a 'that' or 'that feeling, whatever it is'. The expression 'or something like that' can be very useful in such situations. It is as if the therapist is pointing to a part of the patient's inner life as a part of the landscape. It may as yet have no name, but it can be identified as a 'that' or an 'over there', and the process moves on from there (Gendlin, 1967). Out of his experience in the client-centred model, Gendlin (1981, 1996) developed his school of focusing which now has an international membership. Focusing invites the patient to attend inwardly to a bodily felt sense, to go into that felt sense, to see what words emerge in connection with it, and to wait for a 'felt shift' – new meanings which, in the long term, may contribute to structural personality change.

Therapies across the humanistic spectrum are many and diverse. They include gestalt, transactional analysis (TA), psychosynthesis, the human potential movement, the encounter group movement and many others. The humanistic model used most often in primary care is client-centred or person-centred therapy, with or without the integration of other therapies such as gestalt and TA. Some integrative psychotherapies (Albeniz and Holmes, 1996) incorporate insights from the client-centred model. Client-centred therapy is conducted both short and long term (House, 1997), but some therapists find the imposition of time limits problematic because this therapy is usually by definition patient-led – termination occurs when the patient feels ready to do so.

Traditionally, humanistic therapists have taken the view that assessment or diagnosis is unnecessary and may be detrimental to the therapeutic process. Rogers argued that assessment puts the therapist in a 'one-up' position and implies that only the expert can accurately evaluate the person seeking help. Other humanistic therapists take a different view. Those humanistic therapists who use transactional analysis as a theoretical base undertake a detailed script analysis (Berne, 1972) in initial interviews, which is a form of assessment or case formulation. Proponents of process-experiential therapy, whose roots are in the Rogerian model and gestalt therapy, have developed a process-experiential form of case formulation (Goldman and Greenberg, 1997):

- Identification of areas of puzzlement about emotional reactions to situations, with a willingness to explore those feelings with another person.

- An unclear 'felt sense' of the situation, and a readiness for focusing.

- Conflict splits in which one aspect of the self is critical or coercive toward another, indicating readiness for a two-chair dialogue.

- Self-interruptive splits in which one part of the self interrupts or constricts emotions, suggesting readiness for a two-chair enactment.

- Unfinished business, a lingering unresolved feeling toward another person, indicating readiness for an empty-chair dialogue.

- Shame or insecurity about some aspect of experience, suggesting a need for empathic   affirmation from the therapist.

Psychodynamic and humanistic models of psychotherapy are closer in emphasis to one another than either of them is to CBT. Wheeler and McLeod (1995) offer a thoughtful analysis of the similarities and differences between client-centred and psychodynamic models. Both are exploratory, operate through conversation, emphasize the importance of the therapist–patient relationship as a vehicle for promoting understanding, work with the person-in-relationship, require that therapists have had a personal therapy as part of their training, and are broad-based approaches that have tended to incorporate practitioners with different shades of opinion under the same banner. Among the most important differences are an emphasis on conscious vs. unconscious process, expression vs. an understanding of feelings, and accepting patients where they are vs. looking for what is hidden. The major difference from our standpoint occurs in the matter of assessment: person-centred therapists often do not make a detailed initial assessment, whereas assessment is an essential part not only of the psychodynamic formulation but also of the cognitive-behavioural working hypothesis and the sequential diagrammatic reformulation of cognitive-analytic therapy. In Chapter 4 we address the risks of not taking a history and making an assessment at the beginning of therapy.

GROUP, COUPLES AND FAMILY THERAPIES

Group therapies

Clinical psychologists in primary care frequently offer time-limited structured CBT groups for anxiety, stress, depression and anger management. In some settings psychologists contribute to cardiac rehabilitation groups and group sessions for patients with diabetes or hypertension. Some of the short-term cognitive-behavioural group work which has been done in specialist cancer hospitals (Harman, 1991) could profitably be moved to the primary care setting. Time-limited group work has been offered to women with histories of childhood sexual abuse. Thomas, Costello and Davison (1997) describe the usefulness of long-term, slow-open group-analytic work in a primary care setting. Piper, McCallum and Azim (1992) have developed an influential and carefully researched model of brief group psychotherapy for patients who have lost a significant other through death, separation or divorce. Cummings (1997) describes brief psychoeducational groups in primary care combining treatment, information dissemination, and behavioural techniques directed at lifestyle change. These time-limited groups have been offered to adult children of alcoholics, agoraphobics, borderline personalities, chronic schizophrenics, and people with perfectionistic personalities. Similar groups have been offered to people with diabetes, asthma, airways disease, hypertension, ischaemic heart disease and rheumatoid arthritis. Unfortunately, the only outcome measure reported is a reduction in medical utilization rates, so we do not know at present the nature of the psychological change produced or its durability.

Couples therapies and psychosexual counselling

Many counsellors in primary care have had a Relate (marriage guidance) training and are skilled to see couples. Interpersonal and psychosexual problems focused on the spouse or partner account for a substantial proportion of the GP's psychological caseload. Somatizing repeat attenders often have marital and sexual problems, and can benefit from brief couples therapy. A number of innovative approaches to couples work have appeared in recent years, for example, Bader and Pearson (1988), Lachtar (1992), Scharff and Scharff (1991), Strean (1980, 1985). Strean describes immature forms of love – love as dependency, sadistic love, love as a rescue fantasy, compulsive love, love for the unattainable object (unrequited love), celibate love, critical love, loving the partner's parents, and revengeful love – any of which may lead to extramarital affairs and marital breakdown. Sager et al. (1983) describe common profiles in marriage: equal partners, romantic partners, parental partners, childlike partners, rational partners, companionate partners and parallel partners. Each of these behavioural patterns presents difficulties and may lead to instability. Bader and Pearson's (1988) model of marital dynamics is derived from Margaret Mahler's developmental stages of symbiosis, practicing, differentiation and rapprochement.

In 1982 the British Medical Association published a useful leaflet entitled 'Sex Problems in Practice', which advises GPs to follow four steps in the treatment of psychosexual problems:

- Let the patient talk and offer opportunities to express feelings.
- Listen closely to what is said.

- Assess the degree to which the problem is due to ignorance about sex, cultural taboos and myths, and poor communication in the relationship. If so, simple interventions are suggested.

- Assess the degree to which once sexual failure has been experienced, a vicious cycle has begun involving unrealistic concepts of success and/or undue performance pressure.

When these measures fail to work, when the sexual problem occurs in the context of a conflict-ridden and unsatisfactory marital relationship, or when there are indications of personality disorder or other serious psychopathology, the GP should consider referral. The most influential author in the field of psychosexual problems is Helen Singer Kaplan (1974, 1979, 1983). Sexual dysfunction has immediate causes such as failure to engage in effective sexual behaviour, sexual anxiety, perceptual and intellectual defences against erotic feelings, and failure to communicate openly about sexual feelings and experiences. More complex are the intrapsychic causes of sexual dysfunction, which include repression, oedipal conflict, a constrictive upbringing, or anxiety about intimacy and physical contact. Relationship causes of sexual dysfunction include partner rejection, marital discord, and failure in communication. Learned causes of sexual dysfunction may also play a role. None of these perspectives taken alone is complete.

Kaplan recommends a behavioural approach to treatment with a psychodynamic approach to the resistances that emerge in therapy. Treatment combines prescribed sexual experiences or exercises with psychotherapeutic sessions. Sex therapy can become couples therapy over time if required. Examples of sexual tasks which may be assigned include a ban on intercourse, sensate focus (non-demand pleasuring and massage), the squeeze or stop-start technique for premature ejaculation, masturbation techniques and use of a vibrator in anorgasmia, vaginal dilators and relaxation exercises for vaginismus, muscular exercises to strengthen the pelvic floor in anorgasmia, and bibliotherapy (books for patients to read, and erotic films or videos to watch). The mechanisms of therapeutic action include modification of the destructive sexual system, conflict resolution, and the emergence of unrecognized psychodynamic material.

A complete psychosocial and sexual history is needed for each partner, including a history of the individual and his or her relationships, a history of sexual experiences, a history of the dysfunction, and a clear picture of what is happening now between them and what has been tried. A useful format for assessment requires four hours: (1) a conjoint initial interview with both partners; (2) two individual interviews in which histories are taken; (3) a second conjoint session. Co-therapists, where possible male and female, may facilitate discussion. The nine existing studies of marriage guidance counsellors working in GP surgeries date from the 1970s and 1980s, although the work is continuing. These studies were included in Burton's (1992a) annotated bibliography and will not be reviewed here except to mention two review articles by de Groot (1985) and Corney (1986).

Family therapies

There is an increasing interest in family approaches to psychological problems in primary care. Bor (1995) recently compiled a reference library on psychological counselling in primary health care reflecting his own interest in the family approach. In London, the Highgate Group Practice has established a family therapy clinic in a general practice setting (Graham et al., 1994). Recently Mayer et al. (1996) described the usefulness of the family systems model of observing and sitting in on consultations. This is an approach which is gaining in influence in the UK, having been established for some time in primary care in the USA. Campbell and Patterson (1995) recently undertook an exhaustive review of the effectiveness of family interventions in the treatment of physical illness. They found the model to be of greatest benefit in chronic childhood conditions such as asthma and diabetes, some cardiovascular and neurologic disorders and in obesity. Family models appear to be more effective than individual treatment for some patients with anorexia nervosa.

SINGLE-SESSION THERAPY AND 2+1

Very brief therapies of one to three sessions have been described recently. The 2+1 model involves two weekly sessions followed by another three months later (Barkham and Shapiro, 1990). The model does not claim to help all patients or to be a panacea, but is one means of addressing clinical needs and shortening NHS waiting lists. It can be viewed as a trial intervention and a form of assessment or triage. At follow-up, it may be decided that three sessions were enough, that the patient needs more, or that psychological therapy is not helpful for this patient for whatever reason.

Talmon (1990) has examined single-session therapy – maximizing the effect of the first (and often only) therapeutic encounter. He suggests that many patients are already changing and will require only a single session of treatment. His approach utilizes factors common to many short-term therapies: fostering readiness to change, finding a focus, identifying patients' strengths, and practicing solutions. Simple tasks may be suggested, the patient is assured that further appointments can be made in future and follow-up is built in.

OTHER BRIEF THERAPY MODELS

In *strategic solution focused brief therapy* (Quick, 1996), the therapist evaluates the problem and what is maintaining it, considers what might interrupt the cycle, and determines how change might best be implemented. The word strategic refers to the therapist's task of developing a strategy or plan to interrupt the maladaptive behaviour pattern. Quick's procedure is as follows:

- Problem clarification

    a What's the trouble?

    b What's the highest priority problem?

- Solution amplification

    a 'You wake up tomorrow and the problem is solved. What will be different? What else? What will (name of person in your life) notice about you? How will he(she) be different? What else will be different as a result of these changes?

    b Exceptions: 'Are there pieces of the solution that are already happening? How did you do that?'

    c Scaling questions: grading the problem from 1 to 10 (worst to best) – 'How will you know you're at x + 1?'

- Assessment of attempted solutions

    a 'What have you tried? How did you do that?'

    b 'Did it work?'

- Intervention: 'Would you like some feedback?' (if yes):

    a Validate chief complaint, e.g. 'I don't blame you for feeling distressed.'

    b Compliment, e.g. 'I'm impressed that even in the face

of . . . you've been able to. . .'

c Suggestion (homework): 'If what you're doing works, do more of it. Pay attention to how you do it. If what you're doing doesn't work, stop doing it! Pay attention to how you "turn the problem up and down". Pay attention to how you cope with the problem.'

• Plan for additional service

a 'Do you want to make another appointment? Or should we leave it open-ended?

b Referral plan for other service(s), as indicated.

(Quick, 1996, pp. 12–13)

Psychotherapy abbreviation (Pekarik, 1996) is an approach to brief therapy that can be used by therapists from most theoretical orientations. Therapists are encouraged to retain their preferred style but to adapt their approach to a brief format. It is argued that brief therapy can be done from almost every orientation and that therapy is done best when therapists work from within their preferred school or style. The main features of the model are rapid assessment and case conceptualization, establishing a brief therapy focus, negotiating treatment goals, and adapting standard psychotherapy techniques to a briefer format.

The *interpersonal-developmental-existential model* of Budman and Gurman (1988) identifies five common foci and uses them to provide a decision tree for prioritizing focus selection:

• losses

• developmental dysynchronies, which occur when age or stage of life-related achievements and expectations are not yet met

• interpersonal conflicts

• symptomatic presentations, e.g. habit disorders, sexual dysfunctions, fears and phobias

• personality disorders.

If none of the first four foci is present and character issues are in evidence, then personality is an appropriate, but longer-term treatment focus. Assessment is often abbreviated in this model by restricting it to a few plausible treatment issues. Budman and Gurman's opening chapter contains a table which purports to contrast the dominant values of long- and short-term therapists, but as Miller (1996a) cogently demonstrates, they have for argument's sake created a caricature of traditional therapists' values. Miller offers a third column in his own revised table entitled 'Traditional therapist who focuses on the client's best interests'.

Brief intermittent psychotherapy throughout the life cycle: one of the most committed exponents of brief and ultra-brief therapies is Nicholas Cummings (1991, 1997; Cummings and Sayama, 1995). In this model, the concept of cure is abandoned, therapy is never terminated, only interrupted, and specific techniques are used for specific problems. In the first session the therapist 'hits the ground running' – the first session must be therapeutic. A full history is not taken and DSM-IV diagnoses are not given, but an operational diagnosis is made in answer to the question, 'Why has this patient come for help now?' Cummings argues that at various points in patients' lives, they can be expected to repeat early distress patterns and therefore may need access to therapists across their life span. Brief intermittent therapy is targeted on immediate presenting problems. Help may be sought for one problem in Year 1 and a different problem in Year 3 or Year 10.

We turn finally to the professions offering treatment in the National Health Service in the UK: counsellors, psychotherapists, clinical psychologists, psychiatrists and CPNs. The role of these professionals in primary care was discussed in Chapter 1, and organizational issues will be addressed in Chapter 7. Here we describe the therapeutic models most likely to be used by each of them in primary care settings today.

COUNSELLORS AND PSYCHOTHERAPISTS

There has been considerable debate over the distinction between counselling and psychotherapy. With the recent development of psychodynamic counselling, the boundaries have become more blurred than they were previously. Both counsellors and psychotherapists may use any of the models we have described: psychodynamic, cognitive-behavioural, humanistic, cognitive-analytic, brief and ultra-brief therapies, and group, couples or family models.

In the UK, *counsellors* are most likely to have been trained in humanistic, psychodynamic, couple or family systems models, although others obtain training in cognitive-analytic, brief and group therapies. On the whole, few counsellors are trained in cognitive-behavioural therapy. *Psychotherapists* are most likely to be trained in psychodynamic, humanistic, group, couple or family systems models, although others have training in cognitive-analytic or brief therapies. As is the case with counsellors, few psychotherapists are trained in cognitive-behavioural therapy unless they are also clinical psychologists, in which case CBT will have been part of their training. When the psychotherapist is also a psychiatrist, psychotropic medication may be prescribed as part of treatment and the potential need for hospitalization may be an issue. Patients who are more severely disturbed may become management problems, or need inpatient care may be referred to *consultant psychotherapists*. Within medicine, psychotherapy is a distinct sub-specialty of psychiatry and has a formal training leading to the appointment of consultant psychotherapists. Many consultant psychotherapists undertake a psychoanalytic psychotherapy training and are members of the Association for Psychoanalytic Psychotherapy in the National Health Service (APP).

Dare (1996) assumes that counselling and psychotherapy exist on a continuum with each other, and he defines psychotherapy as follows:

> Psychotherapy is a class of helping activity. It consists of an encounter between people, one (or perhaps two) of whom is the designated helper ('therapist'). A psychotherapist is seen as undertaking a professional activity. (A counsellor may be unpaid and may do something very like psychotherapy and be bound by the same ethical rules.) The person (or people) being helped can be seen alone, in a group, or with a partner, or with one or more members of the family of origin or creation. The characteristic activity within psychotherapy is thought and talk. Psychotherapy is a conversation guided by the therapist with the aim of helping the client or patient with a psychological predicament. The predicament may or may not appear to be the result of an external crisis. Its manifestations may be in the form of symptoms, character problems or existential dilemmas.

> (Dare, 1996, p. 34)

Dare points out that when counselling is directed at a specific area such as careers guidance, the focus is on a particular problem. The emphasis is on information giving and advice, and this activity is very unlike psychotherapy. At the other end of the counselling spectrum, when the subject matter is the patient's psychological problems, this activity 'completely overlaps with the practice of psychotherapy'.

East (1995) also sees counselling and psychotherapy as overlapping activities, but describes counselling as brief treatment focusing on patients' current problems whereas psychotherapy is more concerned with the resolution of longstanding personal issues and may be either brief or long term. Bond (1995) agrees that counselling is about helping people who have the capacity to cope in most circumstances, who are experiencing temporary difficulties or in a psychosocial transition. When issues are more symptomatic of something deeper, psychotherapy may be more appropriate. Rowland (1993) suggests that in counselling there is less emphasis on the transference between counsellor and client, which is true of non-psychodynamic counsellors. In company with others, she tends to see counselling as shorter-term, problem-centred work, suggesting that as such it is better suited to general practice than longer-term psychotherapies.

Jacobs (1994) suggests that the contrast between counselling and psychotherapy tends to take on greater meaning when the model used is psychodynamic. Some psychodynamic psychotherapists see counsellors as not at all the same as psychotherapists despite their apparent similarity, but it is undoubtedly true that some counsellors do work with the unconscious and with symbolization, transference and psychotic elements of the personality. Jacobs suggests that there are subtle differences between the terms 'psychodynamic' and 'psychoanalytic', the latter carrying some baggage of debates about orthodoxy in which psychoanalysts or psychoanalytic psychotherapists are seen as in some way superior. 'Psychodynamic' and 'psychoanalytic' are used virtually interchangeably in this text.

Naylor-Smith (1994) suggests that when counselling is task oriented, as in bereavement or post-traumatic counselling, the patient's life in the external world is the focus. However, in more general terms counselling and psychotherapy are on a continuum. When counselling begins to explore unconscious processes, relates the current trauma to the patient's history, or uses the transference (as in psychodynamic counselling), Malan's triangle of insight is being used and the process grades into psychotherapy. When sessions are more frequent than once a week, and a shift away from day-to-day crises occurs together with a loosening of the patient's defences and the potential for regression to dependence, then this work is clearly psychotherapy.

CLINICAL PSYCHOLOGISTS, PSYCHIATRISTS AND CPNs

Most *clinical psychologists* in the UK are trained principally in cognitive-behavioural therapy, although others undertake training in group, couple or family systems models, brief therapies, cognitive-analytic and psychodynamic therapies. Clinical psychologists may incorporate aspects of Rogerian therapy in their work, but this model is not emphasized in most training programmes.

Most *psychiatrists* approach mental illness from a biological perspective. As physicians, they can prescribe psychotropic medication if needed and arrange for hospitalization or physical treatments such as ECT. An increasing number of psychiatrists have developed an interest in brief therapies that can be used in the outpatient department. When consultant psychiatrists are also psychotherapists, their approaches may include psychodynamic, cognitive-analytic, cognitive-behavioural, group, couple or family models. On the whole, psychiatrists rarely train in the humanistic therapies.

Community psychiatric nurses (CPNs) involved in counselling work frequently have further training in cognitive-behavioural or humanistic approaches.

Parry and Richardson (1997), in their strategic review of NHS psychotherapy services in England, distinguished between three levels of skill in the psychological therapies:

- *Type A*: psychological treatment as an integral component of mental health care (e.g. routine GP care, or care provided by professionals in community mental health teams).

- *Type B*: complete interventions in a set number of sessions but informed by more than one theoretical framework (e.g. the work of many counsellors and clinical psychologists in primary and secondary care).

- *Type C*: complete interventions in a set number of sessions informed by a single theoretical model – formal psychotherapy (e.g. psychoanalytic psychotherapy or cognitive-behavioural psychotherapy practised by specially trained clinical psychologists, psychiatrists or CPNs, and by psychotherapists trained by organizations recognized by the United Kingdom Council for Psychotherapy (UKCP) and the British Confederation of Psychotherapists (BCP)). Formal psychotherapy is only occasionally offered in the primary care setting.

The need for accurate assessment at the primary care level is a very pressing problem. Assessment is poorly taught on many counselling courses in the UK, and it is to this problem that we turn in Chapters 4 and 5.

SUMMARY AND RECOMMENDATIONS

A number of psychotherapeutic models in use in primary care have been described. Brief psychodynamic therapy requires a high degree of skill, knowledge and experience. Short treatment does not imply easy treatment, even for an experienced therapist. Patients who are looking for rapid symptom relief and who do not have much interest in exploring the underlying intrapsychic or historical causes of their problems are likely to be offered psychotropic medication or cognitive-behavioural therapy. CBT is an educative model, helping patients to alter their cognitions and actively problem-solve their way through difficulties. Although it is the most frequently used brief therapy in clinical psychology departments in the NHS, it is not suitable for all patients. Cognitive-analytic therapy (CAT) may be a safe first therapy for most patients including borderlines because the structured setting does not foster the development of intense regressive transferences.

There is always more than one feeling about a situation, and the therapeutic task in the humanistic model is to explore as many of these as possible, on the grounds that decision-making and coping are facilitated by awareness of the full range of feelings. Group, couples and family therapies are important treatment options in primary care and should be available in every locality. Single-session and 2+1 models can be viewed as trial interventions and as a form of assessment or triage. Much primary care work makes use of more than one model in an eclectic or integrative model.

The theoretical models most frequently used by counsellors, psychotherapists, psychologists, psychiatrists and consultant psychotherapists have been described. The Department of Health's Strategic Review of Psychotherapy has distinguished three levels of psychotherapy delivered in the NHS. Type A psychological treatments are an integral component of generic mental health care such as routine GP treatment of psychological problems. Type B treatments are complete interventions in a set number of sessions but informed by more than one theoretical framework. Much counselling in primary care is of this type. Type C therapies are complete interventions in a set number of sessions informed by a single theoretical model. Formal psychotherapy is a Type C treatment and is only occasionally offered in the primary care setting.

'How much counselling or psychotherapy is enough for this patient?' is a pressing question in the present cost-containment climate in health care. UK practitioners have much to learn from the American experiment with managed care. In the managed care environment, the overriding concern has been reduction in medical utilization rates: if a treatment results in a drop in medical utilization rates, it has been 'successful'.

Managed care is effectively a form of externally mandated brief therapy achieved by limiting the number of sessions, placing dollar caps on annual psychotherapy benefits, or adopting case management mechanisms. For those personality disordered and abused patients who are incapable of intimacy, the capacity to trust and become safely dependent on the therapist are crucial outcomes that will not be achieved in 1–6 sessions. When third-party reimbursement requires clinicians either to fabricate a reimbursable diagnosis or actively hide severe pathology, serious ethical questions must be asked.

In managed care, clinicians repeatedly have to justify their treatment plans to a third party, and if continuing treatment is refused, the patient may feel abandoned. Especially for those in whom early loss is a prominent feature, when patients are able to make the ending their own positive step, rather than having to accept an abrupt ending imposed on them by others, therapy is truly finished. Managed mental health care violates patients' rights to privacy, penalizes practitioners who refuse to break confidentiality, exacerbates patients' anxiety by adding the worry about when therapy will end, creates a sense of mistrust between patient and practitioner, and may restrict choice by requiring a change from a known and trusted therapist.

Managed care makes no effort to hide the fact that its sole goal is to bring people back to their premorbid levels of functioning. For some personality disordered patients, that may be a very low level indeed. Emphasis in managed care is on 'medical necessity', although this remains controversial in psychotherapy. In what does medical necessity consist in cases of comorbidity? One to six session contracts will not suffice for patients at the severe end of the spectrum. Evidence of efficacy is lacking in the ultra-brief therapies, especially regarding relapse or recurrence after treatment.

Research shows that time-limited treatment is inferior to psychotherapy in which length of treatment is clinically determined. Optimal results are obtained when the patient – not the managed care company – decides it is time to stop. Appropriately prescribed psychodynamic outpatient psychotherapy is one of the most cost-efficient treatments today, when we consider that 70–80 per cent of the cost of all psychological and psychiatric care is for inpatient treatment. Six sessions can be used with carefully selected patients to motivate them for longer-term therapy and onward referral. Some patients find they need only one or two sessions, and are happy to be discharged at that time.

4

ASSESSMENT FOR SHORT VS. LONGER-TERM TREATMENT

Taken together, Chapters 4 and 5 provide a comprehensive guide to assessment for short- vs. longer-term treatment in primary care. This chapter makes suggestions for structuring the assessment interview, including the problem and the history of the problem, the psychosocial history, 'things to listen for' and the psychodynamic formulation. Chapter 5 examines the relevance to assessment of early loss events, comorbidity, and personality disorder, and offers suggestions on how to decide about treatment modality.

It may be argued that the comprehensive assessment being advocated here seldom takes place in primary care, and is more often characteristic of assessment at the secondary or tertiary level. Our point is that a detailed assessment such as this *in primary care* will avoid several adverse outcomes, the emotional costs of which are borne by patients. The two most important adverse outcomes are inappropriate brief treatment leading to no change, deterioration or relapse; and/or repeated referral of patients to one secondary service after another, each of which rejects the patient as unsuitable for the treatment on offer. In the first situation the patient's condition is not helped, has deteriorated, or shows only short-term gains, leading to the 'revolving door phenomenon' with all the concomitant costs to the service. In the second, patients are likely to draw the conclusion that the problem is unmanageable or hopeless, perhaps as they always feared. This outcome is particularly damaging to borderline patients who experience their feelings as unmanageable much of the time. A third reason for doing a detailed assessment at the primary care level is that it may disclose long undiagnosed severe mental illness. Appropriate referral to secondary psychiatric services can then be arranged.

Surprisingly few books have been written on assessment for counselling and psychotherapy. Mace (1995b) offers chapters on assessment for psychoanalytic, brief psychodynamic, cognitive-behavioural, cognitive-analytic, group, couple and family therapies. Palmer and McMahon (1997) explore assessment for counselling drawing on perspectives from rational-emotive, cognitive-behavioural and multimodal therapies. Lukas (1993) reviews the fundamentals of assessment from a social work perspective. Daines, Gask and Usherwood (1997) outline medical and psychiatric issues for counsellors, and Morrison (1997) offers guidelines for recognizing when psychological problems may mask serious medical disorders. Horowitz (1997) focuses on formulation as a guide for treatment planning from an eclectic perspective and Eells (1997) provides a comprehensive overview of psychotherapy case formulation from a variety of theoretical orientations.

A handful of useful articles have been written on assessment for psychodynamic psychotherapy (Coltart, 1986; Hinshelwood, 1991; Klein, 1990; Milton, 1997; Schachter, 1997), and Berkowitz (1996) addresses assessment issues for counsellors in the primary care setting from a psychodynamic perspective. Accurate assessment is particularly important in primary care because the patient may be sent from one clinician to another until one of them takes the measure of their problems and recommends appropriate treatment. Often a patient is given a series of specialist assessments. Each time the patient is rejected for treatment, potential harm is done (Margison, 1997).

THE REFERRAL LETTER

Most primary care mental health work begins with a referral letter from the GP. Some GPs are excellent at preparing the ground for counselling and give a lot of relevant history as well as a detailed description of the presenting problem. Others send a couple of sentences about symptoms. Even a psychologically-minded GP may have a fraction of the story when the referral is made. The following is an extreme example:

> The GP letter said: 'This young man has stopped going out with his mates to the pub. I wonder if social skills training might help.' The night before the patient's appointment, the counsellor received a telephone call at home from a hospital consultant who had seen the patient that day. 'He was complaining of pain in one of his testicles. We thought there might be a bit of torsion but on examination there wasn't. He said something about tying himself up with rope. He was *extremely* anxious talking about it.' This was the first hint that there was more to this story than social isolation.

Over several assessment sessions the story emerged. The young man, who was very slightly built, had got into the habit of bracing a stepladder securely between his bed and his wardrobe. He then tied a rope around his genitals and hung himself upside down by his genitals from the ladder to the fantasy, 'Here is this nice girl, cutting off my genitals' – a ritualistic attempt at castration. Unfortunately, he had had to alter the gauge of rope because he had been bursting blood vessels in his penis.

The actuality of the patient's difficulties may bear little resemblance to the problem mentioned in the referral letter. As Gustafson has observed about those with longstanding disturbance, 'The surface of these patients can be anything' – depression, anxiety, relationship problems, agoraphobia, grief reactions, substance abuse or psychosomatic symptoms. It is well to bear this in mind when referred a patient who looks on the face of it to be suffering from a monosymptomatic phobia or an apparently simple problem. The situation may be more complex when a full assessment has been done, sometimes dramatically so. A factor to bear in mind is that psychiatric diagnoses and psychological treatment have to be mentioned in medical reports for life assurance, and therefore some GPs may minimize these in referral letters. But whatever mental health treatment is eventually offered, a detailed assessment is essential. Ideally, this assessment is carried out at the primary care level.

PRE-ASSESSMENT QUESTIONNAIRES

Many primary care mental health services use pre-assessment postal questionnaires which the patient is asked to complete before the first appointment. A wide range of questionnaires is in use. The Hospital Anxiety and Depression Scale, Beck Depression Inventory, Symptom Checklist-90 Revised, Brief Symptom Inventory and Inventory of Interpersonal Problems are a few examples. The Areas of Change Questionnaire is useful in couples therapy. Choice of pre-treatment questionnaires will be dealt with more fully in Chapter 6, including a new 34-item CORE measure developed by the Psychological Therapies Research Centre (PTRC) at the University of Leeds (Barkham, 1997) which will soon be in widespread use. Pre-assessment questionnaires are useful as baseline measures of symptomatology before treatment begins, especially when clinically informative subscale scores are available. For example, the Brief Symptom Inventory (Derogatis and Spencer, 1982) includes subscales for psychoticism, somatization, depression, hostility, phobic anxiety, obsessive-compulsive, panic, paranoid ideation, and generalized anxiety. Whether the patient returns the questionnaire may serve as a measure of motivation to attend. Questionnaires prepare patients for what psychotherapy may entail and their contents may help the assessor to focus the interview. They also provide pre-treatment data for audit and research, allow diagnosis and prioritization, save the assessor time, and may help to identify the most appropriate assessor among a team of clinicians (Mace, 1995a).

A personal history questionnaire initially devised at the Tavistock Clinic in London has undergone a number of revisions and is used by many NHS departments up and down the country. When conscientiously filled in by the patient, this questionnaire can save time in assessment interviews and provide very valuable information:

- Please describe the nature of your difficulties as you see them, mentioning how long you have had them and how and when they started, as well as your present condition.

- In what way do your difficulties affect your life generally at the present time?

- What aspects of your life give you satisfaction?

- In what way do you expect treatment to help you? When you imagine yourself having treatment, what form does it take?

- Have you, or anyone in your family, been referred to the psychiatric services before?

- Have you had psychotherapy or psychological treatment previously? If so, could you please give details.

- Please comment on your physical health in general. Have you had any serious illnesses or accidents at any time in your life?

- Do you have any difficulties with your body, the way it functions, the way you feel about it and the way you think it looks?

- Have you ever made a suicide attempt? If so, please outline the circumstances and what happened.

- Are you taking medicines prescribed for you at the moment? If so, can you give details.

- Are you taking, or have you taken, non-prescribed drugs of any kind? Is there any concern about your drinking?

- We would like some details about your family:

    — father: age now (or at death if no longer alive, with date)
        — if dead, your own age when he died
            — occupation, when working

    — mother: age now (or at death if no longer alive, with date)
        — if dead, your own age when she died
            — occupation, when working

- Please tell us something about your father, his character or personality, and your relationship with him.

- Please tell us something about your mother, her character or personality, and your relationship with her.

- Please list your brothers and sisters (including half-brothers or sisters) in order of age, including yourself. Please indicate any stillbirths, miscarriages or abortions of which you are aware.

    — name/age/if dead, your own age when he or she died/occupation

- Could you tell us something about your childhood? Please mention any changes or separations you experienced or any other important early relationships, e.g. with grandparents, aunts, uncles or friends.

- Are you single, living with a partner, married, separated, divorced or widowed? If you are, or have been married or living with someone: for how long? age of husband/wife/partner? His/her occupation?

- If you are married or living with someone, do you have any unhappiness or problems in this relationship? Please try to describe them.

- Please list your children, including any stepchildren, in order of age. Please also indicate any stillbirths, miscarriages or abortions [if dead, your own age when he/she died].

- Please tell us something about your children.

- With which person do you have your closest relationship in life?

- What do you find satisfies you and/or frustrates you in this relationship?

- Do you have any sexual problems or difficulties in your sexual relationships? If so, please try to describe them.

- What are your present domestic circumstances? Do you find them difficult in any way?

- Please tell us something about your social relationships.

- How do you feel when you are in a group of people?

- Please tell us something about your schooling and any later education.

- What is your present employment?

- What are your plans and prospects in your work?

- Please give a brief summary of your previous employment since leaving school (age, employment, dates, reasons for leaving or any other comment).

- Please mention any particular satisfaction or difficulties you have experienced in your working life.

- Please use this space if there is any other information which might be important, helpful or relevant in relationship to your difficulties (or to expand on any of the earlier questions if you had insufficient space).

Other questions which can usefully be added to a pre-assessment questionnaire are:

- How do you see yourself as a person and how do you feel other people see you?

- Relationships are important in everyone's life. Please describe what tends to happen between you and others.

- Do you feel that the problems you have in your life are your responsibility or are they contributed to by other people? If other people, who are they?

- Can you say why you are seeking help now?

(Aveline, 1995)

THINGS TO LISTEN FOR IN
THE ASSESSMENT INTERVIEW

Sequences of feelings

Assuming that the counsellor already has a grounding in Rogerian reflection-of-feelings techniques, sequences of feelings can be useful to note, especially when they occur as part of a pattern in interpersonal relationships. Such patterns will help inform the core conflictual relationship theme:

- Every time *anger* is experienced, it is followed by a feeling of *guilt*.

- As a relationship ends, the first feeling may be *hurt*, then *anger* and then *guilt*.

- As the prospect of intimacy arises, first there are feelings of *need*, and then *fear*.

- The feeling of need may be accompanied by feelings of *shame, devaluation of the other*, or *superiority* over others.

- After a loss, *helplessness* may be followed by feelings of *worthlessness*, intense *fear*, *sadness* and *emptiness*.

- After the loss of a parent who had hurt, controlled and deprived a person, there may be feelings of *guilt*, *anger* and *sadness*.

Metaphors

In speaking about their problems, patients will sometimes use vivid metaphors which can be used to elaborate life themes. For example:

1. A woman describes herself as *walking a tightrope* high above the rest of the world. People below are going about their business and developing relationships. Out of her fear of intimacy and because of two traumatic losses in the recent past, she is living in a kind of splendid isolation high above the fray, where her consuming preoccupation is in keeping herself from falling off the tightrope. It became possible to talk about people below inviting her to come down.

2. A man describes how during the potato famine, tenant farmers in Ireland were evicted to spend the winter in a *hole in the ground*. Men, pregnant women, babies and the aged went to live in these pits with a roof of branches and turf, where few survived the winter. Water poured through the roofs, illness quickly followed, the aged soon died and babies perished. The atmosphere was one of acute deprivation, loss of all those who were loved, lack of food and warmth, and waiting for death. It was possible to explore how this metaphor described this

man's view of his own life: living in a hole in the ground, without love or warmth, waiting to die.

3. A young man describes a dream in which the *white hand of a corpse is reaching out of a coffin* toward him. This metaphor expresses his preoccupation with life as a living death, the powerful pull toward suicide, his repeated nightmares of decomposing corpses, strange events in graveyards at midnight, and words mumbled by the 'flaccid lips of the dead'. This therapy was focused for most of its duration on interesting this young man in going on living.

Metaphors are especially useful when employed to relate past to present experience outside the sessions, and to here-and-now experience with the therapist. Important metaphors may emerge when the patient is asked to report a recent dream. Repeating dreams are of special importance.

Interpersonal issues

Another useful way of listening is in terms of interpersonal issues:

- *Intimacy*
    - excessively intense need for intimacy
    - denial of need for intimacy
    - fear that intimacy will result in abandonment
    - incapacity for intimacy due to excessive preoccupation with self
    - incapacity to maintain an intimate relationship over a period of time
    - capacity for intimacy overwhelmed by aggressive impulses
    - feels undeserving of an intimate relationship
    - choice of partner who is incapable of intimacy.

- *Control*
    - overuse of control
    - lack of control
    - excessive rigidity of control
    - inconsistency of control

— strong need to control others as well as the self

— choice of partner with excessive control or poor control.

- *Dependency*
  — denial of all dependent needs

  — unable to make self vulnerable for fear of abandonment

  — exaggeration of dependent needs

  — guilt and shame about dependency

  — narcissistic rage when dependent needs go unmet

  — inability to choose appropriate persons on whom to depend.

- *Trust*
  — inability to trust others

  — too trusting of others, 'naive'

  — unable to share feelings with others or talk to others

  — feeling that the world is an unsafe place

  — fear that trusting others will result in betrayal

  — choice of untrustworthy partner.

- *Anger*
  — unable to express anger

  — fear of aggressive impulses

  — anger expressed in a violent and uncontrollable fashion

  — anger always followed by a feeling of guilt

  — anger always followed by a feeling of fear

  — fear of retaliation from those with whom one has been angry

  — choice of partner who cannot express anger or deal with anger in others

  — choice of partner who cannot control anger, is violent and abusive.

- *Sexuality*
  — inhibition of sexual desire and of sexual response

— inability to let go and experience orgasm

— denial of sexual needs: cannot accept own sexuality

— incapable of controlling sexual impulses: sexual acting out

— infiltration of sexual impulses with aggression

— inability to integrate sexuality with intimacy

— sexual partner becomes 'all bad' after being used for sexual purposes

— sexual partner inappropriately idealized, 'put on pedestal'

— inability to see sexual partner as a whole person

— acting out interpersonal conflict in a destructive sexual relationship

— choice of inappropriate sexual partners.

- *Self-disclosure*

    — unable to talk about feelings

    — too ready to self-disclose, and to inappropriate people

    — self-disclosure is not accompanied by insight or understanding

    — not interested in understanding feelings or experiences of self or others

    — passive-aggressive response: to say and do nothing is safer

    — choice of partner who is unable to talk about feelings.

- *Boundaries*

    — no boundaries between people: people 'flow into' one another

    — no respect for existing boundaries between people

    — too rigid reliance on boundaries to defend against intimacy

    — choice of partner who has inadequate or too rigid boundary control

- *Rejection*

    — incapable of intimacy because terrified of rejection

— does the rejecting first, before the other can do it

— rejects others contemptuously, as inferior

— responds to rejection with helplessness and hopelessness

— sees self as rejected, unloved and worthless

— misperceives commonplace events as rejection

— choice of rejecting partner.

- *Separation*

    — incapable of separating from parents

    — responds to separation with feelings of helplessness and hopelessness

    — defends against pain of separation by 'feeling nothing'

    — responds to separation with narcissistic rage reaction

    — responds to separation with feelings of guilt

    — responds to separation with feeling of emptiness and inner desolation

    — unable to separate from destructive or abusing partner

    — choice of dependent partner to defend against prospect of separation.

Barriers to love: some causes of the inability to form loving relationships

Common childhood antecedents to this problem include the following:

- Choosing partners who abuse or reject them as their mothers or fathers did.

- Finding oneself unable to separate from parents in order to find a partner.

- Choosing unsuitable partners, people who are already committed to another person or people who show no interest in forming a stable committed relationship with anyone.

- Searching for someone as good as mother or father was and finding no one as a result.

- Searching for someone parents will approve of, without success.

- Sometimes the problem is that the person lacks the basic trust that should have been established early in life, and as a result never allow themselves to become vulnerable in a loving relationship.

- Another common problem is that the child grows up continually preoccupied with the self, which could have been a 'survival kit' in childhood to keep the self sane in the face of mad or destructive parents. However, as adults they are unable to reach out and form a relationship because they never learned, as children, to care for others as well as themselves.

- Or perhaps they have been overwhelmed, overcontrolled and smothered by their mother and, too frightened of ever letting that happen again, withdraw from all intimate relationships out of a fear of suffocation.

- Sometimes parents are so bizarre and strange, or the emotional life of the family so empty that the child decides not to try to get to know anyone else and retreats into their own fantasy world.

- In other cases parents blame the child for having been born, leading to a pathological burden of guilt, chronic low self-esteem and a fear of developing relationships out of a sense of unworthiness.

- Sometimes adults, having failed to find an adequate mother or mother-substitute in childhood, are left with a huge unfilled hole inside themselves and look for someone to mend all of this, making them whole and filling up the emptiness inside: When others fail to do so, as they must, for what is being asked is impossible, the relationship ends in failure.

STRUCTURING THE ASSESSMENT INTERVIEW

There are at least five principal therapist activities in assessment interviews:

- Understanding the problem and its history.

- Assembling a psychosocial history and psychodynamic formulation based on the problem and the psychosocial history.

- Making a preliminary diagnostic formulation.
- Building a therapeutic alliance.
- Forming an impression about therapy modality.

Assessment also involves identifying those who would be at risk from psychotherapy, locating the problem as intrapsychic, interpersonal, or limited to a specific relationship (a pointer toward therapeutic modality such as individual, group, couple or family), excluding major mental or physical disorder, assessing impulse control and dangerousness to self and others, discussing the correctness of therapy now, and matching patient need to therapy and therapist (Aveline, 1995).

There are many advantages to having two assessment interviews, as patients often present differently a second time. With very disturbed or distressed patients, the main goal of the first session may be crisis intervention and support, and assessment may have to be postponed. Sometimes the initial interviews require 3–6 hours on as many days, time well spent when patients present with severe disturbance and longstanding problems. Occasionally assessment can be done in an hour. Boundaries are established around the time that has been offered, the setting, and a particular chair. It can be important not to see patients who arrive early until the time appointed, as they may be testing the reliability of the boundaries on a first visit.

Experienced clinicians come to trust their intuition or 'gut sense' about patients in initial interviews. For example, some patients are motivated to suppress the real reason for their distress, sometimes because a spouse or partner sees the same GP. Occasionally a clinician will listen to a patient's problem and do a history to discover no apparent reason for the patient's unhappiness. If patients realize the facade has come down they may say, 'I haven't told you the real reason I'm upset. I'm having an affair, but my wife doesn't know.' On other occasions the counsellor may have a strong impression that a psychotic process underlies what is being said. Arguments do not hang together, speech is tangential and rambling, and odd turns of phrase or neologisms make their appearance. When these patterns are pronounced and are accompanied by psychotic symptoms, an urgent psychiatric assessment should be arranged. The difficulty in such cases is often that there may be an absence of 'hard' evidence of severe disorder. Consultation with a more experienced therapist may be of help. A patient's emotion may not appear to be genuine, or there is something that does not ring true about a story. However, it is well to remember that therapists occasionally fall prey to tall tales told by charming and plausible antisocial personalities. There may be a striking lack of coherence to the patient's self-presentation, alerting the counsellor to the lack of a core stable self. Sometimes the interviewer feels it is as if there is 'nothing firm or substantial to come up against' in conversation. Not infrequently a borderline or 'as if' personality underlies the surface symptomatology. Finally, obsessionals are very skilled at 'rolling in the fog', as Harry Stack Sullivan was fond of putting it, as soon as the therapist gets close to something central. At precisely the moment that something is about to be clarified, there is a change of subject, or some other matter seems more important to discuss. Many other examples of the use of intuition in initial interviews could be cited. It is important to develop and learn to trust intuitive insights such as these and follow them up with a careful assessment.

Prospective patients may of course also be intuitively assessing the therapist during the initial interview, and there is potentially a good deal of information the patient will want to obtain in the first session: how does therapy work, how does the recommended therapy compare with other treatments, how long does it take, what are the therapist's qualifications, how much does it cost (in the private sector), will the patient be discussed with anyone else, and is what the patient says confidential (Tantum, 1995). Such questions should always be answered fully.

Information on the *limits of confidentiality* should either be available to patients in a pre-counselling leaflet or explained in the initial session. These issues tend to arise when patients are an active danger to themselves or others, appear to be incapable of taking responsibility for their own actions, or are abusing children. If the counsellor is contemplating breaking confidentiality by sharing certain details with the GP, the patient's consent should be sought whenever possible. It is also good practice to discuss the situation with a clinical supervisor or more experienced therapist before taking action.

Some counsellors take the view that all material disclosed during counselling is confidential, and refuse to share any details with GPs. In today's NHS, some GPs find this stance difficult, as the doctor loses track of what is happening therapeutically. GPs may also find decisions about patients' medical care more difficult when information is not shared. Most primary care mental health workers write a letter to the GP following assessment, and regularly update the doctor on progress. If it is the clinician's practice to send an assessment report to the GP, this should be made clear to the patient at assessment: 'It is my usual practice to write to your GP with a summary of this session.' If patients have problems with such a report being sent, they usually voice them immediately. Most patients readily agree to the sharing of information between counsellor and GP.

Occasionally patients ask whether notes are made after sessions and if so whether they are kept securely. Sometimes they ask whether the GP has access to these notes. Most counsellors maintain their own case notes separate from the patient's medical record. Only written communications from the counsellor to the GP will become part of the patient's medical notes. If counsellors in training wish to audiotape or videotape the assessment, or if a one-way mirror is being used, the patient's written consent must first be obtained. The consent form should state when any tape recordings will be destroyed. When patients object to letters being sent to the GP or to audiotapes being made of sessions, this may be a communication to the counsellor about the sensitivity of the material likely to emerge. It is also often a rough measure of the degree of disturbance. Patients with relatively straightforward problems tend not to raise objections to written reports or tape recordings. Personality-disordered patients and especially those with paranoid trends may object vehemently to audiotaping and be very concerned about anything communicated to the GP in writing.

THE PROBLEM AND ITS HISTORY

Therapists usually introduce themselves by name and establish the purpose of the session by saying something like, 'We've had a letter from your GP, so I know a bit about the problem. The purpose of this initial session is to understand the problem in more detail, to learn enough about your history and background so that we can begin to make sense of the problem, and come to a decision about whether we will be able to help.' It may then help to say, 'I would be interested to know how you see the problem.' Sometimes patients will say clearly what the problem is: 'I can't go on buses or in lifts', 'I've gone off sex completely', or 'I don't seem to be able to mix with people.' On other occasions patients will have difficulty formulating the problem and they may say, 'It's everything.' In the latter case, the inability to identify a specific problem is the first clinical indication of comorbidity (more than one problem) and the possibility of an underlying personality disorder.

A detailed description of symptoms is needed, together with what was going on in the patient's life when the symptoms began or worsened, what they have done in an attempt to resolve the problem, and whether they have had previous episodes of treatment. If they were in therapy before, was it helpful and if so how? The timing of symptom onset is particularly important. Was it triggered by a loss (bereavement, redundancy, house move, a close friend moving away, retirement); an upset (problems with children, work stress, marital problems); or a success (promotion, marriage, an honour in the work environment)? Did any particular *event*, however trivial, immediately precede the onset of the symptom? If not, did the precipitating event occur in the previous months or within the previous year? What does the patient believe is the cause of the symptom?

Sometimes there are many problems. A summary of each problem presented enables the process to move forward: 'So the first problem is that you and your husband aren't getting on very well these days. Are there any other problems?' Periodically it helps to list the problems that have been mentioned (e.g. depression, anxiety, marital and relationship problems) and then to say, 'Would you say that summarizes the various problems, or are there others we haven't talked about yet?' Sometimes the most serious problem is revealed only after asking, 'Are there any other problems?' several times. It is then possible to go on to hear the history of that problem, what seems to have triggered it initially, what has been tried to remedy it, what makes it worse or better, and why help is sought now. The patient's overall life situation should be explored, not only what symptoms they are experiencing, but the quality of their relationships at home and at work. Much important information may emerge here. Therapists working within a CBT framework will do a behavioural assessment at this point (Chapter 3). Those working within a schema-focused CBT model will also take a detailed history (see below).

Interviewers need to ask repeatedly, 'Are there any other problems?' because often enough after the first three problems there is a pause and the patient says, 'There is one other thing' – which is the most serious and most important problem of all. In the NHS, rushed assessments have the cost advantage that the clinician never gets to the bottom of what is troubling the patient. A very brief treatment is offered for the first and only apparent problem, and the patient reappears within a few months or a year with the other problems unresolved. As one perceptive clinician commented, 'The problem in the NHS is that you might have to take on the *real* problem if you ask, "Are there any other problems?"' If there are insufficient funds in the budget to take on the real problem, clinicians may settle for a superficial problem and promptly discharge the patient, 'greatly improved'. Pre- and post-therapy measures may show a good result – even marked improvement – but the patient's most important problem may never have been identified, let alone addressed. This scenario happens all too frequently at present on both sides of the Atlantic. Problem areas to be considered include not only the obvious psychological, psychiatric and interpersonal issues, but also medical problems, patterns of substance use, work, financial, housing and legal problems, and issues around leisure activities.

Suicide risk

Suicide risk needs to be assessed in those who are depressed. The patient who is deeply withdrawn may be contemplating suicide. On the other hand some patients known to be depressed become unaccountably cheerful after having taken the decision to end their life, with a lethal plan in mind. The interviewer needs to be alert to hints that suicide is being considered: 'If only I could fall asleep and it would all be over', 'I don't think I can bear this much longer', or 'There's no point in going on.' Such hints should be followed up with a risk assessment: does the patient have a plan, how lethal is that plan, under what circumstances might they carry it out, and how likely do they think it is that they will act on the plan? If there have been previous suicide attempts, it is important to ask what happened, whether they intended unquestionably to end their life or whether it was a cry for help, and whether medical attention was needed. Not infrequently there have been previous suicide attempts of which the GP is unaware. Occasionally patients ask the counsellor not to share this information with the GP, which can put the clinician in a difficult position if patients are currently a risk to themselves and actively suicidal. Patients at greater risk of suicide have a previous history of suicide attempts, have suffered a recent loss (such as bereavement or redundancy), are socially isolated, and face chronic problems such as housing or financial difficulties. An urgent psychiatric assessment may need to be arranged. Those with a lethal plan and a high likelihood of acting on it within the next few days may need to be hospitalized. Close links with the GP and secondary services are vitally important in these cases.

Reflection-of-feeling responses

Rogerian reflection-of-feeling responses are helpful throughout the initial interview, such as 'So what seems to be upsetting you most is . . ., and you seem to be saying you feel very angry about that'. This helps build a therapeutic alliance because the patient begins to feel heard and understood at an emotional level. When you reflect back the wrong feeling it helps to say, for example, 'Oh, so it isn't so much a feeling of anger, it's more a feeling of sheer frustration.' As long as reflections are offered tentatively, they are likely to be received as supportive.

Expectations of therapy

It is important to ask patients what they hope for from therapy. Some are looking for a magical, quick or permanent 'fix' for problems. Sometimes this is couched in questions about hypnosis. If people spontaneously express a dislike of a certain kind of therapy, it is important to make a note of that. For example, some patients will say they would not consider joining a group, or their partner is unwilling to attend couples therapy.

Note-taking

Therapists differ on whether they take notes during the first session. If patients ask, it can be explained that in the initial session you need to collect a good deal of information, and notes will help you understand the problem better. If challenged by very paranoid patients, it is advisable to give up note-taking. Most therapists do not take notes after the initial assessment. An alternative to note-taking is tape recording the session if the patient is agreeable. Some therapists take no notes in the initial session but record the material from memory, after the session.

THE PSYCHOSOCIAL HISTORY

It is worth doing a psychosocial history with every patient, even if the end result is an offer of cognitive-behavioural therapy. The first reason for this is to obtain a view of the patient's development and to arrive at an accurate diagnosis. Without a history it is often impossible to understand the background to the current problem and any comorbid conditions. Chapter 3 will have made it clear that the patient's early history is as important to a schema-focused cognitive therapy as it is to a psychodynamic treatment. Sometimes, with unpsychologically-minded patients, the need for history gathering may need to be explained:

> 'It may seem puzzling to you to talk about the past, but I find that if I know something about a person's story, I can understand the problem better and I am better able to help.'

Another reason for taking a history is that it helps create a therapeutic 'holding environment' (Winnicott, 1965) in which patients begin to feel that their difficulties are contained and at least partially understood. A third reason for taking a history is that implicit in history taking is the idea that present problems are linked to the past. Developmental delays, especially around separation and individuation, can be assessed through the history. The patient's ego capacities are also mobilized in telling the story and making meaning of events (Schachter, 1997). An example of failure to take a history follows:

> A builder was referred for a phobia of heights. Given his need to spend much of his professional life on ladders, the phobia was disabling. His first therapist did only a behavioural assessment and discharged him apparently cured after a handful of sessions. Within a year he was re-referred for 'anxiety on the ground'. The underlying issues had not been addressed in the first therapy. The second therapist took a history and discovered two important facts from the patient's first five years of life. First, as a toddler he had fallen head first onto an electric fire and was severely burned on both his hands. Treatment lasted several months. A short time later he was hospitalized for a life-threatening illness. Both the phobia and 'anxiety on the ground' turned out to be about a basic insecurity derived from early trauma, a need to be in touch with 'terra firma'. The first behavioural treatment had failed because of an inadequate assessment and the complete lack of a psychosocial history.

'You are one of how many children?' is a good first question which can be followed up with ages, occupations and marital status of siblings, and whether they have ever had any 'nervous trouble'. From this information many things are immediately apparent: only children or 'virtually only children' (with six or more years between them and the nearest sibling); siblings who died in infancy; long gaps between children, either from different marriages or because later children were 'mistakes'; children conceived out of wedlock; a schizophrenic sibling; or a sibling who died a suicide. A *genogram* may help to structure this information (Stanion, Papadopoulos and Bor, 1997). Drawing such a diagram of the patient's family may disclose clinically important patterns such as several genera-

tions of suicide, eating disorder, substance abuse, or depression; premature deaths in adulthood; a tendency for marriages to end in divorce; and repeated infertility, stillbirths, or a tendency to give birth to twins.

'Did your mother lose any babies lost along the way?' is a second useful question because it discloses miscarriages, stillbirths, terminations, and babies who died shortly after delivery. Depending on the age of the patient at the time, these details may be very significant. For example, children born within a year of the death of a previous infant may be 'replacement children'. Occasionally they are given the same name as the dead baby. An only child conceived after lengthy infertility treatment may have an overly anxious mother. A child born after a Downs syndrome baby may have a mother who is hypervigilant to any early signs of brain damage. A child whose mother had a stillbirth when they were aged 3 may have had a depressed mother who was temporarily emotionally unavailable.

'What do you know about your birth, the actual delivery?' is an important next question because the baby may have been unwanted, the delivery may have been difficult, and mother and baby may have been in poor health. When patients reply 'Nothing', a useful follow-up question is 'Home or hospital?' Usually the answer to that question is known, and more information follows. Severe birth trauma, a life-threatening delivery, separation from the mother at birth (for example, in a neonatal intensive care unit), a baby born in prison or when father was away in the war may emerge in answer to this question. Some birth stories point to an early rejection, for example, a mother who said to the patient whenever she was angry with her, 'Twas only the whiskey fetched you' (this baby was a 'mistake'). *'Were you and your mother both healthy after the delivery?'* is another helpful follow-up question. A history of post-natal depression in the mother is important because of the mother's emotional unavailability to her child during the early days and weeks of life. Failure of bonding is not uncommon in these cases.

'Did you feel wanted by your parents?' is useful to ask if the answer is not already apparent from previous material. The answer to this question sometimes discloses that parents considered or attempted abortion of the patient (Sonne, 1994). Children who were told they were unwanted, who were told their parents wanted them aborted, or who witnessed their mothers attempting to abort subsequent siblings, may feel they suffer from 'the crime of being born' (Goldman, 1988). Many have histories of repeated suicide attempts. They may have a lifelong tendency to attempt to please their mothers by dying. Such examples may sound extreme, but they occur regularly in clinical work:

'My mother never wanted me. She said having children ruined her life. When I was a little girl she became pregnant again, but she got rid of the baby by jumping downstairs. Day after day I watched her jump, until one day the doctor came and my mother wasn't pregnant anymore.'

'I was the result of a one-night stand. My mother told me how she tried to do away with me, but I wouldn't die. The delivery was very traumatic. Both of us nearly died. Later she told me I had ruined her body, destroyed her career, and made her marry a man she didn't love.'

'My mother tried to do away with me by drinking gin, taking tablets and overworking in a neighbour's garden. After I was born she would often "forget" me, leaving me outside so neighbours would come and remind her that her baby was out there.'

Illnesses, accidents or separations as a child (including illnesses or deaths of parents and siblings, trauma during the war, and hospitalizations) should all be enquired about and followed up. Multiple separations and traumas may be particularly important and should be fully explored:

'I was born during the war. My mother was evacuated and I was born in a nursing home. My father was in France at the time. Mum was very poorly after my birth, and I was looked after by the family who had taken us in. When Father returned, he had been injured and had spent many months in a field hospital. He was silent and cut off from us. When I was only 5, he died. Mum had no money and nowhere to go, so we went to live with her mum. When I was 8, my nan died and we were alone again.'

'My little sister died one morning when she went downstairs to warm herself on the fire. Her nightdress went up in flames and no one could save her. I always blamed myself. If only I'd gone downstairs with her. I used to go downstairs with her, but that morning I didn't.'

'All the houses in our street were flattened by the bomb. My best friend died and his mother with him. We were in a shelter in the back garden. Somehow we survived, but my aunt put her head outside the shelter at the wrong time and had her head blown off.'

'One morning, Mum left. We were only very small. My father found some women in the village to come and help at first, and then our auntie came. My sister and I said, "We must be very, *very* good for Auntie." I think we must have thought mum had left because we'd been bad.'

'I went into hospital when I was 4 with suspected TB. My parents were not allowed to visit, and could only stand at the window and wave. Soon after, my mother died, but I wasn't told for six months. Nan came to look after us, but she couldn't cope, so we went to live with a great aunt who was very strict. When Nan recovered from a stroke, we went back with her, but she was "always dying and always being anointed". I was afraid to go home after school for fear of finding the curtains drawn. Nuns and priests were forever coming to the house to anoint her. Each time we thought she'd breathed her last, she survived. When I was 19 she finally did die, and I couldn't believe it. That *really did* upset me.'

'I had a substitute father who was there for a while but one day he got married. I went to the wedding and cried and cried. I kept saying, "He's mine, he's mine."'

Occasionally patients will describe an early loss and move directly on to a current relationship in which the early issues are apparent:

'I was separated from my mother at 18 months because she had to go into hospital. After this, I'm told I didn't want anything to do with my mother, but then I became very clingy. Mum overcompensated for the separation by overprotecting and fussing me. No one fusses me like my mum. Except maybe my fiancé. He likes teddy bears and has given me several. When I'm angry with him I smash the porcelain ones and cut the heads off the soft toys. Later I try to sew the heads back on. I hate the horrible person who does these things.'

It is helpful to enquire about *childhood relationships with siblings, frequent house moves,* and *physical or sexual abuse or assault* (see also Chapter 5). Particularly sensitive interviewing is required with survivors of childhood trauma and abuse (Saporta and Gans, 1995).

'My brother was six years older than I was, so we were never close. Mum wanted another baby and I wanted a little sister, but none came. Then when I was 12, suddenly I had a little brother and life changed for us completely. I was the one in the middle, I was almost like an only child.'

'My father was in the army. I went to seven different schools by the time I was 13. I gave up trying to make friends because I knew I'd have to leave at the end of the year.'

'When he came back from the pub and Mum was working nights, that was when it happened. He used to come into my bedroom and climb under the covers. He told me this was his special way of loving me, it was very secret, and if I ever told anyone, he would put me in a childrens' home and I would never see my mother again. I never told anyone. Then last year my sister told me he did the same thing to her. If Mum was alive, it would kill her to know what he did.'

In the following case, early loss, sexual abuse, and unresolved guilt occur together. Children who are sexually abused have frequently been rejected at an earlier age by their mothers:

'I was unwanted and illegitimate, and I was separated from my mother at birth. During my first four years I lived with five different people. I found out who my mother was when I was ten. I never knew my father. I later contacted, through a friend, the man whose name was on my birth certificate and was told he said, "She has nothing to do with me." When I was ten my moth-

er wanted me back to look after her new brood, so I
went to live with her and my stepfather. His brother
raped me seven times before I was 15. I barricaded my
bedroom door with furniture but he pushed his way
in and I had to do what he said. I told the police when
they came one night because of violence, but no one
listened to me. Once I took the little ones to the park
and one of mum's kids was killed in a fall in the play-
ground. I was blamed and was locked in a neighbour's bedroom, forbidden to go to the funeral.'

In some cases no overt sexual abuse occurred but there was an unpredictable sexual atmosphere in the home – a father whose sexual behaviour was so indiscriminate and uncontrolled, for example, that a child
could not be certain he would *not* attempt something sexual with her. In
such environments, normal oedipal fantasy is too dangerous for a child
to contemplate:

'He was always out on the town with different
women. Mum had given up caring. She knew what he
was like. He was always talking about the size of
women's breasts or their "vital statistics" – 36-24-36.
When I started growing up he used to leer at me, so
I'd run upstairs. I didn't like the way he looked at me.'

The *earliest memory* (EM), before the age of 3 or 5 if possible, frequently
sheds light on the presenting problem. For example:

EM with no people in it – 'A train was going along at
the edge of a field. That was all.' – presenting problem: no relationships.

EM of severe injury – 'I fell off the wall and split my
head open. I was rushed to hospital.' – presenting
problem: lack of confidence, history of repeated failures.

EM of emotional deprivation – 'Just me and my brother
in an empty room with a crust of dry bread.' – presenting problem: difficulties in relationships and
hunger for affection.

Next, explore and follow up any material relevant to the first five years of life. *'Did you have playmates before school?'* is an especially important question for only children. This information is often helpful when the presenting problem is a lack of ability to sustain relationships – a lonely child with a rich fantasy life and no friends, who found school difficult.

> 'My brother wasn't born until I was seven, so I was on my own until then with Mum. Dad was in the war until I was five. We lived in the country where there were no other kids my age. Mum loved books and had a leather-bound collection she'd inherited from her father. I buried myself in books as soon as I could read. Mum says I was reading storybooks at four. But when I got to school I *hated* it, and was badly bullied.'

> 'My grandparents had strict house rules. My parents could have no visitors and were restricted to a single room in the house. No playmates were allowed in. I made friends with the child next door and we played over the fence for years. We learned to play with a fence between us. A child's imagination is a wonderful thing.'

> 'My mother broke my will when I was a small child. I sought my own solitude from an early age.'

About here it is helpful to enquire about *parents' personalities*. 'What was your mother like when you were growing up? How did you get on with her? What was her most difficult feature?' These questions are repeated for father, step-parents, and other caretakers such as grandparents. If there were multiple caretakers, ages at each separation can be very informative, especially if symptoms began during childhood or adolescence. It is also helpful to ask how conflict and discipline were handled, whether it was possible to confide in parents, whether the patient felt closer to one parent as a child, whether they felt rejected, whether parents were threatening, and whether they suffered sexual or physical abuse at the hands of parents. Some of these questions form part of the Adult Attachment Interview (Main, 1995).

> [mother] 'Mum used to make us sit motionless and silent on chairs while she was reading. We were threatened with rat poison in our food and with being gassed in our sleep at night. I had one pair of under-

pants which I washed at night and tried to iron dry. Mum told me and my sisters, "I hope you're sterile. And if you have children, I hope they have two heads. And when I die I'll haunt you."'

[mother] 'What words can I use? . . . She was a stupid bitch and a whore. She drank half the housekeeping money and she was always down the pub getting screwed by some two-bit piece of low life she'd met. She hit both of us when she was drunk but the worst thing about her was that she was hardly ever *there*. There was usually no food in the house. I used to run down to my nan's on a Sunday morning to get something for breakfast.'

[mother] 'She always wanted a daughter, but actually I think she would have preferred me to be a dog. I looked after her dogs one day and one of the pups was run over, and she didn't speak to me for weeks. I'm not sure about her mental stability. She worked as a nurse in a mental home. I haven't had any contact with her for years.'

[grandmother] 'Her husband's death made her very bitter, but after Mum died, she became a recluse. I became the focus of her life and was made to feel very, very obligated. She was nosy and controlling and interfered with my girlfriends.'

[father] 'He was a bully. In the community everybody thought he was an upstanding man. He was a church-warden and then mayor. But he beat my mum – never badly enough to cause broken bones, so it never came to the attention of the authorities. He tried to kill me many times because I used to stand up for my mum. When I had to have help in my teens he called me mad. He still does.'

[father] 'I was a latchkey child, but one afternoon I came home to find the front door locked from the inside. I looked through the keyhole and saw my father hanging from the banister. A neighbour called the police. My mother was still at work. She didn't find out until suppertime.'

> [father] 'Highly strung, moody, temperamental and
> selfish with a chip on his shoulder, a *very big* chip. He
> could resort to violence. I think he was frustrated and
> unhappy, but I hated him and I used to wish he would
> go away and not come back.'

> [grandfather] 'He was a dour Yorkshireman, not very
> jolly. He took all the decisions in the family and was
> preoccupied with toilets. He also had what you could
> call a superiority complex.'

Sometimes patients will describe overwhelming atmospheres at home
when they were children:

> 'The physical environment of the old house was
> frightening: we had gas light, and the stairs and corri-
> dors were scary. My night light was a candle-like thing
> floating in water, casting flickering shadows on the
> wall. Someone had committed suicide in the house
> years before, and I felt a "negative presence" in the
> place. Mum repeatedly told me she could read my
> thoughts. She was very involved in spiritualism and
> contacting the dead, and she was involved in "auto-
> matic writing". She said she had been contacted by a
> "very high spiritual being". She sometimes spoke in
> foul language. Some of the "automatic writing" was
> in foul language.'

As Holmes (1997a) observes, 'attachment themes often stand out more
clearly at assessment than in the creative confusion of the therapy that
follows'. Parental responsiveness to a small child's emotions is a key
determinant of secure attachment. Early environments may be consistently responsive, consistently unresponsive, or inconsistently responsive. A good assessment interview will focus on early relationships with
parents in sufficient depth to generate hypotheses about the nature of the
patient's early *attachment to caregivers*: securely attached, insecurely
avoidant, or insecurely ambivalent. Not only will such information help
in formulating the case dynamically, it will also assist in forming hypotheses about the transferences that can be anticipated.

A discussion of parents' personalities and responsiveness may lead on
to the question, *'Has there been any "nervous trouble" in parents? parents'
families?'* Inherited mental disorders may emerge – or be actively sup-

pressed by some patients – at this point. When patients recount stories suggestive of severe mental illness it can help to ask, 'Was (s)he ever treated for that problem by a doctor?'

School years: Was the patient successful in making friends? How was their academic performance? Follow up any traumatic events such as severe punishments or bullying. Was puberty early or late? What were the patient's feelings about it, and about masturbation? Was sex education provided in the family, from friends, or at school? What were parents' attitudes toward sexuality?

> 'When I had my first period I didn't know what it was. I thought I must have a terrible disease until I told my mother and she fixed me up with some sanitary towels. That afternoon my aunt came in, sat at the kitchen table and said, "I hear you just sat on an axe." I rushed out of the room. Sanitary towels were very dirty things in our house. My father used to take them down to the bottom of the garden to burn them.'

A survey of adolescent development includes first interest in the opposite sex and any homosexual experiences or concerns. The first important girlfriend or boyfriend and first sexual experiences are helpfully explored at this point. Sometimes a first sexual experience is an abusive one. Antisocial behaviour, trouble with the police and drug or alcohol abuse may feature in some histories, although direct questions may have to be asked in order to disclose them. When all these relationships or experiences are lacking, what was adolescence like for the patient? School leaving age, qualifications, and decisions about a career are usually readily volunteered.

Young adulthood: areas to cover include engagement, marriage, cohabitating relationships, and children; circumstances of courtship; behaviour during engagement and after marriage where relevant; sexual adjustment in marriage or partnership(s); any history of infertility; relationships with partners and children; and relationships at work. Where there have been many jobs or relationships, this part of the history may take some time. If the presenting difficulty is relationship problems, a detailed history of what tends to go wrong in relationships is essential. 'How do your relationships end? Who tends to end them, you or the other person? What has tended to be the "last straw" in your relationships? Does this problem remind you of problems you had with your parents, or of your parents' problems with each other?'

Adulthood: a typical 24-hour day; interests, hobbies, leisure. Adult bereavements: perinatal losses (stillbirths, miscarriages and abortions); deaths of parents, siblings, friends, spouse; separations and divorces; ill health in significant others. Menopause, empty nest syndrome, mid-life crises, retirement, and other crises of adult life. General health of patient, partner and ex-partners, surviving parents, and children; thoughts about old age and death; current life situation, hopes and aspirations.

What was the most difficult time in your life? What got you through that?' This question will give clues to ego strength: does the patient collapse under stress, require hospitalization, make suicide attempts, get divorced, become an offender, attempt a 'geographical solution', or need medication? It may be important to ask specifically about some of these events if the history suggests they are a feature, as they are unlikely to be volunteered. Events particularly unlikely to be volunteered include a forensic history and long-term mental illness.

For couples work, a psychosocial history and a sexual history for each partner is needed. A conjoint initial interview is a good first step, followed by two individual interviews, and a second conjoint interview before deciding on therapy. These assessments thus require a minimum of four hours to complete.

It is important to be guided in the history by what the patient has to say, following up leads and discussing traumatic incidents in detail. *A set sequence of questions is unhelpful,* but the above are areas that should ideally be covered along the way. It is often helpful to ask for a *dream* in the initial session, a technique expertly used by Gustafson (1995a, b) in the formulation process. More generally, the initial interview needs to be conducted in an atmosphere where unconscious material can emerge (Holmes, 1995). Following clinical hunches and intuition, taking an interest in themes and metaphors and the ability to 'listen with the third ear' are important skills in this regard.

Early attempts at interpretation: even in the initial session, it is often possible to draw connections between the presenting problem and the details of the history as they occur, for example, 'So this problem goes at least as far back as your teenage years.' Special attention should be paid to any communications offered with the prefix, 'I don't suppose this matters particularly, but . . .' or 'I don't know if this is relevant, but . . .' or 'I don't know, could it be because of XYZ? That might have something to do with it.' For example, one patient said in her initial session, 'My mother left us when I was 4. That *might* have something to do with it.' This bit of history had everything to do with her presenting problem, which was a 21-year history of dependence on tranquillizers.

The patient's response to initial interpretations can be a good indicator of whether psychotherapy can be of help. For example, 'You described a tyrannical and domineering father, and I notice you have described a colleague you dislike in similar terms.' This interpretation relates a parent to a current significant other in Malan's triangle of insight. Is the patient able to think about this similarity and reflect on it? If not, psychodynamic therapy may not be appropriate or helpful. Positive responses to trial interpretation include a reaction at the feeling level, new associations to material already provided, increased reflectiveness on the meaning of the story presented, and fresh memories:

- 'I never thought about it that way before but it's true, isn't it?'

- [bursts into tears] 'That really hit the nail on the head. It hurt terribly when you said that.'

- 'Yes, and there's something else I haven't told you. I don't know if I can say this next thing.'

Negative responses may include an inability to take in the interpretation offered, concrete thinking, restricted access to feelings, and even hostility or paranoia:

- [looks blankly at the interviewer] 'I don't know what you mean.'

- 'I'm a bit blinded by science here. Could you put that in plain English?'

- 'I told you I can't be getting on with fancy explanations. I just want to be rid of me panics.'

- 'Who do you think you are, saying something like that to me? Take that back, what you just said.'

Some therapists make *transference interpretations* in the initial session. The patient's ego strength, degree of disturbance and level of psychosexual maturity will influence how soon transference interpretations can be made. Early transference interpretations with very disturbed patients can prove upsetting and threaten the therapeutic alliance, especially if negative transferences are interpreted at an early stage. Some transference interpretations that might be offered tentatively include:

'You seem to be finding it very difficult to talk on your own, so you're asking me to take the initiative and ask you questions.'

'So it sounds like your doctor suggested you come along to see me, but you yourself are not convinced that sessions here can be of any help.'

A number of clues to transference may appear in the initial interview.

- *Gratification of dependent needs* may be reflected in requests for a special time, requests for tablets, matches, cigarettes, a glass of water, requests for bus fare, or 'Do you have a tissue?'

- *Fears of not being accepted*: 'How can you listen to people complain all day? Your work must be very depressing.'

- *Omnipotent transference*: 'I *know* you can help me!', 'You *must* know the answer', or consistent reference to the therapist as 'Doctor'.

- *Concern about being understood*: 'Are you married?' 'Do you have children?' 'How old are you?' 'Are you Catholic?'

- *Competitive feelings*: 'Well, you beat me today!' [looking at watch], disparaging remarks about the office or the therapist's appearance, attempts to assess the therapist's vocabulary, reference to the therapist's other patients as if they were siblings, treating the therapist as a child or cautioning him or her about their health.

The assessor may wish to note some of these transference clues without commenting on them. Too much emphasis on transference phenomena in the initial interview may prove difficult if the assessor is not to be the psychotherapist and the patient has to spend some time on a treatment waiting list.

'Why take a history? Doesn't it take too much time?' Many patients presenting with psychological problems to their GPs today have very disturbed early histories. If counsellors focus only on the presenting problem without understanding its origins in the past, they may take on patients for short-term treatment who could be harmed by that form of therapy. What follows is an example of a patient with a very disturbed early history. The presenting problems were psychosexual and relationship problems. The history and interview revealed a severe underlying personality disorder of the borderline type.

The patient's father had several psychiatric hospitalizations as well as prison sentences, grandfather 'killed
himself through drink', an uncle committed suicide,
and two aunts were in mental institutions. On mother's side, 'all of them were abusers'. Grandfather and
uncle were the two principal abusers in the family. The
patient and all her siblings were sexually abused.

She did not feel she was a wanted child. Her mother
was very ill after the delivery and was in hospital for
most of the patient's first year of life. Father was in
prison at the time. Her parents separated when she was
born and divorced when she was 3. She was systematically abused from infancy to 15 by five different people. She 'used to close her eyes and pretend it wasn't
happening'. Mother remarried when the patient was in
her early teens, but her stepfather was 'horrible' and
she left home to escape from him. She has recently registered with a GP in the area, and has had no previous
psychological or psychiatric help except a consultation
with a rape crisis centre after a recent sexual assault.
The precipitating event was that sexual abuse could
now happen to her Adult Body. Previously it had happened only to her split-off Child Body.

Her speech was rambling, digressive and very hard
to follow, and her facial expressions frequently bore
little relationship to the feelings being expressed.
Dissociative defences were heavily used, and the identity diffusion so characteristic of borderline personality disorder was prominent: she had legally changed
her name to that of a rock star spelled backwards.

Such patients may be too disorganized to profit from long-term psychotherapy and may be most effectively managed by a community mental
health team. Those who have sufficient ego strength and adequate social
support may be able to profit from long-term therapy in a setting with psychiatric backup. A primary care counsellor who 'never takes a history
because it takes too much time' might take on such a patient for short-term
work relying on the presenting symptom of 'relationship problems'. Within
one or two sessions, patient and therapist could be well into the wilder-
ness without a map. Dangerous excursions of this kind can be avoided by

taking a complete psychosocial history, understanding enough about diagnosis to recognize the warning signs of severe personality disorder (Chapter 5), having regular supervision with an experienced clinician, and maintaining good links with GPs and secondary services.

NONVERBAL COMMUNICATION

Observations about the patient's nonverbal communication are an important part of the initial assessment. Among those things worth observing are predominant facial expression, tone and pitch of voice, leaning back into chair vs. on edge of chair, coat on or off; or requests to hang coat up vs. tossing coat onto the therapist's chair on entering the room. One patient whose eagerness to undress in front of the therapist prevented her from entering the room, as he stood directly in the doorway to go through his undressing ritual.

Dress and grooming: appropriate or not, hygiene adequate or not; casual or formal, neat or messy, colours worn; slogans on T-shirt; age-appropriate attire or not. Kicking of foot throughout interview or at crucial moments, walking around the room and hiding behind the file cabinet while speaking; arms or legs thrown over the side of the chair; legs sprawled (in adolescent girls); waving arms about, talking with hands, flamboyance; effeminate (men), masculine (women). Tics, twitches and stammers (note the topic being discussed when this happens); grunts, coughs, sniffles. Symbolic behaviour, for example, repeatedly inserting shoelace into the eyelet of a boot during a discussion of sexual frustration.

Eric Berne's (1972) concept of the *script signal* is useful here: a characteristic posture, gesture, mannerism or symptom which alerts the therapist that patients have 'gone into their scripts'. For example, the tilt of the head as played in the games, 'Martyr' and 'Waif'; crossing legs or winding the instep around the lower ankle while discussing sex; blinking, tongue-chewing, jaw-clamping, sniffing, hand-wringing, ring-turning and foot-tapping. Also, some people have to go through certain rituals or make certain gestures before they begin to speak, sometimes in order to apologize for speaking: 'I don't know, but. . .', 'Quite possibly', or '[cough, cough] . . .' The gallows laugh is another important script signal: the misfortune being recounted with a laugh is part of the catastrophe of the patient's script. In the waiting area a loud and ostentatious 'A-*hem*', accompanied by looking at one's watch communicates an angry, 'So *now* she's going to see me'. Or constant 'Poor me' sniffing in the waiting area, announcing the patient's presence and 'patient waiting', 15–20 minutes before the session is due to begin. The most important single word in the assessment interview may be the word 'but', which means 'According to my script, I don't have permission to do that.'

PSYCHODYNAMIC FORMULATION

We described a number of models for the psychodynamic formulation in Chapter 3, many of which were based on an observation of relationship episodes or stories the patient tells about encounters with other people. Perry et al. (1987) list five misconceptions about the psychodynamic formulation:

- It is indicated only for long-term cases.

- It is of value only for inexperienced clinicians in training.

- It must be complete and comprehensive rather than tentative and partial.

- It need not be written.

- The therapist will cling to it in the face of new and contradictory evidence.

The authors advocate committing to paper at least a brief psychodynamic formulation of 500–750 words as a working guide. It can be very valuable to understand the story in dynamic terms even if one is to proceed to a cognitive-behavioural or schema-based treatment. The formulation should place the presenting problem in the light of the history, sketch the dynamic factors that appear to explain the current situation, hypothesize about the formative influence of the patient's early experiences on their current predicament, and predict the likely impact of these factors on treatment. The discipline of the 500-word formulation is well worth cultivating in primary care.

The task of formulating involves identifying the pervasive issues running through the course of the patient's presenting problems, patterns that can be traced back through their personal history. Sometimes events in the psychosocial history are fairly readily linked to the presenting problem. What follows are some common patterns, abbreviated and simplified for the sake of illustration.

1. The dynamic formulation may relate an event in the past such as an early trauma to a current conflict. The present problem may be an unwitting repetition of an early experience, event, or interpersonal relationship.

    - John was repeatedly locked in cupboards as a child by his

psychotic parents. His work requires him to work in narrow ducts in the Underground where he is experiencing terrifying panic attacks.

2. Maladaptive behaviour has been unwittingly copied from parents, or is a response to parental behaviour when the patient was a child.

   - When Chris was a little girl, the only way she could gain attention from her mother was to throw noisy temper tantrums. Under stress at work, the tantrums have reappeared and her employer has suggested she seek counselling.

3. An early conflict in the patient's childhood has endured into adult life.

   - Because Mark's parents were unable to deal with his distress, he withdrew into a world of fantasy in which he was completely in control. Newly married, his need to control everything in the relationship is proving problematic.

4. There has been a developmental arrest leading to the current problem. Certain stages of personality development have been incompletely negotiated, because of stress or trauma at the time (Erikson, 1968; Levenson, 1978).

   - Margaret's father died soon after her mother threw him out of the house for excessive drinking. After his death Margaret returned home to look after her depressed mother, and never left to live her own life. In the GP surgery, Margaret and her mother are a symbiotic unit. One cannot be seen without overwhelming interference from the other, and the resulting stress on staff has led to a referral for counselling.

5. Under the impact of early loss or failures of parenting, childhood solutions or 'survival kits' that were adaptive in the past have persisted into adult life and are now maladaptive.

   - Alan discovered that the most effective way of shutting out the 'madhouse' in which he lived as a boy was to retreat into books. His emotions were habitually suppressed and he took solace in intellectualization. This earned him two doctoral degrees and a high-paying job, but at nearly 40, unable to form an intimate relationship, he has become depressed.

6. Unconscious guilt is hindering the patient's adjustment in adult life. Such guilt may stem from childhood abuse, for which patients blame themselves.

- 'My mother said it would have been better if I had never been born.'

- 'If I had been good, Mummy wouldn't have abandoned us.'

- 'If I had gone downstairs with my little sister that morning, she wouldn't have put her nightdress onto the gas fire, and she wouldn't have died.'

- 'I *know* that I am responsible for the deaths of my two baby brothers.' [both cot deaths]

- Alice was abused by her stepfather for many years. She was blackmailed into silence with 'If you tell your mother, you will never see her again. You'll be sent to a children's home.' Alice blamed herself for the abuse. She chose a violent partner who raped her repeatedly but she was unwilling to seek help for many years because she felt this treatment was only what she deserved.

7. Abused as children, in adult life there is an 'identification with the aggressor'. This time the tables are turned, and someone else becomes the victim.

- Tim's parents were ruthless in their treatment of him, allowing him to be physically and sexually abused by members of the extended family. When Tim's wife developed a gynaecological cancer, he was irate that he was being deprived of sex. As he said to his counsellor, 'A woman is just a life support system for a vagina.'

In arriving at the psychodynamic formulation, special attention should be paid to the nature of the child's relationships with parents, the quality of adult relationships, and any clues to transference reactions gleaned from the first hour. It is important that a careful assessment is made so that patients referred for brief psychodynamic therapy are able to use it effectively. Patients with longstanding psychiatric problems of a severe kind, childhood sexual abuse histories, or sustained childhood trauma will probably need longer-term psychodynamic therapy from a specialist.

Another aspect of psychodynamic assessment is the distinction between oedipal (three-person, neurotic) and preoedipal (two-person, borderline and narcissistic) dynamics (Balint, 1968; Holmes, 1995). When two-person difficulties predominate, very short-term therapy is unlikely to be appropriate. One aid to assessing this question is the Quality of Object Relations Scale (Azim, 1991) which outlines five levels of interpersonal relating in order of their maturity:

- *Primitive organizational level*: a repeated pattern of intense, unstable and destructive relationships. Inordinate attachment to others is manifest either in clinging behaviour or alternating periods of clinging and aloofness. Real or imagined loss, separation or rejection lead to extreme emotional reactions. There is preoccupation with destroying or being destroyed by the other, who is alternately idealized or devalued. Others' significance is based on their usefulness. *Antecedents*: physical/sexual abuse, parental rejection, sudden repetitive separations in childhood, disturbed family communication, and failure in development of self and self-esteem.

- *Searching organizational level*: 'falling in love' with others repeatedly, with a heightened fear of loss, rejection and abandonment. Chronic feelings of anxiety and emptiness in the absence of the other, and self-esteem dependent on their availability (cf. the search for the 'transformational object', Bollas, 1978). *Antecedents*: an intense attachment to a parent or caregiver who was lost, *or* overindulgence by a parent who was lost.

- *Controlling organizational level*: a repetitive pattern of attempts to control or possess others in relationships. Reacts to others' attempts at control with defiance and rebelliousness, *or* with compliance and attempts to be agreeable. Anger or rage when unable to control the other. *Antecedents*: inordinate attempts by caregivers to control the child's actions, thoughts or feelings, or a pattern of excessive punishment.

- *Triangular organizational level*: repetitive involvement in rivalrous triangular relationships, an inordinate tendency to be competitive, and a tendency to see members of the opposite sex as either a lover or a parent. Feelings of triumph over the third party. *Antecedents*: the same sex parent competed with the patient for the affection of the parent of the opposite sex, or the opposite sex parent preferred the patient to their own partner (oedipal triumph).

- *Mature organizational level*: capacity to express love, tenderness and concern for people of both sexes, to manifest assertiveness towards people of both sexes, and tolerance of the bad as well as appreciation of the good in others. Capacity to mourn people who are lost, preponderance of affection towards others and a paucity of rage, anxiety, guilt and

envy. *Antecedents*: good enough preoedipal relationships, healthy resolution of the oedipal complex and choice of a good enough love object.

Only the last two levels are organized at the three-person (neurotic) level.
Primitive, searching and controlling object relations are organized at the
preoedipal, two-person level, and many patients presenting to their GPs
for psychological help today are functioning at these levels. In general, the
earlier the wound, the longer treatment is likely to take – if the patient is
amenable to psychotherapy, and if treatment will not make the patient
worse. Another way of assessing patients' psychosexual maturity is in
terms of their principal defence mechanisms:

Primitive defences	*More mature defences*
Splitting	Repression
Idealization	Reaction formation
Devaluation	Undoing
Introjection	Displacement
Projection	Emotional isolation
Projective identification	Intellectualization
Denial	Rationalization
Regression	Sublimation

A preponderance of more primitive defences is found in psychotic states
and borderline personality disorder. When the object world is split into
'all good' and 'all bad' and projection of the 'all bad' bits into other people is heavily used as a defence, patients are usually functioning in the
borderline spectrum. Very short-term therapy is unlikely to help them,
and may be damaging. A clue to the overuse of splitting as a defence is a
series of relationship episodes in which others begin as 'perfect, everything I ever wanted' but who rapidly become monsters: 'I could kill him.'
People, including the therapist, are seen to flip between the good bin and
the bad bin with alarming rapidity. There may also be a tendency to seg-
regate people into camps in one's internal world: 'People I know get
either a tick or a cross.' If the primary care mental health worker is not
trained in the treatment of borderline personalities, these patients should
be referred for specialist assessment at the secondary level after an
exploratory session.

A *Defensive Functioning Scale* (DFS) has been included in the DSM-IV,
including seven levels of functioning ranging from normal to psychotic
(Blais et al., 1996). At the *high adaptive level* are defences such as affilia-
tion, altruism and sublimation. At the *minor image-distorting* level are
devaluation, idealization and omnipotence. Examples of *major image-dis-*

torting defences are autistic fantasy, projective identification, and splitting of images of self or others. The DFS enables clinicians to incorporate psychodynamic information into their descriptive diagnoses. Although a rigorous assessment of defence mechanisms is unlikely to be made in most assessment interviews, an ability to distinguish primitive from more mature defences is important in the detection of borderline psychopathology.

The dynamic formulation and a conceptualization of the patient's difficulties in object relations terms are often more helpful than a formal diagnosis when it comes to psychodynamic treatment, but diagnosis is important in avoiding certain kinds of insight-oriented therapies with very damaged people. For example, borderline patients with poor impulse control, suicidal or homicidal gestures or ideation, lack of insight into their difficulties, and an inability to take responsibility for their behaviour are poor risks for psychodynamic treatment unless there are significant ameliorating factors in their history or presentation. Therapy may also do such patients harm if they decompensate into a psychotic episode. In general, treatments that are likely to induce regression are unwise if borderline patients are likely to experience a 'malign regression'. In these cases the risk of a transient psychotic episode may be considerable, and a more structured therapy may be safer. A cognitive-behavioural approach to symptoms may be helpful, or cognitive-analytic therapy may be sufficiently structured to prevent an intense, regressive transference. Like brief and ultra-brief therapies, long-term, insight-oriented psychotherapy is not a panacea, and can be damaging to some patients. Some patients whose behaviour is poorly controlled are best managed within a community mental health team and not taken on for formal one-to-one therapy.

If patients press for a diagnosis at the end of an assessment, it may help to put it in descriptive terms, for example:

> 'You have had difficulties in doing any creative work for a long time, your relationships have often been unhappy, and you suffer from a number of physical symptoms which are made worse by your emotional state.'

It is generally unhelpful to say, 'You are a depressive', 'You suffer from an anxiety state', or 'You have a personality disorder.' Some patients come to psychotherapy burdened with diagnoses such as manic-depression, which they have come to think of as a life sentence. Occasionally patients arrive for therapy having been told by their GP that their 'personality disorder is untreatable'. There are two exceptions to this general guideline of not offering diagnoses to patients: confirming depression when it is clear that the patient knows this is the problem, combined with positive statements about how psychotherapy can help; and panic attacks, when the patient seems convinced that these are symptoms of a physical problem such as an impending heart attack. Knowing that other people suffer similar distressing symptoms caused by anxiety can be very helpful.

Other considerations in assessing patients for short vs. longer-term therapy are the extent of early loss in the history, the number of presenting problems (comorbidity), and the presence of personality disorder. These issues are discussed in Chapter 5.

SUMMARY AND RECOMMENDATIONS

Too few mental health workers in primary care take an adequate history. The two most important adverse outcomes of the failure to take a history are inappropriate brief treatment leading to no change, deterioration or relapse; and/or repeated referral of the patient to one secondary service after another, each of which rejects the patient as unsuitable for the treatment on offer. A third reason for doing a detailed assessment at the primary care level is that it may disclose long undiagnosed severe mental illness.

Some GPs are excellent at preparing the ground for counselling, and give a lot of relevant history as well as a detailed description of the presenting problem. Others send a couple of sentences about symptoms. The actuality of the patient's difficulties may bear little resemblance to the problem mentioned in the referral letter. Many primary care mental health services use pre-assessment postal questionnaires which the patient is asked to complete before the first appointment. Questionnaires prepare patients for what psychotherapy may entail, and their contents may help the assessor focus the interview. A personal history questionnaire initially devised at the Tavistock Clinic has undergone a number of revisions and is used by many NHS departments. Its routine use can save the assessor considerable time and it is well accepted by most patients.

When listening to patients during the initial interview, sequences of feelings can be useful to note, especially when they occur as part of a pattern in interpersonal relationships. Such patterns will help inform the core conflictual relationship theme. Patients will sometimes use vivid metaphors which can be used to elaborate life themes. Important metaphors may emerge when the patient is asked to describe a recent dream. Another useful way of listening is in terms of interpersonal issues. The inability to form loving relationships is a common problem. Childhood antecedents of some of these problems can be identified.

There are at least five principal therapist activities in assessment interviews: understanding the problem and its history, taking a psychosocial history and making a psychodynamic formulation, making a preliminary diagnosis, building a therapeutic alliance, and forming an impression about optimal therapy modality. Sometimes the initial interviews require 3–6 hours on as many days. Occasionally they can be done in an hour. The limits of confidentiality should be explained, if not already described in a pre-counselling leaflet. A detailed description of symptoms is needed, together with what was going on in the patient's life when the symptoms began or worsened, what the patient has done in an attempt to resolve them, and whether they have had previous episodes of treatment for this problem. The timing of symptom onset is particularly important. Periodically it helps to list the problems that have been mentioned and then to say, 'Would you say that summarizes the various problems, or are there others we haven't talked about yet?' Suicide risk needs to be assessed in those who are depressed. Rogerian reflection-of-feeling responses are helpful throughout the interview to help the patient feel understood and to begin to build a therapeutic alliance.

It is worth doing a psychosocial history with every patient, even if the end result is an offer of cognitive-behavioural therapy. A number of areas that are optimally covered in the history have been described, and examples given. A set sequence of questions is unhelpful. It is important to be guided in the history by what the patient has to say, following up leads and discussing traumatic incidents in detail. The patient's response to initial interpretations can be a good indicator of whether psychotherapy will help. The patient's ego strength, degree of disturbance and level of psychosexual maturity will influence how soon transference interpretations can be made. Observations about the patient's nonverbal communication are an important part of the initial assessment. A characteristic posture, gesture, mannerism or symptom may alert the therapist that patients have 'gone into their scripts'.

'Why take a history? Doesn't it take too much time?' Many patients presenting with psychological problems to their GPs today have very disturbed early histories. If counsellors focus only on the presenting problem without understanding its origins in the past, they may take on patients for short-term treatment who could be harmed by that form of therapy.

It can be very valuable to understand the patient's story in dynamic terms, even if one is to proceed to a cognitive-behavioural or schema-based treatment. The formulation should place the presenting problem in the light of the history, sketch the dynamic factors that appear to explain the current situation, hypothesize about the formative influence of the patient's early experiences on their current predicament, and predict the likely impact of these factors on treatment. The discipline of the 500-word formulation is well worth cultivating in primary care. Another aspect of psychodynamic assessment is the distinction between oedipal (three-person, neurotic) and preoedipal (two-person, borderline and narcissistic) dynamics. When two-person difficulties predominate, very short-term therapy is unlikely to be appropriate. One aid to assessing the level of object relations is the Quality of Object Relations Scale. Another way of assessing patients' psychosexual maturity is in terms of their principal defence mechanisms. A preponderance of more primitive defences is found in psychotic states and borderline personality disorder.

The dynamic formulation and conceptualization of the patient's difficulties in object relations terms are often more helpful than a formal diagnosis when it comes to psychodynamic treatment, but diagnosis is important in avoiding certain kinds of insight-oriented therapies with very damaged people.

5

ASSESSMENT II: EARLY LOSS, COMORBIDITY AND TREATMENT MODALITY

THE IMPORTANCE OF EARLY LOSS EVENTS

One indicator of the appropriateness of short-term therapy is the extent of early loss issues in the patient's history. Using an attachment perspective, Holmes (1997b) suggests a useful classification system for the timeliness of termination in psychotherapy:

    i   brief involuntary ('too early'),
    ii brief planned,
    iii long-term involuntary ('too late') and
    iv long-term planned.

Just as short-term therapies can be terminated too soon, so too can long-term therapies go on unproductively for too long. Holmes helpfully points out:

> Some patients need long–term therapy; others can be usefully helped with brief, or relatively brief intervention. Some need intermittent therapy – to come for a while and then return. In some cases termination can be planned; in others it needs to emerge as a theme for months or even years before it actually happens. Some people need to stop suddenly, while others do better with a gradual process of weaning.
>
> (Holmes, 1997b, p. 164).

From an attachment perspective, the aim of psychotherapy is to help create a secure base in the patient's internal and external worlds. However, when borderline patients have not had the experience of security, this secure base has to be built up from scratch, which inevitably takes time. Patients' previous experience of loss will inform their fantasies of what it means to be separated from a significant other person. For those with traumatic early loss histories, termination may be the most taxing phase in treatment. A careful history, including an assessment of the severity of early loss experience, is essential at the initial interview stage so that brief involuntary therapy, terminated too early, is not offered to these patients.

Many patients are referred for psychological help following the loss of an important relationship. The intensity of the adult psychological reaction may be genetically linked to an earlier loss in childhood. When the early loss occurred before the child had language to structure experience, or before the personality formed adequately to process the event, a re-enactment in adult life can product emotions that feel unmanageable and bewildering. Encouraged to express their feelings of distress for a few hours, they are then discharged. Too often, assessment is inadequare and the historical roots of the problem are never uncovered. Opportunities to work through the earlier loss and to understand the meaning of current emotions are therefore missed. When depression is the presenting problem, relapse is more likely if the underlying causes have not been addressed. Consider the following precipitating events and their antecedents:

Precipitating event	*Childhood antecedent*
• A beloved sister dies.	• Mother died of cancer when the patient was 4.
• Sudden rejection by lover.	• An unwanted baby, given up for adoption.
• Husband killed in accident at work.	• Twin brother killed by hit-and-run driver, aged 3.
• Termination of pregnancy.	• Patient's mother tried to abort her as a foetus and told her about it when she was a child.
• Severely injured in car accident.	• When patient's birth certificate had to be produced, he discovered that he had been adopted; research disclosed that both parents had been killed in a car crash.

A new measure has been developed for the severity of loss events in childhood and unempathic parental responses to the child. The *Inventory of Early Loss* (IEL, Burton and Topham, 1997) includes loss events from infancy to the age of 20 in

Part I, and unempathic parental responses to the child in Part II. Overall early loss is described by a severity score of *mild, moderate, severe* or *very severe*. The IEL allows for the study of specific types of early loss (e.g. death of mother, parental separation and divorce, death of sibling, separation from mother at birth) and particular types of unempathic parental response (e.g. mother intrusive, father emotionally unavailable, both parents critical) as well as an overall early loss score. The Inventory has been developed from a wide search of the psychoanalytic literature on loss experiences in childhood, broadly defined.

Early loss is an important clinical indicator in assessment for psychotherapy. A number of studies have found a relationship between early loss events and adult depression, suicide, and borderline personality disorder. A growing literature links childhood physical and sexual abuse with the development of borderline personality disorder. Childhood sexual abuse has been studied as a precursor of adult eating disorders, sexual and marital problems, and physical complaints. Although not strictly speaking 'loss' events, unempathic parental responses to the child represent the loss of 'good enough' parenting. Both object relations theory and Kohut's (1977) self-psychology set out the impact of unempathic parental responses on the child in a literature too large and complex to be summarized here. Parents may be physically present but emotionally unavailable, and the lack of adequate parental care has been linked to a wide range of adult psychopathology. Parents' failure in empathic responsiveness to their children is an especially important process in the development of psychopathology in Kohut's self-psychology.

It is sometimes queried whether early events reported by patients have been confirmed by independent witnesses. No attempt can usually be made to confirm information provided by patients in assessment interviews, but it is well known in clinical settings that the question, 'Did it *really* happen?' is often less helpful clinically than 'Does the patient *believe* it happened?' Family myths about events can be vital to understand. For example, the story is told that the patient was conceived only because his parents were drunk after a family wedding. Whether or not that was objectively the case is much less relevant clinically than the fact that this was the story *told* to the patient, and that *feeling* of being unwanted is the clinically relevant datum, not the objectively measured blood alcohol level of the parents on a certain evening. Thus, the data collected in a psychosocial history are always subjective and retrospective, and they are meant to be understood as such without apology.

The first section of the IEL concerns the circumstances of the mother's pregnancy and the perinatal period including birth trauma and separations from the mother at birth. Later separations from parents, serious illnesses or accidents, parents' marital breakdown, deaths of siblings, sexual abuse or assault, serious illness or death of surrogate parents, house moves, and being an only child are also scored in this section. 'Other' early loss or trauma (item 29) includes a wide variety of experiences such as severe bullying at school, loss or death of a childhood friend or beloved pet, a stay in borstal, or war trauma. These events usually emerge as the history unfolds, and may be unusual or unique. Economic deprivation is another form of early loss that is often neglected. Older children in some impoverished families are made to forego childhood to serve as surrogate parents to younger siblings. Others are deprived of higher education because an extra income is needed. These children may be hungry and live in inadequate or unsanitary accommodation. They can be mercilessly teased by classmates for their unkempt appearance and unfashionable clothing. In Part I, ages are recorded, and events are eligible for inclusion if they occurred up to and including the age of 20 years. In general, the earlier the loss, the more severe the score.

The impact of unempathic parental responses on the developing child (Part II) is an integral part of the Inventory because of the child's consequent lack of appropriate parenting. Included in Part II are neglect, physical and sexual abuse, and over-controlling, overly critical, cold, unavailable, violent, mentally disturbed, or unpredictable parenting. Whether other siblings were preferred, and whether the parent wished for a child of the opposite sex are also scored. An 'other' category is used for the many idiosyncratic responses given by subjects in reply to this question. There is also a category for blatant, persistent marital discord between the subject's parents. Items in the Inventory appear in Table 5.1, from which raw scores for Parts I and II can be calculated.

Raw scores are obtained by taking the arithmetic sum of all items ticked. When multiple items occur in the same category, they are multiply scored. For example, three separations from the mother score 3 rather than 1. Some items are commonly associated with others, for example, serious illness or hospitalization of the mother, and separation from the mother. Where both have occurred, both are scored. Because loss events are of unequal impact – some carry greater potential for damage to development than others – rules have been devised for the calculation of *severity* scores. Scoring criteria for the overall severity of early loss (mild, moderate, severe or very severe) are shown in Table 5.2.

Certain early loss events merit an automatic score of *severe* ['automatic 3'] regardless of the presence of other events in the history: trauma in the first year of life including being unwanted and/or birth trauma; transfer of care in infancy or toddlerhood to other caretakers; death or permanent or prolonged separation from a parent or parent surrogate up to and including the age of 10 years; childhood sexual abuse or sexual assault; being blamed for the death of a sibling and/or blames self; long separations from parents due to hospitalization or institutionalization of the child or the parent; life-threatening illness in childhood/adolescence; and being an only child or 'virtually an only child' (that is, a minimum of six years separate a child from the nearest sibling).

There are a number of reasons why the only child is at a fundamental disadvantage, psychologically. Only children are usually the sole recipients of parents' first efforts at parenting. The only child has not had an opportunity to benefit from a moderation of parental response as a result of experience with older children. Only children may have a tendency to live in their own world, with a rich fantasy life. The only child may fail to discriminate adequately between private fantasy and consensually validated reality. By definition, the only child does not have a sibling with whom to play, and imaginary playmates may be created. These developments may subsequently be an advantage if the only child becomes a creative artist, but they are often a disadvantage in *social* development. Because the only child never had to learn to share, narcissistic pathology may develop: entitlement, lack of empathy for the needs of others, ruthlessness, and grandiosity. The only child is never dethroned by a younger sibling. Some only children speak of getting whatever they wanted from parents. This is not always a blessing – 'Such empathic parents!' one might be tempted to say – however, unrealistic expectations may be set in place for adult life.

Other disadvantages of being an only child may be less universal, but are not uncommon in clinical practice. The mother's experience of pregnancy, delivery, and the patient's infancy may have been so traumatic that she tells her child she would never go through it again. In some cases the only child is blamed for having caused the mother pain or disfigurement. In other cases the child may become a narcissistic extension of the mother's damaged self. Some only children are born to mothers unexpectedly late in life, or are the only offspring of second or third marriages at midlife. Other only children are replacement babies for one or more stillborn infants or late miscarriages, a position which is fraught with difficulty. Where longstanding infertility and medical treatment resulted in a single successful pregnancy, expectations of the only child are not infrequently unreasonable: 'After all we went through to have you. . .'

Most items in the IEL can be scored from questions in the psychosocial history (Chapter 4). When the IEL is used for research purposes, the most complete results are obtained by going through the IEL checklist with the patient item by item, after the psychosocial history has been completed. Some of the most important events may be those about which the patient says, 'Oh, I forgot to mention this earlier, but. . .'

Sometimes therapists are uncertain how to ask about childhood sexual abuse during assessment interviews. Unless this history has been volunteered by the patient, one way of approaching the question during the

Table 5.1 Inventory of early loss

Part I. Early loss events	tick:	If yes, age:
1. Unwanted pregnancy	____	
2. Attempted abortion or abortion wanted and refused	____	
3. Baby given up for adoption	____	
4. Rejected by mother at birth	____	
5. Birth trauma (e.g. 'nearly died' at birth)	____	
6. Separation from mother at birth (e.g. Neonatal Intensive Care Unit, physical or emotional illness in mother or baby)	____	
7. Failure of bonding between mother and baby noted	____	
8. 'Failure to thrive' baby	____	
9. Illness or hospitalization of child	____	____
10. Illness or hospitalization of mother (note duration of mother's absence)	____	____
11. Transfer of care from mother to a relative or other caretaker such as an orphanage or foster parents	____	____
12. Separation from mother for other reasons (e.g. evacuated during the war, mother working in another city)	____	____
13. Death of mother	____	____
14. Parental marital separation	____	____
15. Parental divorce	____	____
16. Maternal abandonment threats	____	____
17. Death of sibling	____	____
18. Mother's miscarriages, abortions or stillbirths	____	____
19. Childhood sexual abuse or sexual assault	____	____
20. Child is victim of homicidal attempts (e.g. grandmother who repeatedly tried to smother the baby with a pillow)	____	____
21. Child witnesses violent death of parent, sibling, or significant other	____	____
22. Father absent (e.g. war, prison, abandonment)	____	____
23. Father seriously ill	____	____
24. Death of father	____	____
25. Death of surrogate parent	____	____
26. Serious illness of surrogate parent	____	____
27. Traumatic house moves	____	____
28. Only child, or 'virtually' only child (much older/ younger siblings)	____	____
29. Other early loss or traumatic event (specify)	____	____
TOTAL EARLY LOSS EVENTS	____	

Part II. Unempathic parental responses

	Mother or surrogate	Father or surrogate
Under- or over-feeding	____	____
Neglect	____	____
Physical abuse	____	____
Sexual abuse	____	____
Over-controlling, intrusive, smothering	____	____
Overly critical, strict, harsh punishments	____	____
Cold, emotionally unavailable or unresponsive	____	____
Physically violent	____	____
Mentally ill or abused alcohol or drugs	____	____
Unpredictable or frightening	____	____
Preferred other siblings to the child in question	____	____
Wanted child to be of opposite sex	____	____
Other unempathic parental response	____	____
Blatant marital discord	____	
TOTAL UNEMPATHIC PARENTAL RESPONSE	____	
TOTAL RAW SCORE (Part I + Part II)	____	

Table 5.2 Scoring the severity of early loss

Part I. Early loss events (mild, moderate or severe)

1. *Early loss is not a significant feature of the history*
   - No significant separations from parents or loss of parents or parent surrogates through death or other events.
   - If there are instances of early loss, they are minor, such as a single house move during childhood, or one separation from parents for a few days (e.g. having tonsils out without complications).
   - If there are any instances of early separations, these are brief.

2. *Some early loss of a moderate sort*
   - If parental deaths or separations have occurred, these have taken place when the child was 11–19 years old.
   - Sibling deaths fall into this middle category unless the circumstances were such that the child was blamed, or blamed him/herself for the death. In these latter cases, score 3 for severe.
   - Separations from parents through moderately long hospitalizations fall into this middle category, e.g. hospitalized for 4–6 weeks. Year-long or longer removal from the parental home (special hospital or special school) are scored 3 for severe.

3. *Severe history of early loss events*
   - Automatic 3:
     - death or permanent or prolonged separation from parent or parent surrogates up to and including the age of 10 years
     - childhood sexual abuse or sexual assault
     - long separations from parents due to hospitalization or institutionalization of the child or the parent; life-threatening illness in childhood/adolescence
     - only child
   - History of trauma in the first year of life falls here: unwanted pregnancy, maternal attempt to abort the foetus, severe birth trauma, separated from mother at birth, failure to bond, rejected by mother at birth, period in Neonatal Intensive Care Unit.
   - Transfer of care in infancy or toddlerhood to other caretakers such as relatives, foster parents, orphanage, or child placed in care.

Part II. Unempathic parental responses (mild, moderate or severe)

1. Mild: no unempathic parental responses, or only 1 unempathic response
2. Moderate: several unempathic parental responses
3. Severe: many unempathic parental responses

Overall Early Loss Score (mild, moderate, severe or very severe)

Take into account both Part I and Part II scores. Where the two scores differ, assign whichever score is higher. Criteria for a score of 4 for *Very Severe Overall Early Loss*: multiple scorable items of a severe kind in both Part I and Part II, with consequent high raw scores (raw total is usually in excess of 12). Or, a picture of 'catastrophic' early loss in either Part I or Part II. Or, severe congenital defect or disfiguring accident with lifelong implications. When scores in one part are severe (3) but in another part are mild (1), the overall early loss score is 3 rather than 4 unless the loss in the section scored 3 is of an overwhelming kind.

(From Burton and Topham (1997); reproduced with permission.)

psychosocial history is to say, 'Before we leave your childhood and adolescence behind, did you have any unwanted sexual experiences as you were growing up? Did anyone ever assault you or interfere with you sexually?' As long as it is asked gently and without anxiety on the interviewer's part, this question is usually accepted by patients as a normal part of the assessment process. In the absence of such a history patients tend to say, 'Oh no, never anything like that.' In the IEL, the emphasis is on unwanted sexual experiences perpetrated on the patient by older individuals, not adolescent experimentation with same-age peers. This item includes incestuous relationships with parents, step-parents or siblings, and/or abuse initiated by people outside the household such as grandparents, aunts or uncles, friends of the family, teachers, clergy, youth club leaders, or strangers. The key element is the child's perceived inability to say no, whether because the perpetrator was a trusted person in a position of authority, or someone the child 'looked up to'. Occasionally patients will report sexual experiences that qualify as abuse according to these criteria with the words, 'But it wasn't unwanted; I enjoyed it.' Such events are nevertheless scored.

Sometimes there is a long pause and the patient says, 'Yes, there was something. I've never told anyone about it before', and the story unfolds with considerable emotion. When this happens, additional assessment sessions may be needed to deal with the aftermath of disclosure. Sometimes patients report unwanted sexual experiences in adulthood including rape or sexual assault. Although not scored on the IEL, these incidents are of considerable clinical importance. Occasionally patients will say, 'I thought about writing it in the questionnaire, but I couldn't bring myself to put it down on paper'. In other cases, abuse is denied at assessment but comes to light during therapy. Sometimes this is because the patient has felt unable to report it at the time of the assessment interview, and at other times it is remembered in the course of treatment. The complex problems associated with recovered memories of abuse are dealt with admirably by Mollon (1998).

The IEL is proving useful in assessment for psychotherapy, in clinical work, in the teaching of psychotherapy, in the supervision of trainees, and in research. Early loss experiences are also clinically useful in predicting transferences that can be anticipated in therapy, countertransferences in the therapist, key therapeutic issues, and the risks of re-enacting early traumas inside and outside the therapeutic relationship. A pilot study of the IEL using closed case notes found that patients with more severe early loss had more presenting problems and longer therapies than those with mild or moderate scores. More recent work with the IEL found that 47 per cent of a sample of 201 patients on a Direct Access Service waiting list had *very severe* overall scores (Burton and Topham, 1997). This sample of patients had severe problems (usually several comorbid conditions) including anxiety, depression, relationship problems, and a 20 per cent incidence of personality disorder. Severity of early loss was significantly related to the presence of personality disorder.

How can the IEL be used to contribute to a decision about therapy modality?

> *On the whole, unless there are contraindications to any form of psychological treatment (see below), patients with severe and very severe early loss histories are likely to need longer-term therapy.*

One of the reasons for proposing this guideline is that many of those who have suffered severe early disruption in their attachments are prone to re-experiencing the ending of relationships as an abandonment. The ending of therapy needs to be handled skilfully if the patient is not to be re-traumatized in the transference (Casement, 1990). This is one reason why it can be vitally important that this time the patient does not experience a traumatic ending. This time, the patient can choose their own ending, when they are ready to stop the work. Another common pattern among this patient group are those who abruptly dismiss their therapists in the same way that a caretaker once abandoned them. These patients, too, need very skilful handling to prevent an unhelpful acting-out of the earlier trauma. Some people with disturbed early histories are unable to become appropriately attached to or dependent on another person, and this becomes one of the long-term goals of treatment. Others wish to avoid such attachment at all costs and opt for brief symptomatic treatment or psychopharmacology. The internal world of object relationships tends to be disturbed in those with very severe IEL scores, with a preponderance of primitive forms of object relating and defence mechanisms (Chapter 4). Six sessions are extremely unlikely to be sufficient to effect lasting changes in fundamental difficulties of this kind.

Examples of mild, moderate, severe and very severe early loss histories appear below. Patients 3 and 4 will need longer-term therapy, while patients 1 and 2 may profit from brief focal work.

1. *Mild early loss [presenting problem: examination anxiety]*

   - House move, aged 6.
   - Death of grandmother, aged 15.

2. *Moderate early loss [presenting problem: bereavement reaction]*
- Sister hospitalized with scarlet fever, aged 5.
- Mother hospitalized for hysterectomy, aged 13.
- Parental marital problems, aged 12–18.
- Parental separation, aged 18.
- Father emotionally unavailable.
- Mother overly critical.

3. *Severe early loss [presenting problems: depression, relationship problems]*
- Mother's surgery for breast cancer, aged 4.
- Mother's death from metastatic disease, aged 6.
- Child forbidden to attend the funeral or grieve openly for mother.
- Child looked after first by father and then by a severe and unempathic relative.
- Father remarries, in the patient's teens.
- Idealized memories of dead mother.
- Father violent, threatening and sexually abusive.
- Stepmother cold and unempathic.

4. *Very severe early loss [presenting problems: anxiety, depression, psychosexual problems, alcohol dependence, history of antisocial behaviour and self-mutilation, borderline personality disorder]*
- Unwanted baby.
- Attempted abortion.
- Severe birth trauma, mother and baby both 'nearly died'.
- Mother hospitalized after the delivery with serious medical complications.
- Separation from mother for first 6 months of life, care transferred to grandmother.
- Failure of bonding with mother.
- Father away in armed forces at the time of delivery.
- Father in prison, aged 1–4.
- Illegitimate half-brothers and sister the result of father's 'one-night stands'.
- Demands for money from mothers of father's illegitimate children

- Father compulsive gambler and binge drinker.
- Father physically abusive, aged 5–15.
- Father sexually abusive, aged 13–15.
- Economic and emotional deprivation throughout childhood.
- Mother worked part-time to support family.
- Mother often absent in the evenings when sexual abuse occurred.
- Arrested for shoplifting, aged 15.
- Pregnant after running away with boyfriend, aged 16; hostel for unwed mothers.
- Miscarriage in fifth month of pregnancy.
- Severe marital discord, father physically violent toward mother.
- Mother depressed, dependent on alcohol, emotionally unavailable.
- Father's antisocial and paranoid personality disorders, dependent on alcohol.

If the last two examples appear to be extreme, such histories are common among people seeking help from their GP for emotional problems. Without taking a history, it is not possible to uncover these features of the story which have prognostic importance for treatment modality. The IEL provides a framework within which the severity of loss events in childhood and adolescence can be assessed. *It does not need to be formally scored to be clinically useful.* Optimally, a working knowledge of the IEL undergirds history taking at assessment and aids in a decision about treatment modality.

COMORBIDITY – WHEN THERE IS MORE THAN ONE PROBLEM

The distinction between Axes I and II in the Diagnostic and Statistical Manual of Mental Disorders, Fourth Edition (DSM-IV; American Psychiatric Association, 1994) is an important indicator for choice of treatment modality. Axis I is a description of *symptomatology* (e.g. depression, manic-depressive psychosis, schizophrenia, anxiety disorders, obsessive-compulsive disorder, substance abuse, psychosexual problem, eating disorder, or adjustment disorder). Axis II indicates the presence of an underlying *personality disorder* (e.g. antisocial, avoidant, borderline, dependent, histrionic, narcissistic, obsessive-compulsive, paranoid, schizoid or schizotypal personality disorder). Occasionally, an Axis II personality disorder is the only diagnosis. More commonly it appears as a factor underlying the symptomatology on Axis I. There may be more than one problem (comorbidity) on Axis I, Axis II or both. Patients with a comorbid personality disorder on Axis II are likely to take longer to treat. The following is an extreme example:

> A young woman experiences long episodes of depression, during which she talks of suicide. She is troubled by frequent and severe panic attacks, has gastrointestinal and skin disorders that come and go depending on her mood, and she frequently abuses alcohol. At other times she binges on vast quantities of food and induces vomiting. She is anorgasmic when in one of her short-lived promiscuous relationships, and she has no close friends. Increasingly she has been having time off from a job that she does not enjoy. She describes a number of 'sixth sense' experiences, consults clairvoyants, talks aloud to herself, thinks people on the bus are talking about her, cannot make eye contact with the interviewer, and speaks in a digressive, vague manner. 'My friends call me butterfly brain', she says, but she wants to overcome her problems sufficiently to form a long-term intimate relationship, and she consults her GP.
>
> *Axis I*: episodic suicidal depression, panic attacks, multiple psychosomatic ailments, alcohol dependence, bulimia nervosa, sexual dysfunction (anorgasmia).
>
> *Axis II*: schizotypal personality disorder.

Such a patient would pose significant problems to a managed care company, because how is one to decide which of seven different disorders to treat? If it is argued that the suicidal depression is the only 'medically necessary' condition to treat (to keep the patient alive), what will happen to the six other untreated problems? Further, if the other six problems go untreated, will the suicidal depression not recur, remembering that much Axis I symptomatology is driven by personality disorders on Axis II? Such a patient is most likely to be prescribed antidepressants in a managed care setting, and possibly in some general practices in the UK – a short-term measure that will probably result in a relapse because *many of the symptoms on Axis I are driven by personality problems on Axis II*. Depending on the patient's motivation, psychological-mindedness and ego strength, she may profit from an insight-oriented therapy that will help her deal with the underlying issues from an emotionally deprived childhood, but treatment is likely to take some time and require a very skilled therapist. At present it is more likely that she will receive antidepressants and perhaps a short-term treatment for one of her problems (e.g. CBT for panic attacks). She is then likely to present a few months or a year later asking for help with bulimia, psychosexual problems, or another panic attack. It is also likely that an adequate assessment and formulation of all her problems will not have been done. This is not quality psychological care. Adequate assessment needs to be done at the primary care level, not after the patient has received three or four short-term interventions each of which has led to a relapse. Much of the 'revolving-door syndrome' (patients who continually re-refer themselves after treatment) is due to faulty or absent assessment. The financial costs of repeated episodes of care are borne by the health care system, but the long–term *emotional* costs of poor quality treatment strategies such as these are borne by the patient.

In the past decade, as researchers have become better able to distinguish patients who profit from therapy from those who do not, the phenomenon of comorbidity has come under increasing scrutiny (Clarkin, 1996; Clarkin and Kendall, 1992; Wetzler and Sanderson, 1997). First, we will consider *more than one symptom on Axis I* of the DSM-IV – depression plus anxiety, for example. Major depression occurs along with generalized anxiety or panic disorder up to 60 per cent of the time in primary care. Time to recovery for depressed patients with a comorbid anxiety disorder is longer than for those without (Brown et al., 1996). Most patients with an anxiety disorder have at least one additional disorder. Nearly half of those with post-traumatic stress disorder also suffer from major depression, and more than one-third from phobias and alcohol dependence (Sleek, 1997a). Alcohol abuse occurs in 32 per cent of those with affective disorders (mainly depression) and in 24 per cent of those with anxiety disorder (Mueser, Bellack and Blanchard, 1992). Many of the randomized controlled outcome trials of psychotherapy (Chapter 6) have attempted to exclude comorbidity, for example by studying patients who present solely with depression, but in clinical settings such patients are infrequently seen. Comorbidity is extremely common in clinical practice and treatment needs to address the full range of patients' problems (Sanderson and McGinn, 1997).

We turn next to *Axis I + Axis II comorbidity* – that is, symptomatology on Axis I with a comorbid personality disorder on Axis II. It is estimated that approximately one out of 10 adults in the general population and over half of patients in treatment suffer from a personality disorder (Magnavita, 1997). Between 30 and 40 per cent of patients diagnosed with depression also have a personality disorder (Shea, Widiger and Klein, 1992). In the NIMH collaborative study of depression, 74 per cent of patients with major depression had a comorbid personality disorder (Shea et al., 1990). Between 27 and 65 per cent of panic disorder patients (with or without agoraphobia) have a comorbid personality disorder (Brown and Barlow, 1992). It is now well established that patients with an underlying personality disorder do more poorly in a wide variety of therapies – including psychotropic medication used alone – than other patients (AuBuchon and Malatesta, 1994; Diguer, Barber and Luborsky, 1993; Hardy et al., 1995; Patience et al., 1995; Shea et al., 1990). These patients also have more severe symptoms, and are more likely to relapse after brief treatment (Sanderson and McGinn, 1997).

PERSONALITY DISORDERS

Personality *disorder* needs to be discriminated from personality *traits* or *style*. When personality traits are inflexible and maladaptive and cause *clinically significant distress or impairment in social, occupational or other important areas of functioning*, they constitute personality disorders (American Psychiatric Association, 1994). Sperry (1995) provides detailed contrasts between personality style and disorder for each of the DSM-IV personality disorders. To cite one example, in the case of obsessive-compulsive personality disorder, there is a restricted ability to express warm emotions, excessive perfectionism, an insistence that others submit to one's way of doing things, indecisiveness, and an excessive devotion to work to the exclusion of pleasure:

> A hard-driving executive works 14-hour days, is exces-
> sively cold and punitive when a member of his staff
> makes a mistake, takes weeks to decide on a course of
> action, insists that all work is carried out in the way he
> demands, and is unable to enjoy a joke. He is a cold and
> distant husband and father who is seldom at home, and
> he has difficulty taking a holiday. If a son wants to
> study a subject that is not approved, he is ordered to
> do as his father says. When on the annual holiday,
> father times the family's departure for 2 am to avoid
> heavy traffic, and he must arrive at certain service sta-
> tions on the way within 10 minutes of the time he
> arrived there the preceding year. Father stands next to
> the car with a watch and notes his arrival time in a

diary. Holidays for this family are times of major trauma and upset, and are never enjoyable.

The personality traits described in this example are all pathological, persistent and pervasive, applying equally to home, work and leisure functioning.
In DSM-IV, three clusters of personality disorder are described:

- *Cluster A ('odd-eccentric'): paranoid, schizoid and schizotypal personality disorders.* These patients are isolated and aloof, have few relationships, restricted emotions, peculiar ideas, and are suspicious and wary.

- *Cluster B ('dramatic-erratic'): antisocial, borderline, histrionic and narcissistic personality disorders.* These patients are emotional and make an impression on the interviewer, but they have erratic, unstable behaviours, chronic difficulties in interpersonal relationships, heightened and labile emotions, lack insight, and are impulsive and manipulative.

- *Cluster C ('anxious fearful'): avoidant, dependent and obsessive-compulsive personality disorders.* Under pressure, they tend to submit, evade or withdraw; they worry and ruminate, and are anxious or passive/avoidant.

Patients with Cluster C personality disorders rarely need intensive or residential treatment, but those with Cluster A and especially Cluster B disorders can be cause for considerable concern at the primary care level, especially if the personality disorder goes undiagnosed. Severe childhood physical or sexual abuse is associated with Cluster B personality disorders (Raczek, 1992). Some combinations of symptomatology are particularly risky. For example, patients with borderline personality disorder, major depression and alcohol abuse have a very high rate of completed suicide (Stone, 1993). Other depressed borderline patients make suicidal gestures not intending to die, but with a fatal result.

The rigorous assessment of personality disorder for research purposes involves the use of a patient self-report questionnaire followed by a semi-structured interview (Widiger and Alexrod, 1995), of which the SCID-II is probably the most reliable (First et al., 1995; First, 1997). Few primary care clinicians have time to administer a complete semi-structured interview, but it will be worthwhile to briefly explain the SCID-II methodology. The pre-administered self-report personality questionnaire (PQ) is used as a screening tool to save the clinician time. Each of the 113 questions on the PQ corresponds to an initial diagnostic criterion interview question in the SCID-II. For example, question 89 in the PQ is 'Do your relationships with people you really care about have lots of ups and downs?', which corresponds to the initial question for the first criterion in borderline personality disorder. In this case the patient endorsed that question:

> 89. You've said that your relationships with people you really care about have lots of ups and downs. Tell me about them . . . Were there times when you thought they were everything you wanted and then other times when you thought they were terrible? How many relationships were like this?

(First et al., 1995, p. 86)

The first criterion for borderline personality disorder is a pattern of unstable and intense interpersonal relationships characterized by alternating extremes of overidealization (perceiving the other as 'all good' or perfect) and devaluation ('all bad'). From the patient's answer to this question, the clinician scores one of four possible answers: ?, 1, 2 or 3, in which 3 = either one prolonged relationship or several briefer relationships in which the alternating pattern occurs at least twice. To qualify for a diagnosis of each of the personality disorders, a stated minimum number of symptoms must be scored at the '3' level. It is possible for patients to suffer from more than one personality disorder, that is, comorbidity also exists on Axis II.

How is this methodology to be applied at the primary care level? The short answer is that it will not often be rigorously applied outside research studies, but mental health workers need sufficient understanding of personality disorders to make a judgement about the safety of brief and ultra-brief therapies. If patients are referred with anxiety or depression, is there a comorbid personality disorder, especially a Cluster A or B disorder? If so, brief therapies are likely to be inappropriate. Failing to diagnose a comorbid personality disorder may result in unsuccessful treatment and possibly harm the patient.

There are a number of features that clinicians can learn to listen for that signal the possible presence of a personality disorder (Fong, 1995):

- While Axis I disorders are acute symptomatic *states*, Axis II personality disorders are *traits with stability over time*: 'How long has this been a problem?' or 'With how many people has this happened?' are helpful questions.

- Axis I problems are *ego dystonic* – that is, they are perceived as not part of the self and as inherently distressing. Axis II problems are *ego syntonic*, an integral part of the self: the patient says, 'That's just the way I am.' Not infrequently other people complain about the personality disordered patient, while the patient says it's everyone else's problem:

'Nothing the matter with me, mate; *he's* the problem!'

- There is generally *social and occupational impairment of functioning* in personality disorders, for example, very few friends and many changes of job in a short space of time, almost always because of interpersonal conflict. Others are usually blamed.

- Patients with personality disorder use the *same maladaptive coping patterns* over and over again; they appear not to learn from experience.

- After initial progress in short-term work, counselling may come to a sudden stop.

- There is an almost total *lack of awareness of the effects of their behaviour on others*: 'Who, *me*? Is *that* what they said I did?'

- The problems are *acceptable to the patient but not to those in close contact with them* such as partners, friends or employers.

- There is often a pattern of *noncompliance* with treatment.

- The patient enters into intense *conflictual relationships with institutional systems*. Some may have been struck off their GP's list while others are lifelong letter writers or threaten lawsuits on flimsy grounds.

- *Cognitive impairments* may be evident such as derealization, paranoia, projections and magical thinking; judgement is impaired, and insight into personal difficulties is lacking.

- *Emotionality* may be intense and/or labile – there is a longstanding inability to modulate emotion, and subjective distress about this state of affairs is frequently absent.

- There are stable patterns of impairment in *interpersonal and occupational relationships*, whether the patient is a parent, long-term intimate friend, student, or worker. Others are likely to see the patient as demanding, intolerant, competitive, or oppositional.

- There is commonly a particular vulnerability to *stress-related syndromes*, especially in Clusters B and C: autonomic nervous system symptoms, cardiovascular problems, and gastrointestinal symptoms.

Cluster A patients will not seek a relationship with the counsellor and will not desire social support. Cluster B patients are emotional and will attempt to make an impression on the counsellor, but they are often unreliable reporters of events. Cluster C patients tend to be passive, anxious, tense, and compliant to any suggestion (Fong, 1995). Because personality disorders are ego syntonic, many patients are pressed into therapy by partners, friends, or employers. The vital first step of motivating the patient to acknowledge a problem may prove difficult. Other patients are propelled into treatment because of Axis I symptoms such as overwhelming anxiety or disabling depression. Many of these patients are not interested in thoroughgoing change at the personality level, and are seeking only symptom relief. Some of them will be helped by short-term focal therapy or CBT. If the Axis I problems are driven by personality problems on Axis II, however, the therapeutic result may not be long-lasting.

Trainings in counselling and clinical psychology are often weak on diagnosis and clinical assessment outside the mainstream model being taught. Primary care mental health workers, whatever their training, need to acquaint themselves with the main criterion symptoms of the DSM-IV personality disorders, abbreviated summaries of which appear below. Although the number of criteria required for diagnosis may differ slightly from one personality disorder to another, in each case the most important criteria are listed first.

> *Antisocial Personality Disorder*. A pervasive pattern of disregard for and violation of the rights of others since adolescence: failure to conform to social norms, deceitfulness, impulsivity, aggression, reckless disregard for self or others, consistent irresponsibility, and lack of remorse for the harm done to others.

> *Avoidant Personality Disorder*. A pervasive pattern of social inhibition, feelings of inadequacy and hypersensitivity to criticism, beginning by early adulthood and present in a variety of contexts: avoids work activities involving interpersonal contact, unwilling to get involved with others unless certain of being liked, restrained in intimate relationships because of fear of ridicule, preoccupied with being criticized, inhibited in new situations because of feelings of inadequacy, views self as socially inept, and is unusually reluctant to take personal risks or engage in new activities.

> *Borderline Personality Disorder*. A pervasive pattern of unstable interpersonal relationships, self-image and emotion, and marked impulsivity beginning by early adulthood and present in a variety of contexts: frantic efforts to avoid real or imagined abandonment, unstable and intense interpersonal relationships alternating between idealization and devaluation, identity disturbance, impulsivity in at least two areas that are self-damaging, recurrent suicidal or self-

mutilating behaviour, affective instability, chronic feelings of emptiness, inappropriate intense anger, and transient stress-related paranoid ideas or dissociative symptoms.

Dependent Personality Disorder. A pervasive and excessive need to be taken care of that leads to submissive and cling-ing behaviour and fears of separation, beginning by early adulthood and present in a variety of contexts: difficulty making decisions without an excessive amount of advice and reassurance, needs others to take responsibility for most areas of life, difficulty expressing disagreement, difficulty initiating projects on one's own, goes to excessive lengths to obtain nurture and support from others, feels uncomfortable or helpless when alone, urgently seeks another relationship when a close relationship ends, and is unrealistically preoc-cupied with having to take care of oneself.

Histrionic Personality Disorder. A pervasive pattern of exces-sive emotionality and attention seeking, beginning in early adulthood and present in a variety of contexts: uncomfort-able when not the centre of attention, inappropriately sex-ually seductive, rapidly shifting and shallow expression of emotions, uses physical appearance to draw attention to the self, excessively impressionist style of speech, self-dra-matizing and theatrical, suggestible, and considers relation-ships to be more intimate than they actually are.

Narcissistic Personality Disorder. A pervasive pattern of grandiosity in fantasy or behaviour, need for admiration and lack of empathy, beginning by early adulthood and pre-sent in a variety of contexts: a grandiose sense of self-importance, preoccupied with fantasies of unlimited success, power, brilliance, beauty, or ideal love, believes that he or she is 'special' and can only be understood by other special people, requires excessive admiration, has a sense of entitlement, exploits and takes advantage of others to achieve own ends, lacks empathy, is often envious of others, and shows arrogant, haughty behaviour or attitudes.

Obsessive-Compulsive Personality Disorder. A pervasive pat-tern of preoccupation with orderliness, perfectionism and control at the expense of flexibility and efficiency, begin-ning by early adulthood and present in a variety of contexts: preoccupied with details, rules, lists, order or schedules to the extent that the major point of the activity is lost, shows perfectionism that interferes with completing tasks, excessively devoted to work to the exclusion of leisure and friendships, overconscientious and inflexible about morality, unable to discard worn-out or worthless objects, reluctant to delegate tasks, adopts a miserly spending style, and shows rigidity and stubbornness.

Paranoid Personality Disorder. A pervasive distrust and suspiciousness of others so that their motives are interpreted as malevolent, beginning by early adulthood and present in a variety of contexts: suspects without sufficient basis that others are exploitative or deceptive, preoccupied with unjustified doubts about the trustworthiness of friends or associates, reluctant to confide in others because of fear that the information will be used maliciously, reads hidden demeaning or threatening meanings into benign remarks, persistently bears grudges, perceives attacks on their character that are not apparent to others, is quick to counterattack, and has recurrent suspicions regarding partners' sexual fidelity.

Schizoid Personality Disorder. A pervasive pattern of detachment from social relationships and a restricted range of emotional expression in interpersonal settings, beginning by early adulthood and present in a variety of contexts: neither desires nor enjoys close relationships, always chooses solitary activities, has little if any interest in sexual experiences with another person, takes pleasure in few if any activities, lacks close friends or confidants, appears indifferent to the praise or criticism of others, and shows emotional coldness or detachment.

Schizotypal Personality Disorder. A pervasive pattern of social and interpersonal deficits, reduced capacity for close relationships, and cognitive or perceptual distortions and eccentricities of behaviour, beginning by early adulthood and present in a variety of contexts: ideas of reference, odd beliefs or magical thinking that influence behaviour, unusual perceptual experiences, odd thinking and speech (e.g. vague, overelaborate or stereotyped), suspiciousness or paranoid ideas, inappropriate or constricted emotionality, behaviour or appearance that is odd, eccentric or peculiar, lack of close friends or confidants, and excessive social anxiety associated with paranoid fears rather than negative judgments about the self.

(American Psychiatric Association, 1994)

CHOICE OF TREATMENT MODALITY

Patients with mild anxiety or depression, adjustment reactions, distress secondary to physical illness, and uncomplicated bereavement reactions may be helped by brief unstructured Rogerian client-centred counselling. GPs who wish to improve their generic counselling skills may find Rogerian methods particularly useful in the consultation. Even single-sentence reflections of feelings can have a markedly supportive effect on distressed patients. Elements of Rogerian technique are probably present in all forms of counselling, but many patients in primary care need more structured and detailed treatments such as psychodynamic, cognitive-behavioural (CBT) or cognitive-analytic therapy (CAT).

Some of the factors to look for in assessing suitability for psychodynamic therapy are intelligence level, psychological-mindedness, insight into problems, severity of pathology, and an ability to learn from an understanding of relationships, including the transference; an ability to use trial interpretations and psychodynamic formulations; and for brief therapy, a focal problem as opposed to diffuse problems across the whole of life. Patients who are looking primarily for symptom relief or a 'quick fix' to problems may be better helped by a cognitive-behavioural approach.

If it is primarily a cognitive problem (e.g. negative automatic thoughts in depression) or an uncomplicated anxiety symptom, cognitive-behavioural therapy may be helpful. CBT is also the treatment of choice for obsessive-compulsive disorder, some forms of sexual dysfunction, and certain psychosomatic illnesses associated with anxiety or depression. General indications for CBT include access to negative automatic thinking, an ability to link thoughts and emotions, monitor emotional issues, understand and accept the cognitive conceptualization of emotional distress, and take responsibility for behaviour. Those who insist that their problems reflect only a chemical imbalance or a bad upbringing, who are unable to see how negative thoughts affect mood and are unable to accept that changes in thinking can effect changes in feelings are unsuitable for CBT but may benefit from psychotropic medication. Those who cannot make eye contact and are anxiously defensive or hostile may not be able to build an alliance with the therapist. A longstanding history of relationship problems may also bode ill for the therapeutic working alliance. Long-term dysfunction is likely to indicate an underlying personality disorder, and an inability to maintain a focus is a contraindication for CBT. Patients who attempt to control the interview, change topics frequently, speak in vague terms, over-intellectualize, externalize their problems onto other people, or go off on tangents may also have difficulty using this model (Segal et al., 1995). However, some cognitive-behavioural therapists are now focusing their efforts on working with personality-disordered patients by addressing their dysfunctional core schemas in longer-term treatment (Chapter 3).

If the patient brings primarily relationship problems, group treatment might be considered if available. However, social isolates and patients functioning at a schizoid or paranoid level are unlikely to benefit. Those who are antisocial, addicted, or have had a recent psychotic illness or manic episodes should not be offered group treatment (Knowles, 1995). If it is primarily a couples or psychosexual problem and the partner is willing to attend, couples or sex therapy may be recommended. Family therapy is generally indicated when the problem is due to a family dilemma, or the identified patient has symptoms that are a manifestation of a disturbed family as a whole (Lieberman, 1995). However, not all localities offer family therapy.

Finally, treatment may not be offered. No treatment is offered to patients who might present a danger to the therapist, whom psychotherapy would make worse, for whom there are more cost-effective treatments, or who are unwilling or unable to complete a course of therapy (Tantum, 1995). Gustafson suggests that those who will get worse the more therapy they are given include those who develop a malignant regression in treatment (Chapter 3). These patients are not offered formal one-to-one therapy, but provision needs to be made for the management of psychiatric emergencies. Some patients are told to come and do not want counselling, or consistently externalize their problems onto others or their own physical health problems. A few patients have inadequate English and an interpreter is unavailable. Patients may be unmotivated to work on their problems, may be incapable of developing a therapeutic relationship, are unable to recognize that counselling is not about being told what to do, are looking only for 'support', or are hoping the counsellor will collude in labelling a family member as psychologically ill (Burton, Henderson and Curtis Jenkins, 1998). Others have no insight into their condition due to a severe personality disorder or psychotic state, and still others have undiagnosed medical problems such as hypothyroidism, pernicious anaemia or pancreatic cancer, all of which can mimic psychological disorder (Bond, 1995; Daines, Gask and

Usherwood, 1997; Morrison, 1997). Boundary issues may preclude the therapist seeing a given patient. The newly referred patient may be a close relative of an existing patient, the therapist may have personal knowledge of the family and have shared social connections, and occasionally patients referred are already in couples or group work elsewhere.

REFERRAL TO OTHERS

Patients who are unlikely to benefit from brief therapy include those who seek immediate gratification and insist that brief therapy must deliver rapid results, those whose lives are too busy and hurried to attend sessions, those who are severely damaged and unsupported, and those who are unwilling to collaborate or accept responsibility (Feltham, 1997). Patients with dependent personalities who form attachments that cannot be resolved are unsuitable for short-term work and may need to be referred on. Patients with most personality disorders, eating disorders, a history of childhood sexual abuse or severe addiction are likely to need specialized treatment at the secondary level, although services for these problems are inadequate in many parts of the country and primary care counsellors are increasingly being asked to see patients with these problems.

Chronic and complex psychopathology is likely to need longer-term therapy (Steenbarger, 1994; Tillett, 1996). The Complexity and Severity of Problems Index (CASP, Durham, 1997) is being used to predict which patients are vulnerable to relapse after short-term treatment and may profit from longer-term therapy. Thus far, vulnerable patients have had more than one diagnosis on Axis I, have received previous psychiatric treatment, experience severe symptoms, are single, have lower socio-economic status, poorer social adjustment, and a high score on the Psychoticism subscale of the Brief Symptom Inventory. Comorbidity on Axis I of the DSM-IV is a key variable – when there is more than one problem, short-term treatment may not give a lasting result.

The match between therapist skill and patient need is another reason for referring on. The patient referred may be inappropriate to the counsellor's level of competence and would be better helped by another form of therapy, perhaps long term. Others may need HIV counselling, psychosexual counselling, or a referral to social services, a drug and alcohol service, a learning disabilities service, child care facilities, or single parent organizations (Berkowitz, 1996). Mental health workers in primary care need to be thoroughly acquainted with local resources, statutory, private, and voluntary.

Where there is evidence of dementia, an organic brain syndrome, danger to self or others, a psychotic process or suicidal depression, a psychiatric assessment is needed and inpatient treatment may be required. Some patients currently on psychotropic medication may need to have their medication reviewed by a psychiatrist. Unfortunately it is not uncommon for primary care counsellors to be referred such patients from time to time. The appropriate step in these cases is to liaise with the GP so that a psychiatric referral can be arranged.

SUMMARY AND RECOMMENDATIONS

One indicator of the appropriateness of short-term therapy is the extent of early loss issues in the patient's history. Most items in the Inventory of Early Loss (IEL) can be scored from questions in the psychosocial history. Early loss experiences are clinically useful in predicting transferences that can be anticipated in therapy, countertransferences in the therapist, key therapeutic issues, and the risks of re-enacting early traumas inside and outside the therapeutic relationship. Patients with more severe early loss tend to have more presenting problems and longer therapies than those with mild or moderate scores. Severity of early loss is significantly related to the presence of personality disorder.

On the whole, unless there are contraindications to any form of psychological treatment, patients with severe and very severe early loss histories are likely to need longer-term therapy. One of the reasons for proposing this guideline is that many of those who have suffered severe early disruption in their attachments are prone to re-experiencing the ending of relationships as an abandonment. The ending of therapy needs to be handled skilfully if the patient is not to be re-traumatized. Another common pattern among this patient group are those who abruptly dismiss their therapists in the same way that a caretaker once abandoned them. Some people with disturbed early histories are unable to become appropriately attached to or dependent on another person, and this becomes one of the long-term goals of treatment. Others wish to avoid such attachment at all costs and opt for brief symptomatic treatment or psychopharmacology. The IEL provides a framework within which the severity of loss events in childhood and adolescence can be assessed. It does not need to be formally scored to be clinically useful.

Comorbidity is another consideration in deciding on treatment modality. There may be more than one problem on DSM-IV Axis I, Axis II or both. Patients with a comorbid personality disorder on Axis II are likely to take longer to treat. Many of the symptoms on Axis I are driven by personality problems on Axis II. Adequate assessment needs to be done at the primary care level, not after the patient has received three or four short-term interventions each of which has led to a relapse. Much of the 'revolving-door syndrome' is due to faulty or absent assessment. The financial costs of repeated episodes of care are borne by the health care system, but the long-term *emotional* costs of poor quality treatment strategies such as these are borne by the patient.

When personality traits are inflexible and maladaptive and cause clinically significant distress or impairment in social, occupational or other important areas of functioning, then they constitute personality disorders. Primary care mental health workers need sufficient understanding of personality disorders to make a judgement about the safety of brief and ultra-brief therapies. If patients are referred with anxiety or depression, is there a comorbid personality disorder, especially a Cluster A or B disorder? If so, brief therapies are likely to be inappropriate. Failing to diagnose a comorbid personality disorder may result in unsuccessful treatment and possibly harm the patient.

There are a number of features that clinicians can learn to listen for that signal the presence of a personality disorder. Axis I disorders are acute symptomatic states, whereas Axis II personality disorders are traits with stability over time. Axis I problems are ego dystonic – they are perceived as not part of the self and as inherently distressing. Axis II problems are ego syntonic, an integral part of the self. There is generally social and occupational impairment of functioning in personality disorders. Patients with personality disorder use the same maladaptive coping patterns over and over again; they appear not to learn from experience. There is an almost total lack of awareness of the effects of their behaviour on others. The problems are acceptable to the patient but not to those in close contact with them such as partners, friends or employers. These patients tend to enter into intense conflictual relationships with institutional systems. Cognitive impairments may be evident and emotionality may be intense or labile. Trainings in counselling and clinical psychology are often weak on diagnosis and clinical assessment outside the mainstream model being taught. Primary care mental health workers, whatever their training, need to acquaint themselves with the main criterion symptoms of the DSM-IV personality disorders.

A decision about treatment modality is often complex. Elements of Rogerian technique are probably present in all forms of counselling, but many patients in primary care need more structured treatments such as psychodynamic, cognitive-behavioural (CBT) or cognitive-analytic therapy (CAT). Guidelines are provided for those most suitable for psychodynamic or cognitive-behavioural therapy. If the patient brings primarily relationship problems, group treatment might be considered if available. If it is primarily a couples or psychosexual problem and the partner is willing to attend, couples or sex therapy may be recommended. Family therapy is generally indicated when the problem is due to a family dilemma, or the identified patient has symptoms that are a manifestation of a disturbed family as a whole. Guidelines are suggested for those to whom no psychotherapy should be offered, and reasons for referring to others are summarized.

6

DOES IT WORK? SERVICE EVALUATION AND AUDIT IN PRIMARY CARE

PSYCHOTHERAPY OUTCOME STUDIES

Since Eysenck's (1952) challenge to the efficacy of psychotherapy forty-five years ago, the verdict is now in: psychotherapy works (Shapiro's preface to Roth and Fonagy, 1996; Sperry et al., 1996; Strupp, 1997). However one consistent finding over many years has been the *equivalence paradox* – when different psychotherapies are compared, all are found to be about equally effective, or in the words of the Dodo, 'Everyone has won and all must have prizes' (Luborsky, Singer and Luborsky, 1975). What is far from clear, however, is which therapies work best for which patients. This question is presently being vigorously researched.

There are three kinds of outcome in psychotherapy (Lyons et al., 1997): *clinical outcomes* (a drop in symptom level or improved quality of life); *medical utilization outcomes* (a drop in consultation rate or use of inpatient facilities); and *patient satisfaction* (a satisfied customer). Many managed care companies in the USA have concentrated on medical utilization rates and patient satisfaction. Some HMOs have even started withholding part of their payment to clinicians until cost-effectiveness has been demonstrated. In the UK, clinical outcomes and patient satisfaction have generally received more attention than medical utilization rates, but data collection is far from uniform around the country (Parry and Richardson, 1996).

For many years the so-called 'gold standard' for demonstrating the *efficacy* of psychotherapy has been the randomized controlled trial (RCT). Patients with a single disorder (screened to exclude comorbidity) are randomly assigned to treatment and control conditions. Therapists are trained and supervised to administer a model of therapy which has been operationalized in a manual. Adherence to the manual is regularly monitored. RCTs identify potentially useful interventions but they do not demonstrate *effectiveness* in clinical practice. Effectiveness of a treatment is about its utility in clinical settings with patients who present with complex problems, treated by therapists who by and large are not using manualized treatment packages. 'At best, the yield of RCTs can address *"what works for whom"* in the most *ideal* set of circumstances, delivered by the most *ideal* practitioners, to the most *ideal* patients, with the most *ideal* specificity and severity of problem' (Mellor-Clark, 1997).

Seligman (1995) argues that psychotherapy as conducted in the field differs from RCTs in at least five ways:

- It is not always of fixed duration.

- It is self-correcting, discarding unsuccessful techniques or modalities for others.

- Patients can actively choose therapists and therapeutic forms rather than being assigned.

- Patients often have multiple problems requiring interactive choices between therapist and client.

- Field studies often focus on improvement in general functioning while efficacy studies focus on specific symptoms.

There are other problems when the methodology of RCTs is applied to patient populations (Sperry et al., 1996):

- Sample sizes are never sufficient to control for the multitude of possible confounding variables.

- Within-cell variation can be considerable, with patients responding differently to the same treatment.

- Although patients may be randomly assigned, therapists almost never are.

- Some patients in the inferior treatment may achieve better outcomes than some patients in the superior treatment, and vice versa.

- It is virtually impossible to avoid missing data because patients routinely fail to provide complete information at all data points or drop out of therapy.

- The inclusion/exclusion criteria make it difficult for practitioners to know whether their patients are of the same type as the patient who would have qualified for inclusion in the study.

Black (1996) recently observed that RCTs are not a panacea for all inquiry into best health care, and suggested that naturalistic studies have been denigrated without justification. A better research methodology for demonstrating the *effectiveness* of psychotherapy in the field is the systematic, naturalistic experiment in clinical settings, sometimes known as a *field trial*.

Manualized therapies for DSM-IV disorders are being presented as state-of-the-art in the field, but some clinicians believe their recommendations are premature (e.g. Strupp, 1997). Drozd and Goldfried (1996) argue that although empirical evidence of their effects in actual clinical settings is lacking, proponents of manualized therapies suggest that standardizing clinical procedures ensures that patients receive treatments that have been empirically validated in controlled trials. Treatment manuals do not guarantee competent intervention, and recent studies suggest that manualized training may not benefit the therapeutic alliance. Henry et al. (1993) found that therapists' relationship skills declined following manualized training even though their technical skills improved. Therapists who adhered best to the treatment guidelines tended to be more controlling, hostile, and prone to negative interactions with patients. In these respects manualization may not represent progress. Adhering to manuals is also likely to interfere severely with creative processes in treatment and the discovery of new experiences, which to many therapists are hallmarks of successful practice.

Roth and Fonagy's (1996) critical review of psychotherapy research has brought a number of these issues into focus. They examine the efficacy of psychological therapies in relation to selected DSM-IV diagnoses, but the criteria by which they identify therapies with clear evidence of *efficacy* limit the generalizability of their findings:

- Independent replicated demonstration of superiority to a control condition or another treatment condition, *or* a single high quality randomized controlled trial.

- The availability of a clear description of the therapeutic method (preferably but not necessarily in the form of a therapy manual), of sufficient clarity to be usable as the basis of training.

- A clear description of the patient group with whom the treatment was applied.

(Roth and Fonagy, 1996, p. 364)

They suggest that 'RCTs provide the *only valid* – albeit limited – source of evidence for the efficacy of various forms of psychological treatment' (p. 19, italics added). However, they admit that it is 'unlikely that data from trials can be transferred directly into the clinical context. For example, existing manualized treatments used in clinical trials that focus on a specific disorder are likely to pay little attention to comorbid conditions' (p. 31). They point out that *absence of efficacy is not the same as evidence of ineffectiveness.* There are a number of innovative and some well-established therapies such as psychodynamic and eclectic therapies for which evidence of efficacy in the form of RCTs is deficient or lacking. However, Luborsky et al. (1993b) compared psychodynamic therapies to other therapies including cognitive-behavioural therapy (CBT) and found no differences in outcome (the equivalence paradox). Wallerstein (1995), reporting on the 30-year Menninger study of 42 patients in psychoanalysis and psychotherapy, concluded that structural personality change was possible in both expressive and supportive therapies. A recent meta-analysis (Crits-Christoph, 1992) suggests that psychodynamic therapies are as effective as CBT for a range of problems. To merit inclusion, each study had to test the efficacy of a manualized psychodynamic therapy against that of a comparison group such as a waiting list control, nonpsychiatric treatment, another psychotherapy, medication, or another form of dynamic therapy. Evidence for patients deriving benefit from psychodynamic therapies is not lacking if the reviewer looks beyond RCTs.

Roth and Fonagy acknowledge that psychodynamic therapies are particularly effective in cases of comorbidity and complexity, and are often helpful with patients suffering from personality disorders. They also observe that psychodynamic insights are being integrated into cognitive-behavioural approaches (e.g. Persons, 1989; Safran and Segal, 1990). Unfortunately, there are statements in Roth and Fonagy's review that could lead to premature withdrawal of funding from some of the under-researched therapies. For example, 'There is no doubt that the relative paucity of good-quality outcome evidence for psychodynamic therapies hampers arguments for their retention' (p. 46). This statement may be taken at face value by some purchasers while the sentence that follows it is ignored: 'However, it is beholden on payers to measure carefully what evidence is available.' The authors have previously stated that RCTs provide the *only valid* source of evidence for efficacy, therefore a conservative purchaser may be inclined to cut funding. This would be a very regrettable outcome of the review, but there are already signs that such measures are being taken in the case of counselling in primary care, another 'under-researched' treatment.

The implications of the review's conclusions are far-reaching. Roth and Fonagy acknowledge that there are problems with meta-analyses of RCTs. For example, these reviews may:

- omit single-case studies, studies of questionable methodology and trials of patients with mild or subclinical symptoms

- assume that outcome measures are on an interval scale with insignificant skewness or kurtosis (which may not be the case)

- be biased due to the tendency for authors and editors to publish only positive results

- miss important studies by failing to supplement computerized searches with manual searches of the literature, and may omit foreign language literature

- include studies of poor quality and those with biases from selective attrition

- fail to weight the means for sample size

- make unwarranted assumptions of homogeneity in combining studies statistically

- average effect sizes across multiple measures within some studies

- compare incommensurable studies.

(Roth and Fonagy, 1996, pp. 23, 362–363)

Despite these failings, meta-analyses are being used to generate *clinical guidelines* for the treatment of certain DSM-IV disorders, and claims are made that these recommendations constitute sound, *evidence-based* practice (e.g., Fonagy and Target, 1996). Examples of such protocols include the American Psychiatric Association's (1993) practice guidelines on depression, the Depression Guideline Panel of the Agency for Health Care Policy and Research (1993), and the American Psychological Association's list of empirically validated treatments (Task Force on Promotion and Dissemination of Psychological Procedures, 1995). These guidelines and the meta-analyses driving them are surrounded by controversy (Garfield, 1996; Matt and Navarro, 1997; Munoz et al., 1994; Persons, Thase and Crits-Christoph, 1996; Schmidt, Tanner and Dent, 1996; Schulberg and Rush, 1994). And yet, as Roth and Fonagy put it:

> Whether or not psychotherapy researchers or clinicians
> approve, research evidence now influences which
> forms of therapy are reimbursable for which present-
> ing conditions . . . As research evidence begins to be
> collated, there is a temptation to turn to these findings
> as though they provide a definitive answer, without
> noting the cautions researchers almost universally
> attach to them . . . In research trials, greater adherence
> [to manuals] can sometimes be shown to relate to
> improved clinical efficacy. An uncritical reading of this
> work could lead to the erroneous conclusion that
> greater effectiveness would be achieved simply by
> insisting that therapists adhere to a manual.
>
> (Roth and Fonagy, 1996, pp. 38, 40, 42)

Garfield (1996) suggests that those supporting 'empirically validated' psychological therapies have made premature recommendations. A significant problem with following protocols or guidelines is that not all patients with the same diagnosis require identical treatments. The patient's personality, life situation, ethnic identity, expectations about therapy, previous therapy, and perception of the therapist may vary significantly. Therapists may also wish to select features from different approaches in tailoring the treatment to the individual patient. The vast majority of therapists have become to some degree eclectic in orientation. The UK Department of Health's review of psychotherapy (Parry and Richardson, 1996) has taken a cautious line on validated therapies:

> It would be premature and unjustified to imagine that
> certain treatments have been 'validated'. The NHS
> Executive will not therefore publish a list of 'effective'
> therapies on which funding decisions should be based.
>
> (Parry and Richardson, 1996, p. 42)

The reasons given for this approach include:

- the importance of non-technical factors in psychotherapy outcome such as therapist competence, patient characteristics, non-specific factors, the patient's ability to form a therapeutic alliance, and social support available

- the fact that many treatments such as psychodynamic therapy are under-researched

- efficacy in RCTs is very different from effectiveness in clinical settings

- the quality of outcome measurement remains unsatisfactory

- it remains a matter of clinical judgment based on assessment and case formulation whether a guideline should be applied to a particular patient.

(Parry and Richardson, 1996, p. 42–43)

The review also takes the position that 'cookbook' approaches to purchasing particular treatments for specific diagnoses are not recommended. Purchasing predefined packages of treatment for specific diagnostic groups overlooks the very high rate of comorbidity in patients requesting help. At the same time, the review makes it clear that the NHS will not continue to provide any therapy or service which refuses to evaluate its work.

Psychotherapy is not a minor intervention whose effects are always benign. Strupp, Hadley and Gomes-Schwartz (1977) review the negative effects of psychotherapy, including both the exacerbation of presenting symptoms and the appearance of new symptoms (e.g. symptom substitution, psychotic episodes, suicide, deterioration of relationships, withdrawal, severe or fatal psychosomatic reactions, dissociation, substance abuse and criminal acting out). Therapy can become a substitute for action or lead to sustained and unproductive dependency on the therapist. Some patients may attempt to 'over-reach' themselves, undertaking life tasks without adequate psychic resources. Others may become disillusioned with therapy, lose confidence in themselves and in others, and generally lose hope as a result of treatment. One factor associated with negative effects is an inaccurate or deficient assessment, especially the failure to take a history or adequately to assess the patient's ego strength. For example, borderline patients inappropriately taken on for insight-oriented psychotherapy may decompensate into a psychotic state, act out, or attempt suicide.

A variety of deficiencies in therapist training and/or personality can contribute to negative effects, including lack of empathy, exploitativeness, hostility, obsessionalism, seductiveness, greed, pessimism, narcissism and lack of self-awareness. Patient factors related to negative effects include low or absent motivation, poor ego strength, and deeply entrenched masochistic personality traits. Deficiencies of technique associated with negative effects include false assumptions about the efficacy of therapy, inappropriate or nonexistent therapeutic goals, misplaced focus, mismatch between patient and therapist, technical rigidity, overly intense therapy, the misuse of interpretations, dependency-fostering techniques, too much or too little rapport, countertransference distortions, communication problems, and failure to maintain professional distance (especially sexual involvement with the patient). Breaches in confidentiality, prolongation of therapy after an impasse is reached, and destructive labelling of patients are additional factors associated with negative outcomes. Negative effects require special attention in the case of brief therapies and need urgently to be researched, especially at long-term follow-up (Strupp, Hadley and Gomes-Schwartz, 1977).

One contentious issue in deciding which therapies to purchase is the *length of treatment* needed by a particular patient. Managed care in the USA is currently promoting brief and ultra-brief therapies, largely on cost-containment grounds. Longer-term therapies have been under-researched (Denman, 1995). Particularly needed are comparative studies of short- vs. longer-term treatments. Such research is extremely labour intensive and requires many years of data collection. Drop-out during treatment and failure to attend follow-up sessions can seriously affect findings. These problems are magnified when outcome is measured only pre- and post-treatment instead of throughout therapy. Outcome measures such as personal questionnaires need to be capable of capturing uniquely individual (idiographic) issues, as well as standardized measures such as the Beck Depression Inventory used by all patients (nomothetic). Large group sizes are needed, and outcome measures need to be relevant to the goals of long–term therapy. Some such measures exist, as we shall see in the next section, but they have been under-utilized. Research in this area is a particularly pressing need if long-term therapy is not to vanish completely from the NHS. In any case, its availability is now very limited in the public sector in the UK.

It it is now well known that the more disturbed the patient, the harder it is to make therapeutic gains (Barkham et al., 1996; Luborsky et al., 1993a). The most frequently cited meta-analysis of length of treatment in psychotherapy is the *dose-effect* study of Howard et al. (1986). Fifteen samples covering a period of more than 30 years contributed data on 2,431 patients in individual outpatient psychotherapy. Approximately 15 per cent of patients could be expected to have improved prior to the first session, 25 per cent had improved after one session, 50 per cent after 8 sessions, and 75 per cent after 26 sessions. Fifty-two weekly sessions were the maximum effective dose for uncomplicated depression and anxiety without borderline personality disorder or comorbid conditions. Where these were present, longer treatment was required. The authors concluded that cases that had not shown any measurable improvement by 26 sessions should be subjected to clinical review.

By contrast, Kopta et al. (1994) examined ten datasets of outpatient psychotherapy attendances and found that among patients presenting with acute distress, there was 68–95 per cent improvement by 52 sessions (about a year). For patients with chronic distress, 60–86 per cent had improved by 52 sessions. Patients with characterological symptoms showed only 30–59 per cent improvement by 52 sessions. The typical outpatient in their study required 58 sessions to have a 75 per cent chance of symptomatic recovery – about 7 months more therapy than estimated by Howard et al. (1986). A number of methodological problems have been identified in the Howard study (Berman, 1996; Kadera, Lambert and Andrews, 1996). One of the most important problems is that Howard did not apply the *criteria for clinically significant change* developed by Jacobson and Truax (1991), whereas Kopta did employ the criteria. Unfortunately, some purchasers and managed care companies have been citing the flawed Howard study as if it provided the definitive dose-response curve for psychotherapy.

Kadera, Lambert and Andrews (1996) used session-by-session measures to test the dose-response curve on a continuous basis throughout therapy. At 8 sessions, 22 per cent of patients had recovered and at 13 sessions 44 per cent had recovered. Whereas Howard would predict that 50 per cent of patients are measurably improved by 8 sessions, the more recent study found only 22 per cent were recovered by that time. The two studies are in agreement that by session 26 about 75 per cent of patients can be expected to have significantly recovered. The session-by-session data indicate that few patients changed in a steady, linear fashion. Only session-by-session tracking can identify the ups and downs of therapeutic change over time and accurately identify the point of sustained recovery. If linearity is assumed between pre- and post-treatment measures, the session at which recovery occurs can be quite dramatically incorrect, and therapy may be terminated prematurely.

Barkham et al. (1996) further tested Howard et al.'s (1996) suggestion that symptomatic improvement in the dose-response curve was negatively accelerated (i.e., tails off at 26 sessions). Using data from 212 depressed patients who had been randomly assigned to receive either 8 or 16 sessions of time-limited psychotherapy, they found that change in particular symptoms was roughly linear rather than negatively accelerated. Symptoms of acute distress responded quite rapidly to treatment whereas characterological and relational variables changed more slowly.

On the whole, the research in this area has shown that more therapy is generally better than less therapy, yet some patients benefit from 5 sessions while a number go on for years without change. Therefore more research is needed to identify those who can profit from brief treatment. In an Employee Assistance Programme (EAP) sample in the USA, the modal number of sessions per patient is 1, and the average number of sessions is 3, in keeping with the trend toward ultra-brief therapies in EAP and managed care environments (Lambert, 1997). Lambert's team now employs a 45-item self-report Outcome Questionnaire (OQ, Lambert et al., 1994) which includes subjective discomfort, interpersonal problems, social role performance, quality of life, suicidality, substance abuse, and workplace violence. Users of the OQ must be licensed. A cut-off score for the OQ discriminates between patients who are dysfunctional and those who are not. Patients defined as having 'improved' have moved 15 points below the cut-off score on the OQ. Patients are asked to arrive 5–10 minutes early to complete the OQ prior to every session. Data are scanned onto computer and graphically displayed, so that assessment becomes a regular part of treatment.

Borderline patients have very unstable OQ scores over time, with many ups and downs. Also, different parts of the OQ change at different rates: symptoms generally improve faster than interpersonal problems or social role performance, for example. More disturbed patients require more treatment. Patients are grouped according to four predictors of outcome:

- OQ pre-treatment score (severity of symptomatic state).

- Developmental history (previous psychotherapy, hospitalizations, medication).

- Diagnosis by level of severity (childhood sexual abuse and comorbidity are considered).

- Level of functioning (work and overall functional status).

Up to 20,000 patients a year who use EAPs are being tracked in the emerging database. Those scoring 1-1-1-1 on the above four predictors are 'easy' patients, while 4-3-3-3 are more difficult patients whose treatment will take longer. Expectancy tables for the 180 possible patient types have been compiled. At assessment, patients can be profiled according to their expected outcomes, and their actual progress plotted against expected gains over time. A hypothesized dose-response curve for a 1-3-1-1 patient, for example, can be called up on a computer. If the patient is not responding as quickly as expected, a case manager will ask the therapist what needs to be changed, because the patient is not doing as well as would be expected for other patients of this type.

One problem with Lambert's research is the frequent inaccuracy of diagnosis, especially regarding cormorbid personality disorders. Most clinicians are hesitant to give Axis II diagnoses because EAPs will not pay for treating them. The precise nature of patients' symptomatology is therefore in doubt. Another question is the impact of showing patients their OQ scores on a weekly basis. It can be assumed that patients are rewarded in various ways for improving. One wonders how deteriorating scores are handled with patients. Hopefully, therapists will use deteriorating scores to attend to the therapeutic alliance or make other adjustments in treatment. Therapist compliance with weekly OQs has been excellent, possibly because the EAP tells the therapist, 'If your patients fill in their OQs every week, we won't case manage you.' When therapists view the questionnaires positively, their patients are more willing to accept them.

Another problem with EAP research in the USA is that major users of mental health services who move EAPs when they change jobs may be lost to long-term follow-up. Their medical notes do not move with them when they register with a new GP, as is the case in the UK. One of the pressing needs in psychotherapy outcome research is *long-term follow-up* to track relapses and recidivism over time (the 'revolving-door phenomenon'). A good result may appear to have been achieved in 5 sessions on the basis of post-treatment scores, but if the patient returns the following year so seriously deteriorated that hospitalization is required, this is not a good long-term outcome. Such research is expensive, but urgently needs to be done. What are the *long-term effects* of brief and ultra-brief therapies? The answer to that question is not known at present.

The UK Department of Health's Strategic Review of Psychotherapy (Parry and Richardson, 1996) observes that American dose-response studies need to be replicated in the UK. The optimum length of treatment for different conditions is not yet established, so there is little sense at present in purchasers imposing an arbitrary cap on the number of sessions. The right dosage of psychotherapy depends on the severity and complexity of the condition. Some GP fundholders have been setting caps on the number of sessions, although few English health authorities stipulate lengths of treatment in their contracts with providers at the present time.

OUTCOME MEASURES

Howard et al. (1996) argue that there are three fundamental questions in psychotherapy outcome research: (1) Does the therapy work under special experimental conditions? (2) Does it work in clinical practice? and (3) Is it working for this patient? Question (1) is the efficacy question; (2) is the effectiveness question; and (3) is the immediate question posed by the clinician: 'Is what I am doing helping this patient now, this week?' Outcome measurement has advanced considerably since the early pre-treatment/post-treatment comparison studies. With only two points of data per case, a great deal of information is lost regarding changes over the course of therapy. Also, when patients drop out of treatment and no post-treatment measurement is possible, substantial amounts of missing data flaw the study and hamper interpretation. If data are collected continuously over the course of treatment, not only is the missing data problem addressed but much can be learned about patient change during therapy. Equally important is the practitioner's need to know during therapy whether that treatment is working for a particular patient. Continuous tracking of progress allows this kind of information to be fed back to the therapist, for the patient's benefit.

Froyd, Lambert and Froyd (1996) reviewed 348 outcome studies from 1983 to 1988 and found 1,430 measures in use of which 830 were used only once, and for 278 no psychometric properties or data were available. Similarly, Ogles, Lambert and Masters (1996) identified published reports of more than 1,000 different outcome measures in psychotherapy research, but only a handful had been used in more than one study.

The COMPASS system widely used in the USA includes items tapping Subjective Well-being, Current Symptoms and Current Life Functioning. The sum of these 3 subscores is the *Mental Health Index* (MHI) which is tracked throughout treatment. The clinician rates the patient's condition using a Clinical Assessment Index, and a 12-item Therapeutic Bond Scale is also used (Sperry et al., 1996). The COMPASS approach to the managed care 'medical necessity' question is to determine whether a patient's MHI score is more likely to belong to the distribution of patient or non-patient scores. It has been found that an MHI T-score below 60 represents a need for treatment, or 'medical necessity'. Expected courses of recovery can be estimated based on patients' initial clinical characteristics. Severity of disorder pre-treatment is calculated by a weighted formula that includes the following:

- age, gender, ethnicity, employment status, education, marital status
- parent/nonparent status, living alone/not living alone
- presenting problems and their duration; amount of prior

psychotherapy

- level of distress when telephoning for an appointment
- perceived importance of treatment and perceived difficulty of being in treatment
- level of confidence that treatment will be successful
- expectations for likely outcome of treatment
- Subjective Well-being at intake (scale score)
- Symptoms at intake (full-scale score plus 7 subscales)
- Life Functioning at intake (full-scale score plus 6 subscales)
- Mental Health Index at intake (composite score)
- DSM-IV diagnosis, Axis I (provided by therapist)
- presence or absence of Axis II diagnosis (by therapist)
- does/does not meet criteria for diagnosis of Depression (from self-reported symptoms)
- does/does not meet criteria for Substance Abuse
- patient functioning at intake (Global Assessment Form score from therapist)
- life functioning at intake (six functioning domains rated by therapist)
- therapist assessment of patient psychological status at intake
- therapist assessment of patient level of distress at intake
- therapist's intake assessment of patient potential for improvement during treatment.

(Lyons et al., 1997, p. 179)

From this calculation, a patient's expected treatment trajectory over time can be estimated. When actual scores are plotted against estimated scores, treatments that are in difficulty can be identified. Further, patients who no longer have a 'medical necessity' for treatment can be identified, as their MHI scores have returned to the normal range. An obvious problem with this system is that some of the enduring difficulties which people with personality disorders experience may persist despite apparently 'normal range' MHI scores. 'When is treatment finished?' is an important question for relapse prevention. In managed care, reimbursement ceases when MHI T-scores are higher than 60.

The plethora of outcome measures in use in the UK has led to the development of a standardized CORE outcome measure (Mellor-Clark and Barkham, 1998). It is brief (34 items), in simple language (patients need only 5 years of education to understand it) and response choices are clear. This measure has subscales for:

- Subjective Well-being (current distress and self-esteem).
- Symptoms (depression, anxiety, trauma, physical manifestations).
- Life/Social Functioning (close relationships, social relationships, work/ leisure, quality of life).
- Risk/Harm (to self, to others).

This CORE measure was developed at the Psychological Therapies Research Centre (PTRC) at the University of Leeds, funded by the Mental Health Foundation. In addition to the 34-item version intended for use pre- and post-treatment, two short versions of 17 items each are recommended as alternating repeated measures to tap patient change on a session-by-session basis. In this way outcome measurement becomes continuous outcome monitoring. The CORE measure, together with pre- and post-treatment record forms including the Health of the Nation Outcome Scales (HoNOS, Wing, Curtis and Beevor, 1996) are being used in an ongoing study of counselling in primary care at the PTRC funded by the Counselling in Primary Care Trust. The twelve Health of the Nation Outcome Scales (HoNOS, Wing, Curtis and Beevor, 1996) score each of the following on a 5-point Likert scale ranging from 0 = no problem to 4 = severe problem:

1. Overactive, aggressive, disruptive behaviour.

2. Non-accidental self-injury.

3. Problem drinking or drug-taking.

4. Cognitive problems.

5. Physical illness or disability problems.

6. Problems with hallucinations or delusions.

7. Problems with depressed mood.

8. Other mental/behavioural problems: main problem + 4 other relevant problems.

9. Problems with relationships.

10. Problems with activities of daily living.

11. Problems with living conditions.

12. Problems with occupation or other activities.

The items most often applicable to primary care are 7, 8 and 9, although other items may be relevant in individual cases. Item 8 in its original form allowed only one problem to be rated, preventing any measurement of comorbidity. The PTRC forms allow up to five problems to be recorded for any one patient. This arrangement also allows progress on all five problems to be assessed at the end of treatment. When patients present with many problems (e.g. depression, anxiety, relationship problems, eating disorder, and personality disorder), short-term therapy may reduce levels of depression and anxiety, leaving the other problems untouched. This system allows the status of all five problems to be recorded at the beginning and end of treatment.

Good quality outcome studies and clinical audit depend on detailed up-to-date databases. In the UK, resources are often lacking for the maintenance of such databases at a local level, especially in the primary care setting. The project launched by the PTRC takes much of the day-to-day labour out of data collection and analysis. Clinicians require only about five minutes to complete simple double-sided forms at the beginning and end of treatment, and patients complete a CORE measure every six sessions. Other outcome variables can be added on a local basis. The computer-scannable forms can be processed in Leeds at the rate of 40 per minute, and data returned to clinicians in a timely fashion at a reasonable cost. Meanwhile a national database will grow in parallel with some of the projects we have described in the USA. When large numbers of patients' data are on computer, treatment trajectories can be estimated for particular diagnoses in addition to other variables predictive of outcome. Actual performance can be measured against expected scores, and therapies can be adjusted when the need arises. Over a period of years, the result will be a high-quality field trial of counselling in primary care, which is sorely needed. Such well-designed trials are likely to be more informative than RCTs in primary care. The tools making up the CORE evaluation system can be obtained from the PTRC free of charge, and guidelines are provided for those practitioners who wish to analyse their own data. Alternatively, the forms can be analysed and benchmarked by PTRC for an annual fee. Readers wishing to join the evaluation project may contact the PTRC at the University of Leeds.

A number of other outcome measures can be used to supplement the Outcome Questionnaire, the CORE measure, or the Mental Health Index, if the researcher wishes to measure certain symptom complexes in greater detail, estimate cost effectiveness, or pursue variables of interest to psychodynamic therapy (Nelson-Gray, 1996). The *Beck Depression Inventory* (BDI, Beck, Steer and Garbin, 1988) is widely used, as is the *State-Trait Anxiety Inventory* (STAI, Spielberger, 1983). Some primary care services are using the 14-item *Hospital Anxiety and Depression Scale* (HADS, Zigmond and Snaith, 1983). The *General Health Questionnaire* (GHQ, Goldberg, 1978) is a screening measure for psychological morbidity and is unsuitable for outcome studies. The *Brief Symptom Inventory* (BSI, Derogatis and Spencer, 1982; Derogatis and Melisaratos, 1983) has clinically useful subscale scores for psychoticism, somatization, depression, hostility, phobic anxiety, obsessive-compulsive, panic anxiety, paranoid ideation, and general anxiety. The BSI is an abbreviated, 53-item version of the original 90-item *Symptom Checklist 90-Revised* (Derogatis and Cleary, 1977). An easily administered six-item *Quality of Life Questionnaire* (Burton et al., 1993) appears in the Appendix.

The *Inventory of Interpersonal Problems* (Horowitz et al., 1988) has spawned a 32-item short form of the same measure, the *IIP-32* (Barkham, Hardy and Startup, 1996) with subscale scores for:

• Hard to be assertive	• Too dependent
• Hard to be sociable	• Too caring
• Hard to be supportive	• Too aggressive
• Hard to be involved	• Too open

This measure may be particularly appropriate for psychodynamic therapies aimed at an improvement in interpersonal relationships. In American clinics with specialized resources such as the Austen Riggs Center, pre- and post-treatment Rorschach tests can be administered, providing detailed information on thought disorder and level of object relationships in patients with severe personality disorders. The Thematic Apperception Test can be used to measure changes in defence mechanisms from primitive to more mature, and Human Figure Drawings may illuminate changes in degree of differentiation and organization pre- to post-treatment (Blatt and Ford, 1994). Significant constructive changes occurred in 90 patients over an extended period of inpatient treatment which included psychodynamically oriented psychotherapy four times weekly. Research of this kind into long-term psychodynamic psychotherapy with severely disturbed patients urgently needs to be undertaken in specialist UK centres. Another measure relevant to psychodynamic therapies is the *Quality of Object Relations Scale* (Azim, 1991; Piper et al., 1991). Five levels of object relationship (primitive, searching, controlling, triangular and mature) can be coded by clinicians trained in the instrument with good inter-rater reliability. This measure is very suitable for use in outpatient services offering psychodynamic treatment.

Malan and Osimo (1992) devised a scoring system for short-term dynamic psychotherapy outcomes. The patient's state at assessment is taken as baseline. Actual changes are compared with the criteria which have been set for total resolution, and are weighted according to the clinical importance attached to them. The score is the proportion of the original disturbance that is resolved regardless of the initial severity. It is a judgement of the degree to which there has been overall resolution, combined with a judgement about the adaptiveness of the patient's condition at discharge. No change is indicated by 0, complete resolution of all difficulties scores 4, and deterioration is indicated by -1. If serious problems in relationships with the opposite sex remain at the end of treatment, the patient cannot score more than the halfway mark of 2. Two clinicians score patient change at the end of treatment, and the mean score is recorded. Malan and Osimo provide a number of illustrative examples. Sigrell et al. (1998) provide an excellent examples of an outcome study using Malan's outcome measure. Ten patients in long-term therapies ranging from 18 to 48 months were seen to have improved, with scores ranging from 2 to 4. Improvement criteria were tailored to each patient's psychodynamic formulation and presenting problems. A simpler method of scoring improvement on the patient's three principal problems appears in the Appendix (Burton et al., 1993). In this case, improvement on each problem (including interpersonal problems, if these are a feature) is scored by the therapist on a 5-point Likert scale.

Many services today are pressed to provide evidence of *cost-effectiveness* (Rowland and Tolley, 1995; Tolley and Rowland, 1995). A recent review of the economic impact of psychotherapy suggests that it has a beneficial impact on a variety of costs for patients with the most severe problems such as borderline personality disorder. Psychotherapy is a good investment in these cases, reducing the frequency and duration of hospitalization, and allowing an earlier return to work. The economic impact of psychotherapy on less severe disorders such as depression is not so apparent because hospitalization does not enter the picture as often

(Gabbard et al., 1997). The work of Cummings (1997) focuses on the reduction in medical utilization rates as a result of brief psychotherapeutic interventions. The *Keele EAP Evaluation Scale* (McLeod and Worrell, 1997) includes a measure of the *work* efficiency of employees. This measure is of great interest to employers as it has profound cost implications for companies:

> Given the stresses/problems you are having to deal with at this time, in percentage terms how effective or efficient do you feel you are at present at work?

> 0% | 10% | 20% | 30% | 40% | 50% | 60% | 70% | 80% | 90% | 100%

A number of primary care studies have assessed whether counselled patients use fewer psychotropic drugs, consult their GP less often, or use fewer expensive hospital-based psychiatry services (Tolley and Rowland, 1995). Several cost benefits have been found for primary care counselling, although many studies suffer from methodological problems. Tolley and Rowland provide detailed guidance on conducting cost-effectiveness studies. The cost of not treating patients can be estimated by detailing the adverse outcomes that can be expected if the patient goes untreated. For example, there are costs attached to psychiatric breakdown, suicide attempts, further psychotropic medication, inappropriate health-care-seeking behaviours, AIDS risk behaviour, marriage or family breakup or divorce, children taken into care, unemployment, dependence on social services, physical or sexual abuse of children, risk of offending, or social isolation (see the Appendix for a checklist to be used at assessment). Annual data from such an *'at risk of . . .' checklist*, if employed routinely in primary care services, can be used to argue for the cost-effectiveness of counselling or psychotherapy.

A similar procedure has been used by the Henderson Hospital in arguing for the cost-effectiveness of their inpatient service for severely personality disordered patients (Dolan et al., 1995). The Henderson's population are typically single, unemployed young people: 75 per cent have made a suicide attempt; >50 per cent have had adult convictions; 25 per cent have had juvenile convictions; and 10 per cent have served a prison sentence. The average cost to the public of a patient in the year prior to hospitalization was £14,000. The cost of one year's treatment at the Henderson was £25,000, and the annual cost in the year after discharge was only £1,300. It can be seen that the treatment paid for itself in two years.

Patient satisfaction questionnaires are widely used both in the USA and the UK. An example appears in the Appendix. Some managed care companies use patient satisfaction questionnaires instead of symptomatic change scales, which is not sound practice. For example, the relationship between clinical improvement and patient satisfaction was not statistically significant according to a study conducted by Compass (1995). Patient satisfaction is no longer a sufficient outcome measure for counselling and psychotherapy. The CORE measure serviced by PTRC mentioned above is a good example of the minimum data set that any primary care service should be collecting, and throughout therapy rather than just pre- and post-treatment. Patient satisfaction may also be of interest, but should not be substituted for clinically significant change measures.

PRIMARY CARE OUTCOME STUDIES

We turn now to outcome studies in the primary care setting. Much has been written on this subject, but a number of studies are now out of date and suffer from methodological problems (see Burton, 1992a for a review of older work). Roth and Fonagy (1996) apply the same RCT criterion of efficacy to counselling in primary care as to other psychotherapy outcome studies. There are few RCTs, and those that exist are in their judgement of poor quality, as is an early meta-analysis by Balestrieri et al. (1988). One major problem with Roth and Fonagy's chapter on counselling in primary care is that very few of the studies are actually of services delivered by counsellors. Most of the clinicians cited in that chapter are social workers, psychiatrists, GPs, nurse practitioners, health visitors, psychotherapists, clinical psychologists, psychiatric nurses or nurse behaviour therapists. It is therefore difficult to apply their critique to the work of those who are presently offering 'counselling in primary care'.

Three recent RCTs deserve mention. Scott and Freeman (1992) randomly assigned patients to psychotropic medication prescribed by a psychiatrist, CBT from a clinical psychologist, counselling and case work from a social worker, or routine care from a GP. Marked improvement occurred in all groups over 16 weeks. Advantages of specialist treatments over routine GP care were small, but specialist treatment cost at least twice as much as routine GP care. Psychological treatments were however most positively evaluated by patients. King et al. (1994) assigned patients to nondirective counselling or to routine care from the GP according to patient preference. Patients who had seen their GP had a better outcome at 6 months than those who had received counselling. The sample was very small – 19 patients chose counselling and only 5 chose to see their GP, so it is difficult to draw any conclusions. Gournay and

Brooking (1994) compared patients seen by CPNs and GPs and found no differences in outcome between the two groups.

From the evidence available, it would be premature to conclude that counselling in primary care 'doesn't work' – as *potential efficacy is not the same as actual effectiveness in practice.* Many of the studies in this area fail to define counselling adequately, and heterogeneous patient groups make it difficult to draw firm conclusions about differential effectiveness across diagnostic groups. Nonspecific factors in counselling and psychotherapy need to be controlled for when counselling is compared to routine GP care. GPs may be providing elements of support, empathy, and attention which have therapeutic effects of their own. Some may also use reflection-of-feelings techniques in their consultations with patients, so it should not be surprising when further examples of the equivalence paradox are found (Corney, 1990).

Friedli and King (1996) review descriptive studies of counselling in primary care as well as RCTs. They find it difficult to draw conclusions from the descriptive studies because of the absence of control groups. Most of the RCTs suffer from small sample sizes, poorly defined treatments, inadequate evaluation and short timescales for follow-up. The authors call for urgent research into which form of counselling is best for which type of patient. The UK Department of Health's Strategic Review of Psychotherapy (Parry and Richardson, 1996) echoes this call for further research. An American review of RCTs of psychosocial treatments in primary care (Brown and Schulberg, 1995) found evidence to support the efficacy of psychosocial treatments. However, many of the studies cited had methodological problems, for example, only 8 out of 18 RCTs had selected patients using a structured diagnostic assessment procedure. Many patient samples were heterogeneous, and studies limited to single diagnostic categories had the most consistently positive outcomes. Inadequate information was available comparing attrition patterns in treatment and control groups, and a diverse array of outcome measures was used. Those studies which demonstrated a medical cost offset as a result of counselling showed inconsistent effects across studies, which may have been the result of heterogeneous patient samples.

Several other studies have been published recently. Boot et al. (1994) randomly assigned patients to counselling or routine GP care. Those who received counselling showed greater improvement on the General Health Questionnaire than those who saw their GP. Unfortunately, however, the GHQ is not an adequate change measure for psychotherapy research. Fewer of those counselled were prescribed psychotropic medication by their GPs, or were referred to psychiatrists or clinical psychologists for secondary care. Higher patient satisfaction was found in the counselled group. Gordon and Graham (1996) evaluated the work of three practice counsellors offering brief, 6-session interventions with the SCL-90R and HADS. Clinical improvement was highly significant across all outcome measures used. The patients referred had significant psychiatric problems, and counselling was effective in reducing symptomatology. However, some of the more disturbed patients needed to be referred on to specialist secondary services. Therefore, while it can produce cost savings at the primary care level, counselling may also create new demands on secondary care.

Fletcher, Fahey and McWilliam (1995) assessed the impact of counselling on GP prescription of psychotropic medication in a cross-sectional study of general practices in Oxfordshire. The highest level of prescribing was found in those practices with a counsellor in the surgery. It is possible that practices with higher prescribing costs were more aware of their patients' psychological difficulties, or had lists with higher psychological morbidity. The provision of counselling might have uncovered need among patients which led to increased prescribing, or practices might have identified a need for counselling but it was too early to observe effects on psychotropic drug prescribing. The relationship between counselling and psychotropic drug prescribing appears to be complex. Sibbald et al. (1996b) compared a sample of 354 practices with counsellors and 216 matched practices without counsellors, and found no differences in psychotropic drug prescribing between the two groups.

Sharp et al. (1997) randomly assigned 149 patients with panic disorder to medication, placebo, medication plus CBT, placebo plus CBT, and CBT alone. All treatment groups showed statistically significant advantages over placebo, but the groups employing CBT showed the most robust and consistent response. Time spent with the patient was controlled for in the medication-only and placebo-only groups, so that patients received the same amount of attention as those who received CBT. The authors conclude that short-term CBT can be effective in the treatment of panic disorder and agoraphobia in primary care. All experimental groups received only 9 sessions of treatment. Mynors-Wallis et al. (1997) randomly assigned a heterogeneous group of primary care patients to problem-solving therapy from a trained community nurse or routine GP care. There was no difference in clinical outcome between those who had received the problem-solving intervention and those who had routine GP care. However, those who had received the problem-solving therapy had fewer disability days and fewer days off work. Evidence of efficacy from RCTs in primary care is thus slowly beginning to appear.

Several significant but as yet unpublished studies provide additional information. Readers are referred to Mellor-Clark and Barkham (1998) for a more comprehensive analysis of the unpublished literature on counselling in primary care. Coe, Ibbs and O'Brien (1996) evaluated the cost-effectiveness of primary care counselling in Somerset. Counselling services were introduced to 29 general practices resulting in 37 per cent more patients being treated for emotional problems in practices with attached counsellors, a 43 per cent lower referral rate to community mental health teams, and a slight drop in outpatient psychiatry referrals compared to a 65 per cent rise in referrals in practices without a counsellor. The authors conclude that practice-based counselling services can provide a more efficient model of delivering mental health services to many patients in primary care, and reduce the number of referrals for specialist psychiatric care. These findings are in contrast to those of Gordon and Graham (1996) who found that counselling in primary care can create new demands on secondary care. When detection rates are improved and more disturbed patients receive treatment, some patients are likely to need more intensive long-term treatment at the secondary level.

Nettleton (1996) describes a one-year pilot project of counselling in primary care in the Scottish Borders. One counsellor working in three practices saw 110 patients over the year, and patient satisfaction with the service was high. Most patients received 6 sessions or less. Scores on a General Well-being Index improved over treatment and correlated with patient satisfaction. Hemmings (1997) randomly assigned 188 patients to a practice counsellor or routine GP care in East Sussex. Patients in both groups had improved considerably at 3 months and a 4-month follow-up. The counselled group was significantly less likely to be referred to secondary mental health services. Patient satisfaction with counselling was high. The counsellors and a representative GP from each practice met monthly for an action learning group led by an external facilitator. Good results in the GP group may have been due in part to counselling skills acquired in the action learning groups.

Baker et al. (1996) evaluated the work of 22 counsellors in primary care treating 385 patients with a variety of psychological problems in Dorset. Symptoms decreased both in number and severity during counselling, and a 6-month follow-up showed that these gains were sustained over time. Self-esteem, work functioning, home management, social life and leisure activities also improved. Patient and GP satisfaction with the service were high. The presence of a counsellor did nothing to reduce psychotropic medication prescription rates. Referrals to psychiatry declined and referrals to clinical psychology and CPNs increased during the study period, but these changes were unrelated to the presence of a counsellor in the surgery. The Dorset group are launching an RCT to test their findings against a control group consisting of GP routine care. It will be important in this trial to monitor the behaviour of GPs during routine consultations in order to specify which nonspecific factors may be operating in the control group. Otherwise, if another example of the equivalence paradox appears, it will be difficult to interpret the results.

A major problem in psychotherapy research is identifying an appropriate placebo attention control group. Burton and Parker (1995) found that women awaiting mastectomy who received a 30-minute 'chat' from a surgeon the night before surgery were virtually indistinguishable on outcome measures from those who had received a 30-minute reflection-of-feelings intervention from the surgeon. It is difficult to know what would constitute an adequate placebo attention control. The effects of time, attention, support and empathy can be considerable, and may account for the now numerous studies which fail to show statistically significant differences between routine GP care and various forms of primary care counselling.

CLINICAL AUDIT

Outcome studies are often confused with clinical audit. Part of the reason for this is that a single computer base of patient data is often used for both activities. However, the two enterprises are quite distinct (Parry, 1992). Clinical audit is about setting a standard and measuring the extent to which actual practice conforms to the standard. First, a clear standard for some aspect of the service is adopted (e.g. no patient will wait more than three months for an initial assessment). Second, an indicator is defined which will be measured (time from referral to time of first appointment). Third, a target is set (95 per cent of patients will be seen within three months of referral). Finally, the monitoring method is defined: how will data be collected? by whom? and at what frequency? The *audit cycle* is the following sequence:

> Select a topic, accept a standard of practice, observe your practice, compare your practice with the standard, and implement change.
>
> (De Lacey, 1992).

Thomas (1996) discusses how clinical audit can have a positive impact on counselling services. Detailed help with the audit process can be found in Firth-Cozens (1993), Kogan and Redfern (1995) and Mellor-Clark and

Barkham (1998). Fonagy and Higgitt (1989) provide a useful list of the kinds of activities that might be audited in counselling or psychotherapy:

- Speed of dealing with referrals.
- Availability of a range of therapies.
- Depth and quality of initial assessment.
- Clarity of diagnosis, formulation and treatment plan.
- Handling of untreated cases.
- Type and length of treatment.
- Quality of recordkeeping.
- Level of training of therapists and of supervision provided.
- Adequacy of liaison with GPs.
- Management of crisis situations.
- Frequency of negative response to therapy.
- Follow-up arrangements.

(Fornagy and Higgitt, 1989, p. 134)

PRACTICAL SUGGESTIONS FOR SERVICE EVALUATION

These principles for the measurement of treatment outcomes are worth remembering:

- Not everything can be measured at the outset.
- A perfect solution is not possible.
- It is essential to start with the most important things to measure.
- The outcome measure should not be limited to a specific form of treatment.
- The outcome measure should have immediate practical uses that build in value.
- The system should be based on established science that is theoretically sound.

(Sperry et al. (1996, pp. 19–20)

For those with the local resources to input and analyse their own data, the PTRC pre- and post-counselling forms and the CORE measure are available for general use. Other outcome measures of interest for particular therapies can be added. The Appendix provides a more detailed Patient Record Form completed by the therapist at the time of assessment (Burton et al., 1993). A few sections of the original form have been added or amended using superior measures from the PTRC. For example, the sections on employment, ethnicity and relationship factors, current/previous psychological therapy, frequency of counselling, and the nature of ending come from the PTRC. A 6-item Quality of Life Questionnaire and a Patient Satisfaction Form are also included in the Appendix.

The Patient Record Form covers demographic and referral information (with instructions on scoring social class appearing later in the Appendix), a list of problems and personality styles (defined later in the Appendix), predisposing risk factors, and anticipated adverse outcomes if untreated (the 'at risk of. . .' checklist). There is also a space for noting whether the patient needs psychiatric cover during therapy. What follows is a detailed list of possible goals for treatment. At assessment, the therapist ticks all that apply. Predictors of therapy outcome are also scored: motivation, psychological-mindedness, social support available, and quality of intimate relationships. The most appropriate therapy modality is recommended at assessment. At discharge, the therapist rates the amount of change on the patient's three most significant problems using a 5-point Likert scale. Previous research has shown that therapist measures of change correlate positively with patient's answers to the question, 'I think the main problems which brought me to the psychologist have been resolved' (Burton, 1992b).

GAINING STAFF SUPPORT FOR OUTCOME STUDIES

Therapist measures are required both at assessment and termination, and these take time to complete. When patient satisfaction and clinical outcome data are collected on a routine basis, staff may become anxious about comparisons between therapists – now routine in managed care settings in the USA. Staff resistance to service evaluation programmes should not be underestimated. Three varieties of staff response to new technologies have been described: the Eager Adopters, the Hesitant Prove Its Worthers, and the Resisters (Rosen and Weil, 1996). Eager Adopters may be the organization's pioneers. The successful persuasion of Hesitant Prove Its Worthers often depends on how effectively early exposure convinces them that it makes sense, that they can master it, and that it is clinically useful

(Lyons et al., 1997). Resisters are likely to cite concerns about confidentiality, dehumanization of the therapeutic process, reductionism that fails to capture the human experience, and interference with the transference relationship – each of which arguments contains a grain of truth. Some Resisters, who use avoidance as their major coping strategy, may never be persuaded of the importance of service evaluation. Some of these express their view of the process through passive-aggression – forms left blank, and failure to supply missing data when requested.

Mellor-Clark and Barkham (1996) describe counsellor anxieties when an outcome evaluation was undertaken at Relate, in the voluntary sector:

> Some were confused as to why evaluative research needed to take place at all. Several claimed to know their effectiveness because clients rarely complained, attended repeatedly, expressed their innermost feelings and even recommended others to the service. Others felt that clients would be put off attending because they would find the questionnaires intrusive, invasive and insensitive. Administrative staff felt that the burden of co-ordinating research was more than they could handle. Finally, to many, the anticipated benefits appeared nebulous and simply 'pie in the sky' .
>
> (Mellor Clark and Barkham, 1996, p. 86)

The authors' process model for implementing service evaluation is worth following: information exchange between management and external consultants, an inaugural workshop for service participants, working party meetings, evaluation administration meetings, evaluation monitoring meetings, feedback and debriefing workshops, dissemination of findings, and enhancement and improvement. If evaluation is imposed on clinicians, they feel they do not 'own' the process. Once they begin to appreciate how evaluation can improve the service they provide to patients, a substantial part of the consultant's work is done.

It is well to remember that *if you don't evaluate your own service, someone else will do it for you, and use the results for their own political ends* (Curtis Jenkins, 1997b). This reality is occasionally sufficiently persuasive to convince Hesitant Prove Its Worthers of the vital need for ongoing in-house service evaluation.

SUMMARY AND RECOMMENDATIONS

The verdict is now in: psychotherapy works. What is far from clear, however, is which therapies work best for which patients. This question is presently being vigorously researched. There are three kinds of outcome in psychotherapy: clinical outcomes, medical utilization outcomes, and patient satisfaction. For many years the so-called 'gold standard' for demonstrating the *efficacy* of psychotherapy has been the *randomized controlled trial* (RCT). At best, however, RCTs can address 'what works for whom' in the most ideal set of circumstances, delivered by the most ideal practitioners, to the most ideal patients, with the most ideal specificity and severity of problem. A better research methodology for demonstrating the *effectiveness* of psychotherapy in the field is the systematic, naturalistic experiment in clinical settings, sometimes known as a *field trial*.

Roth and Fonagy (1996) suggest that 'RCTs provide the only valid – albeit limited – source of evidence for the efficacy of various forms of psychological treatment.' However they admit that it is unlikely that data from trials can be transferred directly into the clinical context, and they point out that *absence of efficacy is not the same as evidence of ineffectiveness*. There are a number of innovative and some well-established therapies such as psychodynamic and eclectic therapies for which evidence of efficacy in the form of RCTs is deficient or lacking. Unfortunately, there are statements in Roth and Fonagy's review that could lead to premature withdrawal of funding from some of the under-researched therapies. Despite their methodological failings, meta-analyses are being used to generate clinical guidelines for the treatment of certain DSM-IV disorders, and claims are made that these recommendations constitute sound, evidence-based practice.

The UK Department of Health's strategic review of psychotherapy has taken a cautious line on validated therapies: 'It would be premature and unjustified to imagine that certain treatments have been "validated".The NHS Executive will not therefore publish a list of "effective" therapies on which funding decisions should be based.' The review also takes the position that 'cookbook' approaches to purchasing particular treatments for specific diagnoses are not recommended. Purchasing pre-defined packages of treatment for specific diagnostic groups overlooks the very high rate of comorbidity in patients requesting help.

Managed care in the USA is currently promoting brief and ultra-brief therapies, largely on cost-containment grounds. Longer-term therapies have been under-researched. Particularly needed are comparative studies of short- vs. longer-term treatments. It it is now well known that the more disturbed the patient, the harder it is to make therapeutic gains.

The most frequently cited meta-analysis of length of treatment in psychotherapy is the flawed *dose-effect* study of Howard et al. (1986). More recent studies have found that change in particular symptoms during therapy is roughly linear rather than negatively accelerated. On the whole, the research in this area has shown that more therapy is generally better than less therapy, yet some patients benefit from 5 sessions while a number go on for years without change. Therefore more research is needed to identify those who can profit from brief treatment.

Outcome measurement has advanced considerably since the early pre-treatment/post-treatment comparison studies. If data are collected continuously over the course of treatment, not only is the missing data problem addressed but much can be learned about patient change during therapy. The Compass system widely used in the USA includes tracks scores on the *Mental Health Index* (MHI) throughout treatment. Using a weighted formula of pre-treatment variables, a patient's expected treatment trajectory over time can be estimated. When actual scores are plotted against estimated scores, treatments that are in difficulty can be identified. An obvious problem with this system is that some of the enduring difficulties which people with personality disorders experience may persist despite apparently 'normal range' MHI scores.

A standardized CORE outcome measure of 34 items has been developed at the Psychological Therapies Research Centre, University of Leeds, and includes subscales for subjective well-being, symptoms, life/social functioning, and risk/harm. The PTRC project takes much of the day-to-day labour out of data collection and analysis. Clinicians require only about five minutes to complete simple double-sided forms at the beginning and end of treatment, and patients complete a CORE measure every six sessions. A number of other outcome measures can be used to supplement the Outcome Questionnaire, the CORE measure, or the Mental Health Index, if the researcher wishes to measure certain symptom complexes in greater detail, estimate cost effectiveness, or pursue variables of interest to psychodynamic therapy

Patient satisfaction is no longer a sufficient outcome measure for counselling and psychotherapy. The CORE measure serviced by PTRC is a good example of the minimum dataset any primary care service should be collecting, and throughout therapy rather than just pre- and post-treatment. Patient satisfaction may also be of interest, but should not be substituted for clinically significant change measures.

Roth and Fonagy (1996) apply the same RCT criterion of efficacy to counselling in primary care as to other psychotherapy outcome studies. There are few RCTs, and those that exist are in their judgement of poor quality. One major problem with Roth and Fonagy's review of counselling in primary care is that very few of the studies are actually of services delivered by counsellors. More recent outcome studies of counselling in primary care are reviewed. From the evidence available, it would be premature to conclude that counselling in primary care 'doesn't work' – as potential efficacy is not the same as actual effectiveness in practice. Nonspecific factors in counselling and psychotherapy need to be controlled for when counselling is compared to routine GP care. A major problem in psychotherapy research is identifying an appropriate placebo attention control group.

Clinical audit is about setting a standard and measuring the extent to which actual practice conforms to the standard. The Appendix provides a detailed Patient Record Form completed by the therapist at assessment. Staff resistance to service evaluation programmes should not be underestimated. Three varieties of staff response to new technologies have been described: the Eager Adopters, the Hesitant Prove Its Worthers, and the Resisters. It is well to remember that if you do not evaluate your own service, someone else will do it for you, and use the results for their own political ends. This reality is occasionally sufficiently persuasive to convince Hesitant Prove Its Worthers of the vital need for ongoing in-house service evaluation.

7

ORGANIZATIONAL ISSUES

MENTAL HEALTH SERVICE DELIVERY
IN PRIMARY CARE

> Someone in need of psychological therapy cannot yet
> rely on the NHS to deliver the right intervention at
> the right time in the right place. Services are frag-
> mented . . . Whether you end up having an outpatient
> appointment with a psychiatrist, primary care coun-
> sellor, a clinical psychologist . . . seems alarmingly
> arbitrary. On which shore you wash up is not gener-
> ally determined by who is able to offer the most
> appropriate help for your problem. It depends as
> much on which GP you see, who happens to know
> whom, or where you live.
>
> (Parry, 1995, pp. 164–165)

The provision of psychological help in primary care is at best haphazard
and at worst may depend on which clinician is the first to pick up the telephone when the GP places a call. Some GPs, keen to make a prompt referral for an acutely distressed patient, may ring everyone on their referral
list – psychiatrist, psychotherapist, group analyst, crisis team manager, specialist service for eating disorders, addictions or childhood sexual abuse,
clinical psychologist, CPN, practice counsellor, counsellor in the voluntary
sector, or a psychotherapist in private practice. It is not unknown for some
GPs to make multiple simultaneous referrals of patients, a fact which comes
to light only after the patient is seen by the first clinician offering an assessment. Such 'scattershot' referrals clog the network and are considered bad
practice, but they are understandable when GPs are unable to contain the
emotional situation themselves and are faced with lengthy waiting lists in
every NHS service to which they have access. Waiting times of up to 130

weeks are not uncommon in some services.

It is this situation, in part, which has driven GPs to hire practice counsellors. On the doorstep, counsellors 'can be called upon when needed' – but only if they keep treatment slots open for emergencies, and not all counsellors are able to do this because of the demands on their time and their own lengthening waiting lists. Approximately half of practice counsellors work part-time, so they may be on the GP's doorstep only two days a week. Also, many counsellors are unable to deal with psychological emergencies. Some GPs have used counsellors as if they were in-house psychiatrists or clinical psychologists, sending them disorganized borderline patients or those with psychotic problems, severe addictions or longstanding forensic histories. Some counsellors lack the assessment skills to come to an accurate diagnosis of the problem, and some do not have the freedom to refuse referrals. In a recent study of 90 counsellors in primary care, 11 per cent were expected to offer counselling to all patients referred regardless of the severity of the presenting problem (Burton, Henderson and Curtis Jenkins, 1998). This is a serious clinical issue because GPs' ability to accurately diagnose their patients' psychological problems differs enormously. A counsellor may be inappropriately asked to contain a psychiatric emergency with occasionally tragic results. For example:

> Mr. A's marriage broke down and he became severely depressed. His GP referred him to a primary care counsellor. There was minimal information in the referral letter. Five days after the referral a second letter arrived saying, 'I am very sorry to report that Mr. A took his own life last week. He was found in his room in the YMCA on Saturday morning.' Had the counsellor been able to see this patient on the Friday before he died, would it have been possible for her to accurately assess the suicide risk? In this case we could not know. The extent of risk was apparently not obvious to the GP on the Wednesday.

It happens to the most seasoned clinician that suicidality is occasionally missed and tragedy results. However, the risk of such events is greatly increased when patients are inappropriately referred, or when the assessing clinician lacks the assessment skills or the secondary service links to make an urgent psychiatric referral when it is needed. Parry and Richardson (1996) in their strategic review of psychotherapy services in the NHS report that many respondents were concerned that counsellors were being asked to see patients whose psychological problems were inappropriate for their level of skill.

It has sometimes been argued that counsellors can handle many if not most of the psychological problems presenting in primary care, cutting the bill for secondary mental health services in the process. This has turned out to be a fantasy. Clinical psychologists in one locality who were monitoring the work of primary care counsellors under their supervision found that patients referred had significant mental health problems, and the counselling they received reduced their psychiatric symptomatology. However, some of the more severely disturbed patients needed onward referral to specialist teams, creating new demands on secondary care (Gordon and Graham, 1996). Similarly, the increase in primary care counselling in the Southampton area in the past five years has been accompanied by a doubling of the referral rate to the psychological therapies service (Clark, Hook and Stein, 1997). Primary care counselling is not a cheap alternative to secondary mental health care. It may in the long term turn out considerably to expand the range and therefore the total cost of mental health care. How can psychological care at the primary care level best be organized to facilitate early assessment and assignment to an appropriate clinician? This is the question to which we now turn.

AN INTEGRATED COUNSELLING AND PSYCHOTHERAPY SERVICE

The extent to which counsellors and clinical psychologists are now working together in the NHS is reflected in the number of Departments of Clinical Psychology now calling themselves, for example, Departments of Clinical Psychology and Counselling Services. The internal market in the NHS has led to a situation in which professions that once worked collaboratively have been pitted against one another in the battle to secure service contracts. On the positive side, an entire issue of *Clinical Psychology Forum* in March 1997 was devoted to clinical psychologists and counsellors working together in the NHS. Hall (1997) described her experience as a counsellor working in a clinical psychology department. Some psychologists were concerned that hiring counsellors would threaten their job security. Others worried that counsellors would select the most rewarding cases, leaving them with the intractable ones. Some counsellors were concerned about being seen as second-class providers. None of these fears was realized in Hall's department. Instead, counsellors introduced new and valuable perspectives, attitudes to other professions changed, and counsellors' insistence on supervision led to an increased use of formal supervision by all members of departmental staff. A general practitioner writing in the same issue (Cocksedge, 1997) provides a list of problems appropriate to counselling and those appropriate for mental health services (psychologists, psychiatrists and psychotherapists). His classification is consistent with the Camden and Islington MAAG (1996) guidelines (Chapter 3):

Problems appropriate for counselling services	Problems appropriate for mental health services
Mild to moderate problems	*Moderate to severe problems*
Depression	Schizophrenia and related disorders
Relationship difficulties	Mania/hypomania
Anxiety	Depressive disorders
Bereavement	Cognitive impairment or dementia
Emotional and psychological difficulties	Risk of suicide, violence or self-neglect
Response to physical illness	Hypochondriasis
Life cycle developmental issues	Obsessive-compulsive disorder
Problems of adjustment	Post-traumatic stress disorder
Response to trauma	Eating disorders
Sexual difficulties	Personality and behaviour disorders
	Severe anxiety

These are of course only rules of thumb. Sometimes what looks like an 'adjustment problem' masks a complex collection of difficulties. Some complicated bereavements require long-term treatment, especially when the death was violent, sudden or traumatic. Some sexual difficulties, especially in the presence of longstanding marital problems, point to an underlying personality disorder. When is anxiety mild and when is it severe? When is depressive affect part of a clinical depression requiring medication? When has an immediate 'response to trauma', unresponsive to treatment, become post-traumatic stress disorder? All of these issues refer us back to the central issue of this book: the need for careful and thorough assessment at the primary care level.

One model of good practice involves a system in which referrals are centrally received by the Psychology in Primary Care team and allocated for specialist assessment at a clinical meeting. Patients are seen by a psychologist or counsellor in one or two assessment interviews, and assigned for treatment to a counsellor or clinical psychologist as appropriate. Some GP referrals marked 'for counselling' are on the face of it inappropriate for the counsellor to assess or treat:

- 'This patient tells me her daughter has just remembered being sexually abused by her grandfather. The patient now remembers that she was similarly abused by him.' This woman was referred to a clinical psychologist for assessment. After a period of individual treatment, she joined a group for survivors of childhood sexual abuse.

- 'This man recently completed a prison sentence for sexually abusing his two daughters. He is beginning to be concerned that he may abuse again. He is also drinking heavily.' This man was referred to the community mental health team for a psychiatric assessment.

- 'This young woman with anorexia nervosa has for the first time said she is willing to talk to a counsellor. She presently weighs 6.5 stone.' This patient was referred to a psychiatrist with a special interest in eating disorders.

Occasionally clinical psychologists assess patients referred 'for counselling' and refer them on for urgent treatment by a psychiatrist, consultant psychotherapist, or other specialist in secondary care.

Some GP referrals marked 'for the psychologist' are mild problems appropriate for short-term counselling:

- 'This woman's husband died last year at the age of 79 after a short illness. She is having difficulty coming to terms with his loss.' This patient responded well to short-term bereavement counselling.

- 'I have known this patient for many years and she has always struck me as being very stable. However, today she told me that she is becoming increasingly anxious when she visits her son and his young family.' This patient was assessed by a counsellor. After the assessment interview the patient felt sufficiently helped that she did not require any further treatment.

Some GP referrals are returned without an assessment having been carried out because it is evident from the referral material that specialized secondary services are required:

- 'This woman's husband recently left her after a 25-year marriage. Her daughter (separated since the birth of her second child) has recently been diagnosed with leukaemia. My patient is a brittle diabetic with multiple medical problems. She has not been sleeping and has made two half-hearted suicide attempts in the past ten days. She has refused antidepressant medication but has requested counselling. She refuses to see a psychiatrist or psychologist. Can you see her within the week, please?'

- 'This man consulted me today after having spent the previous night in police custody. He had assaulted his wife severely enough to cause several broken bones. She is recovering in hospital; the two small children are with their grandmother. There have been several episodes of grievous bodily harm over the past three years, usually in the context of alcohol. He never thought he would strike his wife. This time he has requested counselling.'

- 'This young woman was recently discharged from a therapeutic community where her self-mutilation improved as did her preoccupation with violent suicide. I enclose a copy of the consultant's discharge summary. Unfortunately she has returned to living with her boyfriend who is addicted to heroin. He is well known to the psychiatric services. She has experimented with hard drugs in the past and I am concerned that renewed association with her boyfriend may have a tragic outcome. An urgent assessment is requested.' [handwritten postscript: 'The boyfriend needs to be treated cautiously if he should accompany the patient. He is paranoid and I am told he carries a large kitchen knife at all times.']

It is clear in these cases that the referral for 'counselling' is misguided. The second and third cases suggest the need for assessment in a psychiatric outpatient department with forensic backup. All three patients require prompt referral to secondary psychiatric services. If a counsellor should agree to see such patients on a one-off emergency basis, good links with appropriate secondary services are vital. The first case is difficult because of the patient's refusal to see a psychiatrist or psychologist. She is probably a danger to herself and a third suicide attempt might succeed. If a counsellor were to assess her, it might be with a view to helping her see the need for psychotropic medication, and reassuring her about psychiatry and clinical psychology. Close liaison with the GP on such a case would be essential. These referrals may seem unusually difficult to the reader, but such patients are regularly seen by GPs and then passed on to primary care counsellors or clinical psychologists in some parts of the country.

Miller (1997) describes a Direct Access Psychology Service model in which clinical psychologists, psychotherapists, counsellors and assistant psychologists work together to provide a range of treatments in GP surgeries, outpatient settings and home visits. In some settings, CPNs or counselling psychologists may join such teams, and psychoanalytic psychotherapists and consultant psychiatrists may serve in back-up roles. The skill mix achieved in this way can be greatly beneficial to patients and is appreciated by referring GPs.

Ohanian (1997) has developed a well-integrated interdisciplinary model for delivering a range of psychological services in primary care. The impetus for the Brief Intervention and Counselling Service (BICS) in Hounslow was the withdrawal in 1995–6 of CPNs from primary care settings, and their return to community mental health teams to concentrate on severe and enduring mental illness. Patients who had been seen by CPNs in primary care were being referred to other professionals, leading to a sudden and unmanageable referral overload. The treatment offered is assessment plus 6–8 sessions of 45 minutes each. One failure to attend (DNA) is counted as a session, and two cancellations (CNCs) count as a session, in a system that is explained to patients at the outset. The mean number of sessions is 4. Referral criteria include anxiety, stress, panic, and phobias; depression, including grief reactions; mild habit disorders; psychosomatic problems; interpersonal problems at home or at work, and adjustment to life crises. Most problems are usually of recent onset. Referral criteria are circulated to all local GPs. Excluded are disorders at the moderate to severe end of the diagnostic continuum:

- Enduring mental illness, learning disability, drug or alcohol dependency.

- Those with complex problems such as post-traumatic stress disorder, eating disorders, and childhood sexual abuse.

- Those whose primary needs are related to financial problems, unemployment or homelessness.

The Hounslow BICS is an outreach arm of the Psychological Treatment Service. Other teams within the Psychological Treatment Service include the Specialist Service for Trauma and Eating Disorders, the Psychotherapy Service, and the Clinical Psychology Service (including those working with patients with severe and enduring mental illness in Community Mental Health Teams (CMHTs), those who work with children, and neuropsychologists). Clear definitions are in place of what each service covers. Each sector in the NHS Trust is served by a team including a clinical psychologist, counselling psychologist, counsellor, and nurse therapist. Each sector also has its own CMHT. A version of the 'opt-in' system is used in the BICS, in which patients receive a letter asking whether they would like an appointment. Only if they respond in the affirmative is an appointment offered. In this particular locality most of the short-term treatment in the BICS is cognitive-behavioural. Other therapeutic models are available in other arms of the service. It is worth repeating that a range of treatments should be available in each locality including group, couples and family therapies, and short- and longer-term individual psychotherapies.

Models such as these point to an interdisciplinary future in which case mix and skill mix are carefully balanced so that patients have the best chance of receiving the treatment they require. Adequate assessment at the primary care level is crucial. A wide range of professions will be involved at primary and secondary levels: clinical and counselling psychologists, counsellors, CPNs, nurse therapists, psychotherapists, psychiatrists, CMHTs, crisis teams, and trauma, eating disorder and addiction services all working together with good links maintained among them. The interdisciplinary rivalries that are rife in the NHS can result in poorer patient care. It is to be hoped that the move away from the NHS internal market will take the competitive edge off some of these unproductive territorial battles and allow energies to return more fully to the tasks at hand.

LINKS WITH SECONDARY MENTAL HEALTH SERVICES

It will by now be clear that primary care psychological services will only make an effective contribution to patient care if they work closely with local secondary and specialist services. A recent survey of primary care counsellors in the UK found that many counsellors were unaware of services in the statutory, voluntary and private sectors. More than half the sample (57 per cent) reported they had poor links with secondary services, a serious clinical problem when the urgent referral of psychiatrically disturbed patients is required (Burton, Henderson and Curtis Jenkins, 1998). Counsellors in another recent study also reported an interest in developing closer links with secondary services (Clark, Hook and Stein, 1997). It is essential that all mental health professionals working at the primary care level are able to recognize and appropriately refer patients suffering from severe mental illness. Surprising as it may sound, severe mental illness is not always picked up by the referring GP, who may have spent only a few minutes with the patient.

Every practice counsellor, Primary Care Psychology Service, or Direct Access Service for GPs should compile and annually update a local resource list, so that all clinicians involved in assessment are aware of what services are available and ideally the length of their waiting lists. Some services in affluent areas refer patients who request it to psychotherapists in the private sector. An approved list of private practitioners may be helpful if such referrals take place frequently. Orientation of new counsellors and clinical psychologists should include meetings with key clinicians in secondary services and specialist teams, so that a personal contact is established at the outset. In the rush to ensure that new members of staff take on patients quickly, these vital links are often forgotten. It is an investment of time that is well worth the effort, because the costs of poor communication between primary and secondary care clinicians are borne by patients. Regular meetings of primary and secondary care clinicians working in a locality can also clarify referral criteria and facilitate mutual understanding.

WAITING LIST MANAGEMENT

One of the most difficult problems facing primary mental health care is the management of waiting lists. Many unsuccessful attempts have been made to 'solve' this problem. One recent effort to manage the waiting list in an open-access NHS counselling centre in Oxford was to offer patients who had recently joined the waiting list the option of being seen promptly for up to four sessions. This arrangement was made with the understanding that they could return to the waiting list for longer-term counselling if four sessions had proved insufficient. Of those on the waiting list 57 per cent accepted the offer and attended at least one session. For 25 per cent of these, four sessions were sufficient. For a further 50 per cent it was a useful beginning which helped them plan for longer-term work in private therapy, Relate, or further therapy at the Isis Centre later (Brech and Agulnik, 1996). This 4-session model recalls the 2+1 model of Barkham and Shapiro (1990) discussed in Chapter 3. Only 25 per cent of patients found 4 sessions sufficient, so the 4-session model may best be understood as an extended assessment or triage method, allowing planning for the most appropriate onward referral. A few clients accepted 4 sessions out of a sense of desperation, and most of them felt needy and disappointed at the end of that time. It may be important to devise a mechanism to screen out vulnerable clients from these schemes, because if referral for 4 sessions is left to the patient, the neediest of them – and perhaps those *least* suited to ultra-brief therapies – may grasp at any straw and be damaged in the process.

A number of strategies have been tried for managing waiting lists in clinical psychology, some of them based on avoidance: restricting access by not advertising, discouraging referrals, employing strict referral criteria, emphasizing group work, training other professionals, offering brief treatment or infrequent appointments, or closing waiting lists completely. Two more substantive strategies have received attention in the last few years: assessment prior to placement on a treatment waiting list, and the 'opt-in' model.

Geekie (1995) offered new patients two assessment sessions a fortnight apart, informing them in the appointment letter that there would be a waiting time of some months before they were offered further regular appointments. Stevenson et al. (1997) applied Geekie's model and reduced a waiting list of 71 to 33 in a short space of time. Eighteen patients did not reply to a letter asking if they wished to be seen by a psychologist. Of the 53 remaining, 8 failed to attend the assessment, 5 were discharged after assessment, 2 were referred to other agencies, 5 were offered immediate intervention, and 33 were placed on the treatment waiting list, 9 of whom were 'urgent'. Such a system requires that each clinician set aside a number of assessment hours per week. It carries with it the drawback that the assessor may not be the same person who offers treatment. For some vulnerable patients, this is a significant problem because a transference has already begun to develop and reassignment to another therapist is perceived as at best a rejection and at worst an abandonment. Other patients react with anger when told, 'This is an assessment session.' After a wait of several months, most expect treatment and some are enraged when it is not immediately forthcoming. Finally, by the time treatment is offered, the assessment may need to be repeated because the problem has altered significantly in the intervening months.

The 'opt-in' system has been promoted principally by Seager (1991, 1994) who argues that asking patients to opt in to their own treatment fosters a healthy sense of autonomy and acts as a screening device to assess motivation for psychological therapy. GPs are provided with information booklets about clinical psychology services to give to patients who request help or who are judged by the GP to need it. Along with the booklet is a consultation request form stamped by the surgery to legitimize it as a GP referral, which patients can then send to the psychology department if they decide they want treatment. The request form also enables patients to give some basic information about their reasons for seeking help, if they wish. Only the names of patients who 'opt in' to treatment go on the waiting list. Not only does this system shorten waiting lists, it creates a shorter list of people whose needs and motivations are broadly matched to the services on offer. The 'opt-in' system is a form of written informed consent for psychological treatment. GPs retain their role in discussing and advising to the extent that they wish, but instead of deciding for their patients, the GP can help patients decide for themselves what is needed. GPs have expressed high levels of satisfaction with the scheme (Seager et al., 1995). It would be interesting to see this system applied to in-house practice counsellors who are developing waiting lists. In inner city areas, translations of the information booklet will be required. Some practice counsellors are beginning to use information booklets for patients in the absence of an 'opt-in' referral system.

TEAMWORK AND CLINICAL SUPERVISION

GP surgeries are stressful places for everyone including nonclinical staff such as receptionists, secretaries and practice managers. The clinical pressures on GPs and practice nurses are immense, especially given the short consultation times prevailing at the moment. In addition, primary health care teams are adapting to the new stresses of computerization, meeting screening quotas, and responding to demands for sophisticated evaluation and monitoring from the NHS Executive. Counsellors and primary care psychologists need to work towards becoming an integral part of the primary health care team. Obstacles to effective team work include interpersonal differences, fear of change, intra- and inter-professional rivalries and misunderstanding, differentials in perceived power and status, differences in conceptual approaches and models of health, lack of training in team-working, different management structures and lines of accountability, and competing organizational priorities (Vanclay, 1997). Differences in conceptual approaches to health are particularly important, especially the contrast between the biomedical model still used by some GPs and the biopsychosocial model of counsellors and clinical psychologists. Surprisingly few counsellors in a recent survey cited this issue as particularly important in their places of work, although some said it 'depended on which doctor' (Burton, Henderson and Curtis Jenkins, 1998). Unfortunately it is by no means true that all younger GPs are better schooled in the biopsychosocial approach.

What then are the features of a well-functioning primary health care team (Vanclay, 1997):

- Shared goals and clear objectives.

- Clearly defined, complementary roles understood and respected by all members.

- Clear procedures and agreed protocols.

- Regular and effective communication.

- Support for and recognition of the contribution of all members.

- Commitment by all team members to jointly agreed goals.

- Regular reflection on progress and feedback on performance.

Team-building days are well worth the time and effort, and some clinical psychologists in primary care have placed this kind of consultation exercise high on their professional agenda (Brunning and Burd, 1993; Casey et al., 1994). Although it may prove difficult to integrate part-time counsellors and psychologists into team-building days, the time spent will be richly rewarded in terms of improved communication and enhanced mutual understanding. Regular feedback meetings, lunchtime case conferences or Balint groups, training days and scheduled liaison with GPs also enhance the working atmosphere and improve the quality of patient care. Differing counsellor practices with regard to confidentiality were discussed in Chapter 4. When counsellors or other mental health practitioners begin working in general practices, detailed discussions should take place with GPs on this issue so that everyone is clear about the level of communication that is expected.

Clinical supervision is an increasingly important issue for counsellors in primary care. All counsellors who are members of the British Association for Counselling (BAC) must be in continuous clinical supervision. Counselling in primary care is in many ways a new profession and few of counsellors' current supervisors have personal experience of working in the primary care setting (Burton, Henderson and Curtis Jenkins, 1998). When counsellors work alongside clinical psychologists in primary care, the assumptions underlying their supervision by, say, clinical psychologists, needs to be understood. For if clinical psychologists view counsellors as members of an inferior profession with deficient skills, this bias may unhelpfully enter the supervisory relationship. Worse, if counsellors are competing for the same contracts as their clinical psychologist supervisors, the countertransference problems that are likely to develop on both sides can make the supervision hour a very fraught time indeed.

An initial issue that needs to be addressed in the supervision of primary care counsellors is one of differential power. Clinical supervisors are powerful figures for supervisees, and this power is best worn lightly. When supervision crosses professional boundaries (for example, when counsellors are supervised by psychologists, psychotherapists, psychiatrists or other professionals) the power differential may be magnified. Optimally, supervisor and supervisee learn from one another in the same way that therapists learn from patients (Casement, 1985). Anything that can be done to foster an environment of mutual learning and growth in supervision will ultimately benefit patients. Power relations in the supervisory setting are complex. Others are perceived as powerful by virtue of their formal status (e.g. training); through the process of informal influence; and through their expertise in the primary care setting. Clinical psychologists who have never worked in primary care may possess the first and second but lack the third – direct, hands-on experience in GP surgeries.

A second issue is that counselling supervision involves a number of practical and managerial components which are not always appreciated by psychologists without primary care experience. An understanding of the primary care setting is crucial, because certain problems can arise in the GP surgery which are seldom an issue in a hospital or community mental health centre setting. Differences in the culture of GPs and counsellors may result in problems around patient care, for example, with regard to liaison around psychotropic medication. Other issues include confidentiality – what information to share with the GP and when – and dual transferences, when patients have contrasting reactions to the GP and to the counsellor. Counsellors may be unclear to whom they are accountable, they may not feel part of the primary health care team, receptionists may make appointments for them, and there may not be a room dedicated to counselling work. The case mix may be inadequate, secretarial support may be haphazard, and there may not be a clear treatment contract for each patient. A lengthening waiting list may be a burden and its management may become a crucial issue for morale and effectiveness. Counsellors may not have sufficient time to keep written records and liaise with GPs (Burton, Henderson and Curtis Jenkins, 1998; Clark, Hook and Stein, 1997). They may not have patient information leaflets or pre- and post-counselling evaluation forms. If there is a departmental service evaluation programme in place, counsellors' work may be evaluated alongside clinical psychologists'. If their outcomes are compared to those of psychologists by diagnostic category (for example, who does best with mildly depressed patients), such an evaluation system may affect the supervisory relationship, encouraging splitting and projection.

A third concern in supervision is whether there is enough of it, and whether its provision is reliable. Individual supervision probably occurs optimally once a week for an hour, although many counsellors receive much less supervision than this. Too often counsellors have a large number of patients to present in a single supervision hour. If a weekly hour is insufficient for the caseload, the benefits of an hour and a half may outweigh the cost. Group and peer supervision at less frequent intervals can be of considerable benefit as long as the environment is constructive and supportive. In one recent study, 47 per cent of counsellors paid for their supervision (Burton, Henderson and Curtis Jenkins, 1998); in another, the figure was 100 per cent (Clark, Hook and Stein, 1997). Hopefully this situation will change as GPs become aware of the crucial role that supervision plays in the quality of patient care. Worryingly, the second study cited found that 86 per cent of practice counsellors had regular external supervision, but those from other professions (CPNs, practice nurses, health visitors and GPs) received no supervision at all for their clinical work.

All too often in busy clinical psychology departments, supervision happens 'when it can'. Reliability of the supervision hour is as vital to the clinician as the therapeutic hour is to the patient. Supervisors serve as containers of anxiety for supervisees in the same way that supported mothers become 'good enough' for their infants. An unsupported counsellor may be as damaging to patients as an unsupported mother to her baby. If supervision can be cancelled at a moment's notice because of an urgent administrative meeting, then it may fail to meet the supervisee's need for containment and holding and patients may suffer as a result.

Differences in theoretical orientation may be important in supervision. The training of counsellors working with clinical psychologists varies widely at a local level. Some counsellors are trained in short-term psychodynamic therapy whereas others have a Rogerian or person-centred training. Still others are systemically oriented or favour an integrative model. Similarly, some clinical psychology departments are mainly cognitive-behavioural while others employ a mix of models ranging from psychoanalytic psychotherapy to family therapy, group work, couples therapy, cognitive-analytic therapy and cognitive-behavioural therapy both individually and in groups. When counsellors express a strong preference for clinical supervision with a colleague from their own theoretical orientation, this wish should be respected.

Many counsellors welcome the opportunity to carry a few longer-term cases for their own learning. This wish, when expressed, should be supported by clinical supervisors. For example, supervisors might encourage counsellors to negotiate a 6-session average treatment length, which they become responsible for maintaining in the long term. Counsellors who trained years ago may be more experienced in long-term counselling than some recent graduates who may wish to learn more about longer-term treatment. Optimally, there will be some flexibility in the counsellor's caseload to allow for learning new skills.

Any clinical psychology service contemplating employing counsellors should make adequate provision for their supervision, and the most effective clinical supervisors for primary care counsellors may not be clinical psychologists. In some settings, clinical psychologists may maintain line managerial roles with counsellors while their clinical supervision is provided by senior counsellors with firsthand experience in primary care, or by others whom they see for consultation such as NHS psychotherapists and psychiatrists, as is already occurring in some localities. Those who line manage counsellors and psychologists in primary care might bear in mind three guidelines: excellent communication, consistent support, and the best clinical supervision available.

Possibly because ongoing supervision is required of all members of the BAC, the supervision needs of clinical psychologists have received less attention in the primary care literature. During training, clinical psychology trainees usually receive intensive case supervision of at least an hour and a half per week. During the first two years post-qualification, specialized training courses are likely to be approved by departmental managers. Supervision is regular, and may be intensive. Supervision after those two years have elapsed is much more haphazard. Many departments rely heavily on group supervision in weekly case conferences. Ideally, specialist individual supervision should be available to clinical psychologists at all levels of expertise, if necessary from outside the employing health authority. This may be particularly relevant in the primary care specialty, which is poorly developed in some parts of the country.

FUTURE DIRECTIONS

Epidemiology

Training for GPs at this level needs to include better detection of psychological problems, better ways of managing the 'heartsink' or 'fat file' patient, and more effective use of listening and counselling skills in the consultation. These training efforts need to be provided as continuing education for qualified GPs as well as in medical schools, and thoroughly evaluated. Some improvements could probably be achieved by the introduction of simple measures. For example, the effectiveness of an *at risk checklist* on the cover of patients' medical notes might greatly improve the quality of psychological care at the primary care level and needs to be evaluated.

Multidisciplinary teamwork

In the primary care setting this is likely to become more important in the next decade – clinical and counselling psychologists working more closely with counsellors, GPs, nurses and other members of the primary health care team. The working conditions of primary care counsellors require attention, including better pay, sufficient time for record-keeping, liaison meetings, supervision, and rooms dedicated to counselling work. With the removal of the internal market in the NHS under the present government, some of the dual pressures of clinical and market anxiety may gradually be alleviated. However inter-professional rivalries are likely to continue because they are largely driven by unconscious processes. These unproductive battles need to be continually addressed because they consume energies that are better invested in patient care.

Referral criteria

Referral criteria for different psychological services in primary care need to become more consistent across the country. GPs may need written guidance in their localities such as the example of good practice provided by the Camden and Islington MAAG (1996). More attention needs to be given to patient preference for type of treatment. Too often, patients are fitted into treatments that are on offer instead of being given the most effective therapy for their condition. More responsive services need to be developed at the primary care level for patients from ethnic minorities. Those with personality disorders, addictions, eating disorders, and histories of trauma need improved services at the secondary level. A range of treatment modalities for individuals, couples, families and groups should also ideally be available in each locality.

Assessment skills

The assessment skills of GPs, counsellors and psychologists require improvement. Some of this innovation will need to be made in medical schools and on counselling and clinical psychology courses. Continuing education will need to be made available at the post-qualification level for all the relevant professions in primary care. Training in assessment should include guidelines on the assessment of personality disorders, early losses and comorbidity, since increasingly patients are presenting with a collection of problems deriving from the first few years of life. Applying an elastoplast to the most superficial problem and discharging the patient is no longer sufficient, although regrettably this continues to happen in many places on both sides of the Atlantic. At the same time, long-term therapy is not a panacea either, as there are some patients who fail to benefit from this treatment. One of the assessment skills most urgently required is the ability to distinguish those patients who should be managed in community mental health teams instead of being offered formal psychotherapy.

Brief and ultra-brief psychotherapies

The uncritical headlong rush into unresearched brief and ultra-brief psychotherapies is in urgent need of review. One of the most pressing problems in the UK is the adequate funding of services, both short and long term. Some have asked whether NHS purchasers should pay for psychotherapy in any of its forms in the absence of rigorous cost-benefit analyses (e.g. Fahy and Wessely, 1993), while others have argued that not treating is unethical:

> In the short term it may save money not to use expensive facilities and to make do without the luxury of effective psychotherapy – to muddle through with a mixture of drug therapy, intermittent support, and a blind eye turned to much human misery. (Holmes, 1994, p. 1071)

In the long term, however, the emotional costs of such policies are borne by patients. For example, the abrupt termination of the long–term treatment of a medically ill borderline patient could result in the patient being struck off the GP's list following an episode of acting-out. Following this incident, the patient may be at risk of more adverse outcomes such as serious physical deterioration or loss of accommodation. Such scenarios occur too commonly at present, justified in terms of cost containment.

There is a growing consensus that approximately 15–20 per cent of those who present for psychological help in the National Health Service need to be held in long-term supportive treatment of some kind. In the UK, too often they are seen by trainees rather than the highly skilled clinicians they need. Long-term treatment of some deeply disturbed patients can be very cost-effective when the alternatives are considered. The 'at risk of . . .' checklist in the Appendix is a particularly useful tool in this regard: what are the likely costs to society of *not* treating a particular patient?

Evidence-based medicine

'Evidence-based medicine' has become a fashionable term in purchasing circles, but what it means in the case of psychotherapy is as yet unclear. Curtis Jenkins (1997a) suggests it may be a Trojan horse that is being trundled into general practice with potentially disastrous results. The evidence is far from in for many forms of counselling and psychotherapy, especially some of the treatments being used in primary care. Parry (1997) argues that, 'There is little clinical sense in purchasers imposing arbitrary funding limits, or funding only a preset number of sessions, since the right dosage of psychotherapy varies according to the severity and complexity of the condition.' Yet in many services today contracts accommodate only a preset number of sessions, regardless of individual differences. Very short-term therapies may also pay scant attention to the therapeutic alliance (Roth and Parry, 1997). Again, the costs of these policies are borne by patients.

Treatment outcome

In the matter of treatment outcome, future research directions include:

- basing evidence-based practice in the psychotherapies on a better research foundation than is currently available,

- bridging the efficacy-effectiveness divide by promoting research into psychotherapy *as it is delivered* in the field,

- maintaining updated systematic reviews of effectiveness for all therapies,

- broadening the research base for some commonly practiced

treatments such as psychodynamic therapies,

- studying the application of the better researched therapies to patients with dual diagnoses and comorbidity and those needing long-term care,

- increasing the length of follow-up of patients who have received short- and longer-term treatments,

- identifying those therapy process factors predicting positive outcomes, including therapist competencies,

- devising longitudinal studies of the impacts of training and supervision on outcomes, and

- measuring the cost effectiveness of alternative methods of psychotherapy service delivery.

(Roth and Parry, 1997, pp. 377–378)

Continued attention needs to be paid to distinguishing patients who can profit from short-term therapy from those who need longer-term treatment. Long-term follow-up of patients treated with brief and ultra-brief therapies is particularly urgent, as at present we have little information about the long-term impact of these therapies. 'Revolving-door' patients are an unresolved and costly problem in mental health care. We must ask whether the short-term, symptom-targeted treatment packages currently on offer are increasing their numbers.

American dose-response studies need to be replicated in the UK using the best available methodologies. Contrasting treatment modalities for specific problems in primary care need to be compared as they are delivered, in the field. Better designed studies of psychodynamic therapies both short and long term are particularly urgently needed, together with a refinement of psychodynamic therapy outcome measures.

Patient satisfaction and medical utilization rates are no longer adequate as outcome measures. Objective measures of therapeutic change appropriate to the therapeutic modality being used need to be employed – not just pre- and post-treatment, but throughout therapy. Large databases using high quality standardized questionnaires such as the PTRC's CORE measure need to be assembled in order to develop an ongoing field trial of counselling in primary care (Mellor-Clark and Barkham, 1998).

Professional issues

If GPs become better diagnosticians of psychological problems, the need for high-quality psychological care at the primary care level will increase. There is an enormous amount of work to do, more than enough for all the interested professions. It is unproductive to speculate about which professions will survive with the largest psychological health care contract in primary care. All the professions are needed working alongside one another using a range of well-designed and evaluated treatments, some short term and others long term, all delivered after an appropriately detailed assessment at the primary care level. Of all the skills required in primary care, a thorough and accurate assessment remains the key.

APPENDIX

PATIENT RECORD SHEET

Name _____   GP _____
Address _____   Date of Birth _____
        _____
        _____   Age (at referral) _____
        _____   Male ____   Female ____
Telephone _____   Date of assessment _____
First therapy appointment _____   Date of discharge _____
                                          Therapist's initials _____

Marital Status

	Single	Married	Widowed	Divorced	Separated	Cohabitating
	1	2	3	4	5	6

—— Living alone   ____ Living alone with children over 5
___ Living alone with children under 5   ____ Living as a full-time carer

Education

1 ___ Special Education   4 ___ O level or school certificate
2 ___ Secondary schooling   5 ___ A level or higher school certificate

Occupation
Partner's occupation

1 ___ Full-time paid employment (over 30 hours/week)   6 ___ Full-time student
2 ___ Part-time paid employment (under 30 hours/week)   7 ___ Part-time student
3 ___ Receiving sickness/incapacity/invalidity benefit 8 ___ Retired
4 ___ Unemployed   9 ___ Houseperson
5 ___ Other not specified by the above categories

Social class   Social Classes I and II   Social Classes III, IV and V   (see attached guidelines)
                         1   2

Ethnic background

1 ___ Asian (Bangladeshi)   6 ___ Black (African)
2 ___ Asian (Indian)   7 ___ Black (Caribbean)
3 ___ Asian (Pakistani)   8 ___ White (European)
4 ___ Asian (E. African)   9 ___ Other (specify) _____
5 ___ Asian (Chinese)

Source of Referral

General Practitioner   Specify: _____
Other   Specify: _____
Episode of care: 1 ___ 1st referral
                   2 ___ 2nd or later episode of care
                   Dates of previous referral: _____

Current/previous psychological therapy (please tick all that apply):

Within primary care level only	current	previous	_____	_____
Within secondary care without hospital admission	_____	_____		
Within secondary care with hospital admission	_____	_____		
Within specialist care level	_____	_____		

Other, e.g. private therapy (please specify) _____

Frequency of attendance

More than once weekly _____   Less than once weekly   _____

Weekly   _____   Non-fixed frequency   _____

Ending of treatment

Unplanned ending   *Planned ending*

Due to crisis   _____   Planned from outset   _____

Due to loss of contact   _____   Agreed during treatment   _____

Other (please specify   _____   Agreed at end of treatment _____
                                                     (i.e. penultimate or last session)

Assessment case only: YES   NO
If assessment only, purpose of assessment _____
Number of sessions:
Total number of attendances N = ___
No. of individual sessions N = ___   No. of couples' sessions N = ___
No. of family sessions N = ___   No. of group sessions N = ___
No. of sessions which patient did not attend or cancelled N = ___
Initial rejection of treatment (DNA first session):   YES   NO

Outcome

1. Returned to responsible medical officer after assessment. No contract made.
2. Referred on to another agency after assessment. Specify: _____
3. Therapy terminated by mutual consent.
4. Therapy terminated by therapist. If referred on, specify: _____
5. Therapy terminated by patient.
6. Other. Specify: _____

Change in use of psychotropic medication:
at first appointment   at discharge

Tick if using	more	less	none
Antidepressants			
Benzodiazepines or beta blockers			
Antipsychotics			

Change in symptom scores:

Measure used: _____

Pre-treatment score _____

During treatment scores _____ _____ _____ _____ _____

Post-treatment mean score _____

Presenting problem in psychological terms (please tick all that apply)

____ Monosymptomatic phobia   ____ Agora-/claustrophobia and/or panic attacks

____ Obsessive-compulsive   ____ Habit disorders

____ Psychosexual disorders   ____ Depression

____ Marital/relationship problems   ____ Anger/aggression

____ Psychosomatic   ____ Somato-psychic

____ Stress/generalised anxiety   ____ Post-traumatic stress

____ Eating disorder   ____ Psychotic state

____ Borderline personality disorder   ____ Other personality disorder, i.e. _____

____ Atypical grief reaction

____ Other (specify)

Patient's personality structure in psychodynamic terms:
[A glossary defining the different personality styles is attached]

____ Basically psychologically healthy
     with good ego strength   ____ Passive-aggressive

____ Dependent   ____ Inadequate

____ Psychopathic   ____ Immature

____ Perverse   ____ Neurotic (Obsessional)

____ Depressive   ____ Neurotic (Hysterical)

____ Schizoid   ____ Anxious

____ Narcissistic   ____ Paranoid

____ Other features of the patient's character ____ Borderline
          (specify)_____

Predisposing risk factors:

____ Marital/relationship breakdown   ____ Bereavement/loss of significant other

____ Mid-life crisis   ____ Retirement

____ Illness/operation   ____ Job loss

____ Sexually abused as a child   ____ Rape victim

____ Physically abused as a child

____ Other _____

At risk of:

____ Psychiatric breakdown   ____ Marriage/family breakup/divorce

____ Attempting suicide   ____ Unemployment

____ (Further) psychotropic medication   ____ Dependence on social services

____ Sexual abuse of children   ____ Physical abuse of children

____ Inappropriate health-care
      seeking behaviours   ____ Physical illness

____ AIDS risk behaviour   ____ Risk of offending

____ Isolation   ____ Children being taken into care

____ Other _____

____ Needs psychiatric cover

Goals of treatment: Please tick the principal goals of treatment

____ **TO REDUCE SYMPTOMS** (specify): _____

____ **TO EXPLORE FEELINGS, GAIN INSIGHT or RESOLVE INTRAPSYCHIC CONFLICT** (specify):
      ____ exploration of feelings: _____
      ____ achievement of insight into unconscious processes, e.g. _____
      ____ resolution of intrapsychic conflict, e.g. _____

____ **TO IMPROVE QUALITY OF RELATIONSHIPS** (specify):
      ____ achievement of separation and autonomy
      ____ development of ability to trust
      ____ capacity for empathy
      ____ communication of feelings with others
      ____ ability to give and receive feedback
      ____ appropriate assertion
      ____ increased self-esteem and self-confidence
      ____ formation and maintainance of friendships
      ____ commitment to an intimate relationship
      ____ perception of others as whole objects (e.g. without idealization or devaluation)
      ____ reduction in behaviours expressing grandiosity, envy, or entitlement
      ____ moderation of dependency needs and fears of abandonment
      ____ reduction in need to control others
      ____ moderation of need to compulsively look after other people
      ____ management of aggressive or sadistic behaviour, or victimization of others
      ____ minimization of self-destructive or masochistic tendencies in relationships
      ____ enjoyment of a non-exploitative and mutually pleasurable sexual relationship
      ____ other (specify)_____

TO ACHIEVE STRUCTURAL CHANGE (specify):
      ____ increase ego strength and support adaptive coping strategies
      ____ improve reality testing
      ____ develop more mature and flexible ego defenses
      ____ reduce acting-out behaviours, impulsivity, and re-enactments
      ____ develop resources for coping with unmanageable feeling states

_____ develop a capacity for guilt, where this is lacking

_____ work through excessive guilt, or moderate the demands of a too-strict superego

_____ develop more mature and better integrated superego functioning

TO FACILITATE COGNITIVE CHANGE (specify):

_____ modification of distorted beliefs and 'thoughts that cause problems'

_____ modification of core beliefs and assumptions

_____ decrease frequency of automatic negative thoughts about self, world and future

_____ positively reframe stressful situations and reduce 'catastrophizing' as a cognitive style

_____ develop more adaptive coping mechanisms under stress

TO IMPROVE WORK PERFORMANCE (specify; see also improve quality of relationships):

_____ develop the capacity to work creatively and effectively

_____ work through blocks to creative activity

_____ enhance ability to work collaboratively, as part of a team

_____ develop ability to relax and unwind during leisure time

OTHER (specify): _____

AT THE END OF THE ASSESSMENT PHASE PLEASE RATE:

(a) Motivation to change

Highly motivated	Very motivated	Somewhat motivated	Not very motivated	Not at all motivated
1	2	3	4	5

(b) Psychological-mindedness

Excellent capcity for insight, can make good use of transference	Good capacity for insight, can work in the transference	Some capacity for insight but has difficulty working in the transference	Little capacity for insight, unable to use transference	No insight, concrete thinking; not psychologically-minded
1	2	3	4	5

(c) Social support available

Excellent	good	Fair	Poor	None
Partner, family, friends, colleagues	Partner, family, some friends	Unsupportive partner, some family support	No partner, unsupportive family, few friends	Isolated without family or friends
1	2	3	4	5

(d) Quality of intimate relationships (adapted from Howard, Lyeger and O'Mahoney, 1991)

1 Steady relationship with mutual affection, warmth, support, and effective communication; satisfactory sexual relations; conflicts are minor and rapidly resolved.

2 Steady relationship generally provides affection and support; good communication; occasional conflicts but these are readily resolved; sexual relationship is generally satisfactory to both partners.

3 Relationship sometimes lacks affection, warmth, and support; sexual relations are less than satisfactory or are somewhat lacking in intimacy.

4 Lack of support; only rare, occasional expressions of warmth; sexual interest diminished or excessive without regard to mate's feelings, pleasure, etc.

5 Warmth lacking throughout; no sexual initiative or advances are grossly inappropriate and inconsiderate; risk of physical or sexual violence.

— No information; romantic relationship does not exist due to lifestyle choice (e.g. celibacy) or to other factors (e.g. death of a spouse); or no current relationship and not seeking a relationship.

Appropriate treatment (dependent on availability):

____ Long-term individual psychoanalytic therapy   ____ Long-term group analytic therapy
      (up to two years)

____ Short-term focal psychodynamic therapy   ____ Cognitive-analytic therapy
      (10-20 sessions)

____ Cognitive-behavioural therapy   ____ Relaxation training

____ Assertiveness/social skills training   ____ Brief intervention

____ Time-limited psychodynamic group therapy   ____ Social conflict group

____ Anxiety/stress management group   ____ Cognitive-behavioural group therapy

____ Other group treatment (specify): _____

____ Couples/sexual therapy   ____ Family therapy

____ Other (specify) _____   ____ No treatment

Outcome of treatment

For a maximum of 3 principal treatment goals, please rate the patient's improvement (if there are only 1–2 goals, please rate these here):

Goal no. 1

Fully achieved	Mostly achieved	Achieved in part	Little progress	Not achieved at all
1	2	3	4	5

Goal no. 2

Fully achieved	Mostly achieved	Achieved in part	Little progress	Not achieved at all
1	2	3	4	5

Goal no. 3

Fully achieved	Mostly achieved	Achieved in part	Little progress	Not achieved at all
1	2	3	4	5

Reference No. ____   Date _____

Present Quality of Life

Please rate the extent to which your problems are affecting you in each of the following two ways, by making a circle around the appropriate number on the scale from 1 (extreme) to 5 (no effect):

	1 Extreme	2 Marked	3 Moderate	4 Mild	5 No effect
Disable you (e.g. cause you to avoid people or situations, restrict your ativity)	1	2	3	4	5
Cause you psychological distress (e.g. unhappiness, depression, fears, anxiety, tension)	1	2	3	4	5

Please rate the general quality of the following aspects of your life over the past month by making a circle around the appropriate number on the scale from 1 (extremely bad) to 5 (extremely good).

	1 Extremely bad	2 Bad	3 Moderate	4 Good	5 Extremely good
WORK (including domestic work)	1	2	3	4	5
LEISURE ACTIVITIES (e.g. going out with friends, reading, sport)	1	2	3	4	5
FAMILY RELATIONSHIPS (e.g. with parents, spouse, children, family outings)	1	2	3	4	5
INTIMATE RELATIONSHIPS (e.g. giving and receiving affection, sexual relationships)	1	2	3	4	5

If you would like to make specific comments, please write them over the page.

Thank you for completing this questionnaire.

SCORING SOCIAL CLASS

(Classification of Occupations, HMSO, 1970)

- Where partners' occupations place them in different social classes, use the higher of the two scores.
- Where woman is housewife, or partner is invalid cared for at home, use occupation of working partner to score social class.
- Where patient is retired or unemployed, use occupation before retirement or redundancy.
- Where patient has had several occupations, use that with the highest social class.

Coding:

1 = social classes I and II
2 = social classes III, IV and V

Social Classes I–V: overview and examples

I. Professional, etc. occupations

- Doctors, dentists, pharmacists
- Psychologists, psychotherapists
- Clergy, ministers, members of religious orders
- Solicitors, barristers, judges
- University teachers
- Chemists, physical and biological scientists
- Civil, mechanical, electrical, electronic engineers
- Accountants, surveyors, architects

II. Intermediate occupations

- Primary and secondary school teachers
- Social welfare workers, laboratory technicians
- Authors and journalists, painters, sculptors and creative artists
- Farm managers, market gardeners
- Ship captains, deck and engineering officers
- Aircraft pilots, navigators, flight engineers
- Nurses, radiographers, chiropodists, physiotherapists, occupational therapists
- Proprietors and managers, sales
- Senior government officials, local authority senior officers
- Managers in engineering, building, mining
- Personnel and sales managers

III. Skilled occupations, both manual and nonmanual

- Furnacemen
- Smiths, forgemen, sheet metal workers, machine tool fitters
- Radio mechanics
- Carpenters, joiners, cabinet makers

- Plumbers, gas fitters, bricklayers, masons, plasterers
- Butchers, meat cutters, milkmen, publicans, innkeepers
- Tanners, shoemakers, shoe repairers
- Weavers, knitters, tailors, upholsterers
- Printing press operators, valuers and auctioneers
- Drivers of buses, coaches, heavy goods vehicles
- Clerks, cashiers, office machine operators, typists

IV. Partly skilled occupations

- Fishermen, gardeners, miners
- Assemblers, electrical and electronic
- Machine tool operators, warehousemen, packers
- Hand and machine sewers and embroiderers
- Food processors, waiters and waitresses
- Construction workers, paint sprayers
- Bus conductors

V. Unskilled occupations

- Labourers, building and contracting
- Apprentices, engineering and allied trades
- Dock labourers
- Lorry drivers' mates, van guards
- Charwomen, office cleaners, window cleaners, chimney sweeps

Scored examples:

Local government officer (retired) 1
Cleaner 2
Education assistant; HGV driver 2
Clerk; machine tool fitter (deceased) 2
Dining room assistant 2
Teacher 1
Shop assistant 2
Property developer, self-employed 1
Social worker; housewife 1
Receptionist 2

DESCRIPTIONS OF PERSONALITY STYLES

Neurotic (Hysterical) personality
- self-dramatizing, craving excitement, tendency to overreaction, outbursts or tantrums
- perceived as shallow and lacking in genuineness by others
- egocentric, vain, dependent, prone to manipulative suicidal threats, gestures or attempts
- impressionistic style of cognition: global, diffuse, and lacking in detail; judgement labile
- distractible, suggestible, often naive or deficient in knowledge
- repression the principal defence mechanism
- tendency to conversion reactions: unconscious conflicts transformed into bodily symptoms

Neurotic (Obsessional) personality
- restricted ability to express warm and tender emotions
- perfectionism, rigidity of cognition, inflexibility
- fear of loss of control; fear of dirt, messiness, and disorder, stubbornness, interest in ritual
- insistence that others submit to own way of doing things
- excessive devotion to work to the exclusion of pleasure: work has a 'driven' quality
- impulse seen as an enemy; tyranny of the 'should'; submission to propriety and duty, unusually harsh superego
- defense mechanisms of reaction formation, undoing, emotional isolation, intellectualization indecisiveness, procrastination, great difficulty making decisions.

Anxious personality
- generalized, nonspecific anxiety which is not reality based, phobic anxiety.

Passive-aggressive personality
- resistance to demands for adequate performance, expressed indirectly, e.g. procrastination, dawdling, stubbornness, inefficiency or 'forgetfulness'
- pervasive social and occupational ineffectiveness
- expression of aggression and hostility through passive means.

Dependent personality
- passively allows others to assume responsibility for major areas of life because of inability to function independently
- subordinates own needs to those of persons on whom one depends
- helpless and clinging, appears fearful and timid, shrinks from situations expressing hostility
- lacking in self-confidence.

Inadequate personality
- apparently low instinctual drives
- lack of motivation which is not an accompaniment of depression
- ineffectual, inept in life, poor judgment
- tendency to passivity; gives in to external pressure, drifts
- immature level of object relations.

Immature personality

- pattern of relating which is not age-appropriate

- developmentally arrested in a significant way.

Depressive personality

- melancholic, 'victim of circumstances', nothing good enough, anything good is destroyed, successes are minimized, automatic negative thoughts, pessimistic about the future

- feelings of inadequacy, loss of self-esteem, or self-deprecation

- loss of interest in or enjoyment of pleasurable activities, irritability or excessive anger

- chronic tearfulness, recurrent thoughts of death or suicide.

Psychopathic personality

- failure to accept social norms with respect to lawful behaviour

- inability to maintain enduring attachment to a sexual partner, profound distrust of others

- sense of entitlement used to justify antisocial acts

- aggressiveness, violence, failure to honour financial obligations, impulsivity, recklessness, repeated lying, fabrication, glib

- seeking immediate practical gain or advantage, egocentric, charming, persuasive

- lack of guilt or remorse for antisocial behaviour

- inadequately developed superego functioning.

Paranoid personality

- pervasive, unwarranted suspiciousness and mistrust of people

- furtive, constricted, apprehensively suspicious, devious

- hypersensitive, acutely responsive to rebuff, touchy, guarded

- vigilant for signs in the environment that confirm persecutory world view

- strong sense of external threat: distortion of reality and misperception of cues

- splitting, projection and projective identification: favoured defence mechanisms

- attribution to others of motivations that are repudiated and intolerable in oneself

- cold, restricted affect; often also described as 'borderline' in level of functioning.

Schizoid personality

- emotionally cold and aloof

- indifference to praise or criticism of others

- close friendships with no more than one or two persons

- object relations and defence mechanisms organized at the paranoid-schizoid position

- often also described as borderline in level of functioning.

Narcissistic personality

- grandiose sense of self-importance, exaggeration of achievements and talents

- capable of high achievement, strong need for admiring attention from others

- preoccupation with fantasies of unlimited success or power or ideal love, exhibitionism, inability to recognize limitations, self regarded as unique, special and/or superior

- marked feelings of rage, shame or emptiness in response to criticism, indifference of others, or defeat; deep, sustained feelings of hollowness, meaninglessness, and futility

- entitlement, exploitativeness, relationships that alternate between overidealization and devaluation, including feelings of contempt

- search for objects who mirror the self, including narcissistic object choice in sexual relationships; sexual behaviour may involve perversions, promiscuity and/or lack of inhibitions

- egocentric, lack of empathy for the needs and feelings of others.

Borderline personality

- multiple symptom picture, e.g. anxiety, polysymptomatic neurosis, polymorphous perverse sexual trends, impulse neurosis and addictions

- impulsivity, unstable and intense relationships, intolerance of being alone, physically self-damaging acts, chronic feelings of emptiness or boredom

- outbursts of anger or rage, identity disturbance, affective instability, rapid and dramatic swings from one affect state to another

- magical thinking, ideas of reference, social isolation, recurrent illusions, odd speech, inadequate rapport, suspiciousness, shift towards primary process thinking

- defences and object relationships organized at the paranoid-schizoid position

- primitive defence mechanisms, e.g. splitting, projection, projective identification, idealization, omnipotence, devaluation, introjection, primitive forms of denial

- lack of anxiety tolerance, lack of frustration tolerance, lack of impulse control, demand for immediate gratification, lack of developed subliminatory channels

- tendency to act out under stress, abuse of alcohol or drugs to alleviate anxiety

- incapacity for synthesizing good and bad introjected part-objects, deficiences in ability to experience guilt, little capacity for realistic evaluation of others

- crude expression of pregenital and sexual aims, often severely infiltrated with aggression

- identity diffusion: multiple, contradictory and unintegrated self-images

- need-fulfilling relationships, as-if relationships, or relationships based on part-objects.

Perverse personality

- sadomasochistic behaviour, including 'emotional bondage'

- exhibitionistic or voyeuristic behaviour, paedophilias and incestuous behaviour

- hostile attachment to objects.

Basically psychologically healthy with good ego strength

- good tolerance of stress

- persistence in the face of a negative environment

- mature object relatedness.

PATIENT SATISFACTION QUESTIONNAIRE   Patient code no. _____

Now that you have completed your sessions with the psychologist, we would be grateful to know how you have felt about the help you have received. Your reply can be posted to us in the enclosed stamped addressed envelope.

Please ring the number corresponding to your reply to each question.

1. **When you were referred to us, were you seen as promptly as you felt necessary?**

Yes, very promptly	Fairly promptly	Acceptable wait	No, some delay	No, long delay
1	2	3	4	5

2. **How convenient was the location?**

Very convenient	Mostly convenient	Somewhat convenient	Inconvenient	Very inconvenient
1	2	3	4	5

3. **On the day of my appointments:**

I was almost never kept waiting	Very occasionally I waited a few minutes	The psychologist was sometimes late	The psychologist was usually late	The appointments never began at the scheduled time
1	2	3	4	5

4. **How satisfied were you with the kind of help you received?**

Very satisfied	Mostly satisfied	Somewhat satisfied	Somewhat dissatisfied	Very dissatisfied
1	2	3	4	5

5. **I think the main problems which brought me to the psychologist have been resolved:**

Yes, very much so	Yes, for the most part	Only a little progress	No, problems a little worse	No, problems much worse than before
1	2	3	4	5

6. **How would you describe your relationships with other people now, compared to when you began seeing the psychologist?**

Most of my relationships with other people have improved	Some of my relationships with other prople have improved	No change in my relationships	Some of my relationships have deteriorated	My relationships have deteriorated overall
1	2	3	4	5

7. How would you describe your ability to manage your difficult feelings now, compared to how you were before?

Much better able to manage my difficult feelings	Better at managing difficult feelings most of the time	No change in ability to manage difficult feelings	Difficult feelings are somewhat worse than before	Difficult feelings are much worse than before
1	2	3	4	5

8. If you felt in need of help again, would you choose to see a psychologist?

Yes, definitely	Yes, probably	No, possibly not	No, I don't think so	No, definitely not
1	2	3	4	5

Which part or aspects of your treatment helped you the most?

Which parts or aspects of treatment were least helpful? (e.g. time of appointments, length of treatment, particular aspects of the sessions)

Do you feel there were aspects of your problem which were given the wrong emphasis (either too much or not enough) or misunderstood in your treatment? If so, please tell us something about this:

If you have any other comments or suggestions, please write them here.

Thank you very much for your help.

REFERENCES

Ackley, D.C. (1997) *Breaking Free of Managed Care: A Step-by-step Guide to Regaining Control of Your Practice*. New York: Guilford Press.

Albeniz, A. and Holmes, J. (1996) Psychotherapy integration: its implications for psychiatry. *Brit. J. Psychiatry* **169**, 563–570.

Alexander, P. (1996) Less pessimism concerning primary care psychology: a reply to McPherson. *Clin. Psych. Forum* **91**, 16–18.

Alperin, R.M. (1994) Managed care versus psychoanalytic psychotherapy: conflicting ideologies. *Clin. Soc. Work J.* **22**(2), 137–148.

Alperin, R.M. (1997) Is psychoanalytically oriented psychotherapy compatible with managed care? In R.M. Alperin and D.G. Phillips (eds) *The Impact of Managed Care on the Practice of Psychotherapy: Innovation, Implementation, and Controversy*. New York, Brunner/Mazel, pp. 185–198.

American Psychiatric Association (1993) Practice guideline for major depressive disorder in adults. *Amer. J. Psychiatry* **150** (Suppl 4), 1–26.

American Psychiatric Association (1994) *Diagnostic and Statistical Manual of Mental Disorders* (4th edn). Washington DC: American Psychiatric Association.

Amies, P. (1996) Psychotherapy patients: are they 'the worried well'? *Psychiatric Bull.* **20**, 153–156.

Anderson, E.M. and Lambert, M.J. (1995) Short-term dynamically oriented psychotherapy: a review and meta-analysis. *Clin. Psych. Rev.* **15**(6), 503–514.

Arborelius, E. and Thakker, K.D. (1995) Why is it so difficult for general practitioners to discuss alcohol with patients? *Fam. Pract.* **12**(4), 419–422.

AuBuchon, P.G. and Malatesta, V.J. (1994) Obsessive compulsive patients with comorbid personality disorder: associated problems and response to a comprehensive behaviour therapy. *J. Clin. Psychiatry* **55**(10), 448–453.

Austad, C.S. (1996) *Is Long–term Therapy Unethical: Toward a Social Ethic in an Era of Managed Care*. San Francisco: Jossey-Bass.

Aveline, M. (1995) How I assess for focal therapy. In C. Mace (ed.) *The Art and Science of Assessment in Psychotherapy*, Routledge: London, pp. 137–154.

Azim, H.F.A. (1991) The quality of object relations scale. *Bull. Menn. Clin.* **55**, 323–343.

Bader, E. and Pearson, P.T. (1988) *In Quest of the Mythical Mate: A Developmental Approach to Diagnosis and Treatment in Couples Therapy.* New York: Brunner/Mazel.

Baker, R., Allen, H., Penn, W., Daw, P. and Baker, E. (1996) *The Dorset Primary Care Counselling Service Research Evaluation.* Dorset Healthcare NHS Trust. Unpublished manuscript.

Balestrieri, M., Williams, P. and Wilkinson, G. (1988) Specialist mental health treatment in general practice: a meta–analysis. *Psych. Med.* **18**, 711–717.

Balint, M. (1957) *The doctor, His Patient and the Illness.* London: Pitman.

Balint, M. (1968) *The Basic Fault: Therapeutic Aspects of Regression.* London: Tavistock.

Bamber, M. (1997) An Evaluation of Three Cognitive Models of Depression. *Clin. Psych. Forum* **99**, 3–8.

Banks, M.H., Beresford, A.A., Morrell, D.C., Waller, J.J. and Watkins, C.J. (1975) Factors influencing demand for primary health care in women aged 20–44 years: a preliminary report. *Int. J. Epid.* **4**, 189–195.

Barkham, M. (1997) The development of a core battery of measures for routine evaluation–the Mental Health Foundation project. Paper presented at the BAC Counselling Research Conference, University of Birmingham, 13 June 1997.

Barkham, M. and Shapiro, D. (1990) Towards resolving the problem of waiting lists: psychotherapy in two-plus-one sessions. *Clin. Psych. Forum* **23**, 15–18.

Barkham, M., Hardy, G.E. and Startup, M. (1996) The IIP-32: a short version of the inventory of interpersonal problems. *Brit. J. Clin. Psych.* **35**, 21–35.

Barkham, M., Rees, A., Stiles, W.B., Shapiro, D.A., Hardy, G.E. and Reynolds, S. (1996) Dose-effect relations in time-limited psychotherapy for depression. *J. Cons. Clin. Psych.* **64**(5), 927–935.

Barron, J.W. and Sands, H. (eds) (1996) *Impact of Managed Care on Psychodynamic Treatment.* Madison CT: International Universities Press.

Beaumont, G. (1983) Depression and suicide in general practice. In G. Beaumont (ed.) *Suicide and Depression, Risk and Prevention, A Symposium Sypplement to Psychiatry in Practice.* Proceedings of a symposium held at University Hospital of South Manchester, 19 January 1983, pp. 29–37.

Beck, A.T., Freeman, A. and associates (1990) *Cognitive Therapy of Personality Disorders.* New York: Guilford Press.

Beck, A.T., Rush, J., Shaw, B. and Emery, G. (1979) *Cognitive Therapy of Depression.* New York: Guilford Press.

Beck, A.T., Steer, R.A. and Garbin, M.C. (1988) Psychometric properties of the Beck depression inventory: twenty–five years of evaluation. *Clin. Psych. Rev.* **8**, 77–100.

Bell, D. (1996) Primitive mind of state. *Psychoanal. Psychother.* **10** (1), 45–57.

Bell, L. (1996) Cognitive analytic therapy: its value in the treatment of people with eating disorders. *Clin. Psych. Forum* **92**, 5–10.

Berkowitz, R. (1996) Assessment: some issues for counsellors in primary health care. *Psychodyn. Couns.* **2**(2), 209–229.

Berman, J.S. (1996) Evaluating the rate of change during psychotherapy by following the same clients over time. Paper presented at the Society for Psychotherapy Research conference at Amelia Island, Florida, June 1996.

Berne, E. (1972) *What Do You Say After You Say Hello? The Psychology of Human Destiny*. New York: Grove Press.

Black, N. (1996) Why we need observational studies to evaluate the effectiveness of health care. *BMJ* **312**, 1215–1218.

Blais, M.A., Conboy, C.A., Wilcox, N. and Norman, D.K. (1996) An empirical study of the DSM-IV defensive functioning scale in personality disordered patients. *Compr. Psychiatry* **37**(6), 435–440.

Blatt, S.J. and Ford, R.Q. (1994) *Therapeutic Change: An Object Relations Perspective*. New York: Plenum.

Boardman, J. (1991) Detection of psychological problems by general practitioners. *Update* 1 June, 1068–1073.

Bollas, C. (1978) The transformational object. *Int. J. Psycho-Anal.* **60**, 97–107.

Bond, T. (1995) The nature and outcomes of counselling. In J. Keithley and G. Marsh (eds), *Counselling in Primary Health Care*: Oxford: Oxford University Press, pp. 3–26.

Book, H.E. (1998) *How to Practice Brief Psychodynamic Psychotherapy: The CCRT Method*. Washington DC: American Psychological Association.

Boot, D., Gillies, P., Fenelon, J., Reubin, R., Wilkins, M. and Gray, P. (1994) Evaluation of the short-term impact of counseling in general practice. *Pat. Educ. Couns.* **24**, 79–89.

Bor, R. (1995) BPS Division of Counselling Psychology Reference Library on Psychological Counselling: psychological counselling in primary health care. *Couns. Psych. Rev.* **10**(3), 38–40.

Borus, J.F., Howes, M.J., Devins, N.P., Rosenberg, R. and Livingston, W.W. (1988) Primary health care providers' recognition and diagnosis of mental disorders in their patients. *Gen. Hosp. Psychiatry* **10**, 317–321.

Boswell, E.B. and Stoudemire, A. (1996) Major depression in the primary care setting. *Amer. J. Med.* **101** (Suppl 6A), 3S–9S.

Brech, J.M. and Agulnik, P.L. (1996) Do brief interventions reduce waiting times for counselling? *Counselling* **7**, 322–325.

British Association for Counselling (1993) *Guidelines for the Employment of Counsellors in General Practice*. Rugby: Counselling in Medical Settings Division of the BAC.

British Medical Association (1982) *Sex Problems in Practice*. London: BMA.

Brown, C. and Schulberg, H.C. (1995) The efficacy of psychosocial treatments in primary care: a review of randomized clinical trials. *Gen. Hosp. Psychiatry* **17**, 414–424.

Brown, C., Schulberg, H.C., Madonia, M.J., Shear, M.K. and Houck, P.R. (1996) Treatment outcomes for primary care patients with major depression and lifetime anxiety disorders. *Amer. J. Psychiatry* **53**(10), 1293–1300.

Brown, L.S. (1997) The private practice of subversion: psychology as Tikkun Olam. *Amer. Psychol.* **53**(4), 449–462.

Brown, R.L., Leonard, T., Saunders, L.A. and Papasouiotis, O. (1997) A two–item screening test for alcohol and other drug problems. *J. Fam. Pract.* **44**(2), 151–160.

Brown, T.A. and Barlow, D.H. (1992) Comorbidity among anxiety disorders: implications for treatment and DSM-IV. *J. Cons. Clinc. Psych.* **60**, 835–844.

Bruggen, P. (1997) *Who Cares? True Stories of the NHS Reforms.* Charlbury: Jon Carpenter.

Brunning, H. and Burd, M. (1993) Clinical psychologists in primary care. *Clin. Psychol. Forum* **58**, 27–31.

Brunning, H., Elliott, S., Fleming, W. and Prior, J. (1994) Our money in their hands: marketing clinical psychology to GP fundholders. *Clin. Psychol. Forum* **66**, 24–28.

Budman, S.H. and Gurman, A.S. (1988) *Theory and Practice of Brief Therapy.* New York: Guilford Press.

Burton, M. (1991) Counselling in routine care: a client-centred approach. In M. Watson (ed.), *Cancer Patient Care: Psychosocial Treatment Methods.* Cambridge: BPS Books and Cambridge University Press, pp. 74–93.

Burton, M.V. (1992a) Psychosocial problems in primary care: contributions of psychologists and other professionals, an annotated bibliography. In B. Kat (1992), *On Advising Purchasers: Guidance for Members of the Division of Clinical Psychology of the British Psychological Society.* Leicester: British Psychological Society, pp. 87–130.

Burton, M.V. (1992b) Monitoring psychotherapy outcome in a district psychology service. Annual Conference of the Society for Psychotherapy Research UK, Ravenscar, April.

Burton, M.V. (1997) Counsellors in primary care: supervision issues. *Clin. Psychol. Forum* **101**, 29–31.

Burton, M. V. and Parker, R. W. (1995) A randomized controlled trial of preoperative psychological preparation for mastectomy. *Psycho-Oncology* **4**, 1–19.

Burton, M.V. and Ramsden, R. (1994) A survey of GP referral patterns to outpatient psychiatry, clinical psychology, community psychiatric nurses, and counsellors. *Clin. Psychol. Forum* **74**, 13–17.

Burton, M.V. and Topham, D. (1997) Early loss experiences in psychotherapists, Church of England clergy, patients referred for psychotherapy, and scientists and engineers. *Psychother. Res.* **7**(3), 255–280.

Burton, M.V., Keller, A., Boston, K., Eichhorn, H., Kaethner, L., Ramsden, R., Richman, S. and Spector, J. (1993) The Abbots Langley clinical audit form. *Newsl. Assoc. Psychoanal. Psychother. NHS* **13**, 5–7.

Burton, M.V., Sadgrove, J., and Selwyn, E. (1995) Do counsellors in general practice surgeries and clinical psychologists in the National Health Service see the same patients? *J. Roy. Soc. Med.* **88**, 97–102.

Burton, M.V., Henderson, P. and Curtis Jenkins, G. (1998) Primary care counsellors' experience of supervision. *Counselling*, May.

Camden and Islington Medical Audit Advisory Group (1996). *Counselling and Psychological Therapies: Guidelines and Directory.* London: MAAG.

Campbell, S.M. and Roland, M.O. (1996) Why do people consult the doctor? *Fam. Pract.* **13**(1), 75–83.

Campbell, T.L. and Patterson, J.M. (1995) The effectiveness of family intervention in the treatment of physical illness. *J. Marital Family Ther.* **21** (4), 545–583.

Campkin, M. (1995) The GP as counsellor. In J. Keithley and G. Marsh (eds) *Counselling in Primary Health Care.* Oxford: Oxford University Press, pp. 258–271.

Cape, J. (1996) Psychological treatment of emotional problems by general practitioners. *Brit. J. Med. Psych.* **69**, 85–99.

Casement, P. (1985) *On Learning from the Patient.* London: Tavistock.

Casement, P. (1990) *Further Learning from the Patient: The Analytic Space and Process.* London:Tavistock/Routledge.

Casey, M., Harris, R., McDonald, K. and Todd, G. (1994) Opportunities for consultation. *Clin. Psych.Forum* **65**, 36–38.

Cheston, R. (1995) Symptomatic differences between referrals to clinical psychologists working in primary and secondary care. Paper presented at the British Psychological Society London Conference, December 1995.

Clark, A., Hook, J. and Stein, K. (1997) Counsellors in primary care in Southampton: a questionnaire survey of their qualifications, working arrangements, and casemix. *Brit. J. Gen. Pract.* **47**, 613–617.

Clarkin, J.F. (1996) Treatment of personality disorders. *Brit. J. Clin. Psych.* **35**, 641–642.

Clarkin, J.G. and Kendall, P.C. (1992) Comorbidity and treatment planning: summary and future directions. *J. Cons. Clin. Psych.* **60**(6), 904–908.

Claxton, J. and Turner, A. (1997) Clinical psychology and counselling: a retrospective analysis of GP referrals to a clinical psychology service. *Clin. Psychol. Forum* **106**, 15–18.

Cocksedge, S. (1997) A GP perspective. *Clin. Psychol. Forum* **101**, 22–25.

Coe, N., Ibbs, A. and O'Brien, J. (1996) The cost effectiveness of introducing counselling into the primary care setting in Somerset. Counselling Project Board, Somerset Health Authority. Unpublished manuscript.

Cohen, J.S.H. (1992) Annie – a management and resource problem: discussion paper. *J. Roy. Soc. Med.* **85**(5), 282–284.

Collins, S. and Murray, A. (1995) A pilot project employing counselling psychologists within an adult mental health clinical psychology service. *Clin. Psych. Forum* **78**, 8–12.

Coltart, N.E.C. (1986) Diagnosis and assessment of suitability for psychoanalytic psychotherapy. *Contemp. Psychoanal.* **22**(4), 560–569.

Compass Information Services (1995) Scientific foundation of the COMPASS® System. Philadelphia: Compass Information Services.

Coren, A. (1996) Brief therapy – base metal or pure gold? *Psychodyn.*

Couns. **2**(1), 22–38.

Corney, R. (1984) The effectiveness of attached social workers in the management of depressed female patients in general practice. *Psychol. Med.* **14** (Suppl 6), 47.

Corney, R. (1987) Marriage guidance counselling in general practice in London. *Brit. J. Guid. Couns.* **15**, 50–58.

Corney, R. (1990) Counselling in general practice – does it work? Discussion paper. *J. Roy. Soc. Med.* **83**, 253–257.

Corney, R. (1992) The effectiveness of counselling in general practice. *Int. Rev. Psychiatry* **4**, 331–338.

Corney, R. (1995) Social work involvement in primary care settings and mental health centres: a survey in England and Wales. *J. Ment. Health* **4**, 275–280.

Corney, R.H. (1986) Marriage guidance counselling in general practice. *J. Roy. Coll. Gen. Pract.* **36**, 424–426.

Corney, R. and Jenkins, R. (eds) (1993) *Counselling in General Practice*. London: Tavistock/ Routledge.

Corney, R.H. (1996) Clinical psychologists in general practice: the impact of GP fundholding. *Clin. Psych. Forum* **90**, 27–31.

Corney, R.H., Strathdee, G., Higg, R., King, M., Williams, P., Sharp, D. and Pelosi, A.J. (1988) Managing the difficult patient: practical suggestions from a study day. *J. Roy. Coll. Gen. Pract.* **38**, 349–352.

Counselling in Primary Care Trust (1996) Information pack. Available from CPCT, Majestic House, High Street, Staines TW18 4DG.

Craig, T.K.J. and Boardman, A.P. (1997) Common mental health problems in primary care. *BMJ* **314**, 1609–1612.

Crisp, A. (1996) Future directions of psychotherapy in the NHS: adaptation or extinction? Psychiatry and psychotherapy. *Psychoanal. Psychother.* **10** (Suppl), 11–20.

Crits-Christoph, P. (1992) The efficacy of brief dynamic psychotherapy: a meta-analysis. *Amer. J.Psychiatr.* **149**(2), 151–158.

Crits-Christoph, P. and Barber, J.P. (eds) (1991) *Handbook of Short-term Dynamic Psychotherapy*. New York: Basic Books.

Cummings, N.A. (1991) Brief intermittent therapy throughout the life cycle. In C.S. Austad and W.H. Berman (eds.) *Psychotherapy in Managed Health Care: The Optimal Use of Time and Resources*. Washington: American Psychological Association.

Cummings, N.A. (1995) Unconscious fiscal convenience. *Psychother. Priv. Pract.* **14**(2), 23–28.

Cummings, N.A. (1997) Counselling in primary care: a 35-year perspective from the United States. Paper presented at the Sixth St. George's Counselling in Primary Care Conference, May 1997.

Cummings, N.A. and Sayama, M. (1995) *Brief Intermittent Psychotherapy Throughout the Life Cycle*. New York: Brunner/Mazel.

Curtis Jenkins, G. (1997a) A primare care led mental health service: a vision for the future or ultimate nightmare? Paper presented at the Royal Society of

Medicine, 15 October.

Curtis Jenkins, G. (1997b) Welcome address. First Annual Training Conference, Postgraduate Diploma and Masters Programmes in Counselling in Primary Care. Royal Society of Medicine, 8 November.

Curtis Jenkins, G. and Einzig, H. (1996). Counselling in primary care. In R. Bayne, I. Horton and J. Bimrose (eds) *New Directions in Counselling*. London: Routledge, pp. 97–108.

Daines, B., Gask, L. and Usherwood, T. (1997) *Medical and Psychiatric Issues for Counsellors*. London: Sage.

Dammers, J. and Wiener, J. (1995) The theory and practice of counselling in the primary health care team. In J. Keithley and G. Marsh (eds) *Counselling in Primary Health Care*. Oxford: Oxford University Press, pp. 27–56.

Dare, C. (1996) Evidence – fact or fiction. In Future directions of psychotherapy in the NHS – adaptation or extinction? *Psychoanal. Psychother.* **10**(Suppl), 32–45.

Day, C. (1997) Advances in primary child mental health care: the development and evaluation of the community child and family service. *Primary Care Psychology: Special Interest Group Newsletter* **5**, 31–33.

Day, C. and Wren, B. (1994) Journey to the centre of primary care: primary care psychology in perspective. *Clin. Psychol. Forum* **65**, 3–6.

de Groot, M. (1985) *Marriage Guidance Counsellors in the Medical Setting*. Research Report No. 1. Rugby: National Marriage Guidance Council.

de Lacey, G. (1992) What is audit? Why should we be doing it? *Hospital Update* June, 458–466.

Denman, C. (1995) Questions to be answered in the evaluation of long-term therapy. In M. Aveline and D.A. Shapiro (eds) *Research Foundations for Psychotherapy Practice*. Chichester: Wiley, pp. 175–190.

Department of Health (1994). *Developing NHS Purchasing and GP Fundholding: Towards a Primary Care-led NHS*. Leeds: Department of Health.

Depression Guideline Panel (1993) *Depression in Primary Care, Volume 2. Treatment of Major Depression*. Clinical Practice Guideline no. 5, AHCPR publication 93-0551. Rockville MD: US Dept Health and Human Services.

Derogatis, L.R. and Cleary, P.A. (1977) Confirmation of the dimensional structure of the SCL-90R: a study in construct validation. *J. Clin. Psych.* **33**(4), 981–989.

Derogatis, L.R. and Melisaratos, N. (1983) The brief symptom inventory: an introductory report. *Psych. Med.* **13**, 595–605.

Derogatis, L.R. and Spencer, P.M. (1982) *Brief Symptom Inventory: Administration, Scoring and Procedures Manual*. Baltimore: Clinical Psychometric Research.

Diguer, L., Barber, J.P. and Luborsky, L. (1993) Three concomitants: personality disorders, psychiatric severity, and outcome of dynamic psychotherapy of major depression. *Amer. J. Psychiatry* **150**(8), 1246–1248.

Dolan, B., Warren, F., Menzies, D. and Norton, K. (1995) Are short-term savings worth long-term costs? Paper presented at the Society for Psychotherapy Research Annual Conference, Ravenscar, 20 March.

Donnison, J. and Burd, M. (1994) Partnership in clinical practice. *Clin. Psychol. Forum* **65**, 11–14.

Dosanjh, N., Marshall, H. and Yazdani, A. (1977) Mental health needs of young Asian women in Newham. *Primary Care Psychology: Special Interest Group Newsletter* **5**, 38–39.

Drozd, J.F. and Goldfried, M.R. (1996) A critical evaluation of the state-of-the-art in psychotherapy outcome research. *Psychotherapy* **33**(2), 171–180.

Dunn, M. and Parry, G. (1997) A formulated care plan approach to caring for people with borderline personality disorder in a community mental health setting. *Clin. Psychol. Forum* **104**, 19–22.

Durham, R. (1997) Matching intensity of therapy to complexity of the disorder. Paper presented at the Annual Conference of the British Psychological Society, Edinburgh, 4 April 1997.

East, P. (1995) *Counselling in Medical Settings.* Buckingham: Open University Press.

Eells, T.D. (ed.) (1997) *Handbook of Psychotherapy Case Formulation.* New York: Guilford Press.

Engel, G.L. (1977) The need for a new medical model: A challenge for biomedicine. *Science* **196**, 129–136.

Engel, G.L. (1980) The clinical application of the biopsychosocial model. *Amer. J. Psychiatry* **137**(5), 535–544.

Erikson, E. (1968) *Identity, Youth and Crisis.* New York: W.W. Norton.

Eysenck, H.J. (1952) The effects of psychotherapy: an evaluation. *J. Cons. Psych.* **16**, 319–324.

Fahy, T. and Wessely, S. (1993) Should purchasers pay for psychotherapy? *BMJ* **307**, 576–577.

Fallowfield, L. (1993) The need for counselling skills in general practice. *J. Roy. Soc. Med.* **86**, 425–427.

Feltham, C. (1997) *Time-limited Counselling.* London: Sage.

Ferguson, B., Cooper, S., Brothwell, J., Markantonakis, A. and Tyrer, P. (1992) The clinical evaluation of a new community psychiatric service based on general practice psychiatric clinics. *Brit. J. Psychiatry* **160**, 493–497.

First, M.B. (1997) *User's Guide for the Structured Clinical Interview for DSM-IV Axis II Personality Disorders (SCID-II).* Washington DC: American Psychiatric Press.

First, M.B., Spitzer, R.L., Gibbon, M. and Williams, J.B.W. (1995) The structured clinical interview for DSM-III-R personality disorders (SCID-II). Part I. Description. *J. Pers. Dis.* **9**(2), 83–91.

Firth-Cozens, J. (1993) *Audit in Mental Health Services.* Hove: Lawrence Erlbaum.

Fletcher, J., Fahey, T. and McWilliam, J. (1995) Relationship between the provision of counselling and the prescribing of antidepressants, hypnotics and anxiolytics in general practice. *Brit. J. Gen. Pract.* **45**, 467–469.

Fonagy, P. and Higgitt, A. (1989) Evaluating the performance of departments of psychotherapy. *Psychoanal. Psychother.* **4**(2), 121–153.

Fonagy, P. and Target, M. (1996) Should we allow psychotherapy research to determine clinical practice? *Clin. Psych. Sci. Pract.* **3**(3), 244–249.

Fong, M.L. (1995) Assessment and DSM-IV diagnosis of personality disorders: a primer for counselors. *J. Couns. Devel.* **73**, 635–639.

Forth, C. (1996) Psychiatric disorders. In J. Keithley and G. Marsh (eds) *Counselling in Primary Health Care.* Oxford: Oxford University Press, pp.129–142.

France, R. and Robson, M. (1997) *Cognitive Behavioural Therapy in Primary Care: A Practical Guide.* London: Jessica Kingsley.

Friedli, K. and King, M. (1996) Counselling in general practice – A review. *Primary Care Psychiatry* **2**, 205–216.

Froyd, J.E., Lambert, M.J. and Froyd, J.D. (1996) A review of practices of psychotherapy outcome measurement. *J. Ment. Health* **5**, 11–15.

Gabbard, G.O., Lazar, S.G., Hornberger, J. and Spiegel, D. (1997) The economic impact of psychotherapy: a review. *Amer. J. Psychiatry* **154** (2), 147–155.

Garfield, S.L. (1996) Some problems associated with 'validated' forms of psychotherapy. *Clin. Psych. Sci. Pract.* **3**(3), 218–229.

Gask, L., Sibbald, B. and Creed, F. (1997) Evaluating models of working at the interface between mental health services and primary care. *Brit. J. Psychiatry* **170**, 6–11.

Geekie, J. (1995) Preliminary evaluation of one way of managing a waiting list. *Clin. Psychol. Forum* **85**, 33–35.

Gendlin, E.T. (1962) *Experiencing and the creation of meaning.* New York: Free Press of Glencoe.

Gendlin, E.T. (1967) Therapeutic procedures with schizophrenics. In C.R. Rogers (ed.) *The Therapeutic Relationship and its Impact: A Study of Psychotherapy with Schizophrenics.* Madison: University of Wisconsin Press.

Gendlin, E.T. (1981) *Focusing*, 2nd edn. New York: Bantam Books.

Gendlin, E.T. (1996) *Focusing-oriented Psychotherapy: A Manual of the Experiential Method.* New York: Guilford Press.

Gerrard, T.J. and Riddell, J.D. (1988) Difficult patients: black holes and secrets. *BMJ* **297**, 530–532.

Gill, D. (1996) Frequent consulters in general practice: a systematic review of existing literature, and a five year follow up study in one practice. MSc dissertation in Epidemiology, Institute of Health Sciences, Oxford.

Goldberg, D. (1995) Epidemiology of mental disorders in primary care settings. *Epid. Rev.* **17**(1), 182–190.

Goldberg, D. and Huxley, P. (1980) *Mental Illness in the Community – The Pathway to Care.* London: Tavistock.

Goldberg, D., Sharp, D. and Nanayakkara, K. (1995) The field trial of the mental disorders section of ICD-10 designed for primary care (ICD-10-PHC) in England. *Fam. Pract.* **12**(4), 466–473.

Goldberg, D.P. (1978) *Manual of the General Health Questionnaire.* Windsor: NFER.

Goldman, H.A. (1988) Paradise destroyed: the crime of being born. *Contemporary Psychoanalysis* **24**(3), 420–450.

Goldman, R. and Greenberg, L.S. (1997) Case formulation in process-experiential therapy. In T.D. Eells (ed.) *Handbook of Psychotherapy Case Formulation*, New York: Guilford, pp. 402–429.

Gordon, K. (1998) Themes in the supervision of primary care counsellors. *Clin. Psych. Forum* **111**, 23–26.

Gordon, K. and Graham, C. (1996) The impact of primary care counselling on psychiatric symptoms. *J. Ment. Health* **5**(5), 515–523.

Gordon, P.K. (1995) Characteristics of clients referred to a primary care counselling service. Paper presented at the British Psychological Society London Conference, December 1995.

Gordon, T. (1970) *Parent Effectiveness Training*. New York: Wyden.

Gournay, K. and Brooking, J. (1994) Community psychiatric nurses in primary health care. *Brit. J. Psychiatry* **165**, 231–238.

Graham, H., Senior, R., Dukes, S., Lazarus, M. and Mayer, R. (1994) The introduction of family therapy to British general practice. *Fam.Syst. Med.* **11**, 363–373.

Green, B. (1994) Developing a primary care and community psychology service. *Clin. Psychol. Forum* **65**, 32–35.

Griffiths, V. and Cormack, M. (1993) General practitioners and mental health services: a survey. *Clin. Psychol. Forum* **56**, 19–22.

Groves, J.E. (1978) Taking care of the hateful patient. *New Eng. J. Med.* **298**, 883–887.

Groves, J.E. (ed.) (1996) *Essential Papers on Short-term Dynamic Therapy*. New York: New York University Press.

Gustafson, J.P. (1995a) *Brief Versus Long Psychotherapy: When, Why and How*. Northvale, New Jersey: Jason Aronson.

Gustafson, J.P. (1995b) *The Dilemmas of Brief Psychotherapy*. New York: Plenum.

Hahn, S.R., Kroenke, K., Spitzer, R.L., Brody, D., Williams, J.B., Linzer, M. and deGruy, F.V. (1996) The difficult patient: prevalence, psychopathology, and functional impairment. *J. Gen. Int. Med.* **11**(1), 1–8.

Hall, J. (1997) Counsellors and psychologists: a subjective experience of working together. *Clin. Psychol. Forum* **101**, 18–21.

Hardy, G.E., Barkham, M., Shapiro, D.A., Stiles, W.B., Rees, A. and Reynolds, S. (1995) Impact of Cluster C personality disorders on outcomes of contrasting brief psychotherapies for depression. *J. Cons. Clin. Psych.* **63**(6), 997–1004.

Harman, M. (1991) The use of group psychotherapy with cancer patients: a review of recent literature. *J. Spec. Group Work* **16**(1), 56–61.

Harris, T. (1996) Primary prevention: assessing the relevance of life events and difficulties among primary care attenders. In T. Kendrick, A. Tylee and P. Freeling (eds) *The Prevention of Mental Illness in Primary Care*. Cambridge: Cambridge University Press, pp. 41–56.

Hemmings, A. (1997) Counselling in primary care: a randomised controlled trial. Unpublished manuscript, submitted for publication.

Henry, W.P., Schact, T.E., Strupp, H.H., Butler, S.F. and Binder, J.L. (1993) Effects of training in time-limited dynamic psychotherapy: changes in therapist behavior. *J. Cons. Clin. Psych.* **61**, 434–440.

Heywood, J. (1997) Referring patients for counselling: factors which inform the decisions of general practitioners. Paper presented at the BAC Counselling Research Conference, Birmingham, 14 June.

Higgs, R. (1984) Life changes. *BMJ* **288**, 1556–1557.

Higgs, R. and Dammers, J. (1992) Ethical issues in counselling and health in primary care. *Brit. J. Guid. Couns.* **20**(1), 27–38.

Hinshelwood, R. (1991) Psychodynamic formulation in assessment for psychotherapy. *Brit. J. Psychother.* **8**(2), 166–174.

Hinshelwood, R. (1996) Psychiatry and psychotherapy. *Psychoanal. Psychother.* **10** (suppl) 5–10.

Hoag, L. (1992) Psychotherapy in the general practice surgery: considerations of the frame. *Brit. J. Psychother.* **8**(4), 417–429.

Holden, J.M., Sagovsky, R. and Cox, J.L. (1989) Counselling in a general practice setting: controlled study of health visitor intervention in treatment of postnatal depression. *BMJ* **298**, 223–226.

Holmes, J. (1994) Psychotherapy – a luxury the NHS cannot afford? *BMJ* **309**, 1070–1071.

Holmes, J. (1995) How I assess for psychoanalytic psychotherapy. In C. Mace (ed.) *The Art and Science of Assessment in Psychotherapy*. London: Routledge, pp. 27–41.

Holmes, J. (1997a) Attachment, autonomy, intimacy: some clinical implications of attachment theory. *Brit. J. Med. Psych.* **70**, 231–248.

Holmes, J. (1997b) 'Too early, too late': endings in psychotherapy – an attachment perspective. *Brit. J. Psychotherapy* **14**(2), 159–171.

Hopkins, P., ed. (1972) *Patient-centred Medicine*. London: Regional Doctor Publications.

Hopkins, S.M. (1995) Personal reflections on counselling in primary health care: an approach based in analytical psychology. *Couns. Psychol. Rev.* **10**(4), 5–9.

Horowitz, L., Rosenberg, S.E., Baer, B.A., Ureno, G. and Villasenor, V.S. (1988) The inventory of interpersonal problems: psychometric properties and clinical applications. *J. Cons. Clin. Psych.* **56**, 885–892.

Horowitz, M.J. (1997) *Formulation as a Basis for Planning Psychotherapy Treatment*. Washington DC: American Psychiatric Press.

House, R. (1996) General practice counselling: a plea for ideological engagement. *Counselling* **7**(1), 40–44.

House, R. (1997) An approach to time-limited humanistic-dynamic counselling. *Brit. J. Guid. Couns.* **25**(2), 251–262.

Howard, K.I. and Mahoney, M.T. (1996) How much outpatient therapy is enough? *Behavioral Healthcare Tomorrow* **5**, 44–50.

Howard, K.I., Krause, M.S. and Orlinsky, D.E. (1986) The dose–effect relationship in psychotherapy. *Amer. Psychol.* **41**, 159–164.

Howard, K.I., Lueger, R.J. and O'Mahoney, M.T. (1991) The global assessment scale. Unpublished manuscript.

Howard, K., Moras, K., Brill, P.L., Martinovich, Z. and Lutz, W. (1996) Evaluation of psychotherapy: efficacy, effectiveness, and patient progress. *Amer. Psych.* **51**(10), 1059–1064.

Howe, A. (1996) 'I know what to do, but it's not possible to do it' – general practitioners' perceptions of their ability to detect psychological distress. *Fam. Pract.* **13**(2), 127–132.

Howells, E. and Law, A. (1996) A long-term brief intervention in primary care. *Clin. Psychol. Forum* **93**, 12–15.

Hughes, I. (1997) Can you keep from crying by considering things? Some arguments against cognitive therapy for depression. *Clin. Psychol. Forum* **104**, 23–27.

Jackson, G., Gater, R., Goldberg, D., Tantam, D., Loftus, L. and Taylor, H. (1993) A new community mental health team based in primary care: a description of the service and its effect on service use in the first year. *Brit. J. Psychiatry* **162**, 378–384.

Jacobs, M. (1994) Psychodynamic counselling: an identity achieved? *Psychodyn. Couns.* **1**(1), 79–92.

Jacobson, N.S. and Truax, P. (1991) Clinical significance: a statistical approach to defining meaningful change in psychotherapy research. *J. Cons. Clinc. Psych.* **59**, 12–19.

Jenkins, R. (1992) Developments in the primary care of mental illness: a forward look. *Int. Rev. Psychiatry* **4**, 237–242.

Jewell, D. (1988) I do not love thee Mr. Fell. . . Techniques for dealing with 'heartsink' patients. *BMJ* **297**, 498–499.

Jones, H., Murphy, A., Neaman, G., Tollemache, R. and Vasserman, D. (1994) Psychotherapy and counselling in a GP practice: making use of the setting. *Brit. J. Psychother.* **10**(4), 543–551.

Kadera, S.W., Lambert, M.J. and Andrews, A.A. (1996) How much therapy is really enough? A session-by-session analysis of the psychotherapy dose-effect relationship. *J. Psychother. Pract. Res.* **5**(2), 132–151.

Kakar, S. (1989) *Intimate Relations: Exploring Indian Sexuality.* London: Viking.

Kaplan, H.S. (1974). *The New Sex Therapy.* New York: Brunner/Mazel.

Kaplan, H.S. (1979). *The New Sex Therapy, Volume II. Disorders of Sexual Desire and Other New Concepts and Techniques in Sex Therapy.* New York: Brunner/Mazel.

Kaplan, H.S. (1983). *The Evaluation of Sexual Disorders: Psychological and Medical Aspects.* New York: Brunner/Mazel.

Karon, B.P. (1995) Provision of psychotherapy under managed health care: a growing crisis and national nightmare. *Prof. Psychol. Res. Pract.* **26**(1), 5–9.

Kat, B. (1992) *On Advising Purchasers.* Leicester: Division of Clinical Psychology of The British Psychological Society.

Kat, B. (1994) The contribution of psychological knowledge to primary health care: taking a step back to go forward. *Clin. Psychol. Forum* **65**, 23–26.

Kat, B. (1997a) How many psychologists, counsellors, CPNs etc. are needed, to see how many patients? An approach to research in one practice. *Primary Care Psychology: Special Interest Group Newsletter* **4**, 2–6.

Kat, B., (1997b) The psychology of primary healthcare. *Primary Care Psychology: Special Interest Group Newsletter* **5**, 3–19.

Keithley, J. and Marsh. G. (eds) (1995) *Counselling in Primary Health Care*. Oxford: Oxford University Press.

Kelleher, D. and Islam, S. (1994) The problem of integration: Asian people and diabetes. *J. Roy. Soc. Med.* **87**, 414–417.

Kendrick, A. (1994) How GPs improve their skills in detecting and managing mental health problems. Paper presented at Mental Health Care in 90s and Beyond, Royal Society of Medicine, London, 31 January 1994.

Kennerley, H. (1997) Schema-focused cognitive therapy. *BPS Psychotherapy Section Newsletter* **22**, 27–38.

King, M., Broster, G., Lloyd, M. and Horder, J. (1994) Controlled trials in the evaluation of counselling in general practice. *Brit. J. Gen. Pract.* **44**, 229–232.

Klein, J. (1990) Patients who are not ready for interpretations. *Brit. J. Psychother.* **7**(1), 38–49.

Knight, L. (1995) Explaining what counselling psychology is and what it can offer to GPs in primary health care settings. *Couns. Psychol. Rev.* **10**(4), 2–4.

Knowles, J. (1995) How I assess for group psychotherapy. In C. Mace (ed.) *The Art and Science of Assessment in Psychotherapy*. London: Routledge, pp. 78–89.

Kogan, M. and Redfern, S. (1995) *Making Use of Clinical Audit: A Guide to Practice in the Health Professions*. Buckingham: Open University Press.

Kohut, H. (1977) *The Restoration of the Self*. New York: International Universities Press.

Kopta, S.M., Howard, K.I., Lowry, J.L. and Beutler, L.E. (1994) Patterns of symptomatic recovery in time-unlimited psychotherapy. *J. Cons. Clin. Psych.* **62**, 1009–1016.

Lachtar, J. (1992) *The Narcissistic/Borderline couple: A Psychoanalytic Perspective on Marital Treatment*. New York: Brunner/Mazel.

Lambert, M. (1997) How much outpatient therapy is enough? Paper presented at the Annual Conference of the British Psychological Society, Edinburgh, 4 April.

Lambert, M., Lunnen, K., Umphres, V., Hansen, N.B. and Burlingame, G. (1994) *Administration and* Scoring *Manual for the Outcome Questionnaire (OQ-45.1)*. Salt Lake City UT: IHC Center for Behavioral Healthcare Efficacy.

Launer, J. (1994) Psychotherapy in the general practice surgery: working with and without a secure therapeutic frame. *Brit.J. Psychother.* **11**(1), 120–126.

Lazarus, A. (ed.) (1996a) *Controversies in Managed Mental Health Care*. Washington DC: American Psychiatric Press.

Lazarus, A. (1996b) Cost-shifting and managed care. *Psychiatric Services* **47**(10), 1063–1064.

Lechner, M.E., Vogel, M.E., Garcia-Shelton, L.M., Liechter, J.L. and Steibel, K.R.

(1993) Self-reported medical problems of adult female survivors of childhood sexual abuse. *J. Fam. Pract.* **36**(6), 633–638.

Lees, J. (1997) An approach to counselling in GP surgeries. *Psychodynam. Couns.* **3**(1), 33–48.

Lerner, P.M. (1996) Managed care and the borderline patient: where treatment was, there management will be. In J.W. Barron and H. Sands (eds) *Impact of Managed Care on Psychodynamic Treatment*. Madison CT: International Universities Press, pp.131–152.

Levenson, D. (1978) *The Seasons of a Man's Life*. New York: Knopf.

Lewis, G., Sharp, D., Bartholomew, J. and Pelosi, A.J. (1996) Computerized assessment of common mental disorders in primary care: effect on clinical outcome. *Fam. Pract.* **13**(2), 120–126.

Lieberman, S. (1995) How I assess for family therapy. In C. Mace (ed.) *The Art and Science of Assessment in Psychotherapy*. London: Routledge, pp. 61–77.

Llewelyn, S. (1997) Child sexual abuse survivors and cognitive analytic therapy. Paper presented at the Annual Conference of the British Psychological Society, Edinburgh, April 1997.

Lloyd, K.R., Jenkins, R. and Mann, A. (1996) Long term outcome of patients with neurotic illness in general practice. *BMJ* **313**, 26–28.

Luborsky, L. (1984) *Principles of Psychoanalytic Psychotherapy: A Manual for Supportive-Expressive Treatment*. New York: Basic Books.

Luborsky, L., Diguer, L., Luborsky, E., McLellan, T. and Woody, G. (1993a) Psychological health-sickness (PHS) as a predictor of outcomes in dynamic and other psychotherapies. *J. Cons. Clin. Psych.* **61**(4), 542–548.

Luborsky, L., Diguer, L., Luborsky, E., Singer, B., Dickter, D. and Schmidt, K.A. (1993b) The efficacy of dynamic psychotherapies: is it true that 'Everyone has won and all must have prizes'? In N.E. Miller, L. Luborsky, J.P. Barber and J.P. Docherty (eds) *Psychodynamic Treatment Research: A Handbook for Clinical Practice*. New York: Basic Books, pp. 497–516.

Luborsky, L., Singer, B. and Luborsky, L. (1975) Comparative studies of psychotherapies. *Arch. Gen. Psychiatr.* **32**, 995–1008.

Lukas, S. (1993) *Where to Start and What to Ask: An Assessment Handbook*. New York: Norton.

Lyons, J.S., Howard, K.I., O'Mahoney, M.T. and Lish, J.D. (1997) *The Measurement and Management of Clinical Outcomes in Mental Health*. New York: Wiley.

Mace, C. (1995a) When are questionnaires helpful? In C. Mace (ed.) *The Art and Science of Assessment in Psychotherapy*. London: Routledge, pp. 203–215.

Mace, C. (ed.) (1995b) *The Art and Science of Assessment in Psychotherapy*. London: Routledge.

Mackenzie, B. (1996) The enemy within: an exploration of the concept of boundaries in a GP's surgery. *Psychodyn. Couns.* **2**(3), 390–400.

McLeod, J. and Worrell, L. (1997) The Keele EAP evaluation scale. Paper presented at the BAC Counselling Research Conference, Birmingham, 14 June 1997.

McPherson, F. (1995) Clinical psychology and primary care: a comment on Alexander. *Clin. Psych. Forum* **85**, 36–37.

Magnavita, J.J. (1997) *Restructuring Personality Disorders: A Short-term Dynamic Approach.* New York: Guilford.

Mahtani, A. and Marks, L. (1994) Developing a primary care psychology service that is racially and culturally appropriate. *Clin. Psychol. Forum* **65**, 27–31.

Main, M. (1995) Discourse, prediction, and recent studies in attachment: implications for psychoanalysis. In T. Shapiro and R.N. Emde (eds) *Research in Psychoanalysis: Process, Development, Outcome.* Madison CT: International Universities Press, pp. 209–244.

Main, T.F. (1957) The ailment. *Brit. J. Med. Psych.* **30**, 129–145.

Malan, D.H. (1976) *The Frontier of Brief Psychotherapy.* New York: Plenum.

Malan, D.H. (1979) *Individual Psychotherapy and the Science of Psychodynamics.* London: Butterworths.

Malan, D.H. and Osimo, F. (1992) *Psychodynamics, Training and Outcome in Brief Psychotherapy.* Oxford: Butterworth-Heinemann.

Mann, A. (1993) The need for counselling: the extent of psychiatric and psychosocial disorders in primary care – a review of the epidemiological research findings. In R. Corney and R. Jenkins (eds) *Counselling in General Practice*: London: Routledge, pp. 7–16.

Mann, J. (1973) *Time-limited Psychotherapy.* Cambridge: Harvard University Press.

March, P. (1997) In two minds about cognitive-behavioural therapy: talking to patients about why they do not do their homework. *Brit. J. Psychother.* **13**(4), 461–472.

Margison, F. (1997) Discussant of Glenys Parry's paper, The provision of psychotherapy service. Annual Conference of the British Psychological Society, Edinburgh, 3 April.

Marks, I. (1985) Controlled trial of psychiatric nurse therapists in primary care. *BMJ* **290**, 1181–1184.

Marmor, J. (1953) The feeling of superiority: an occupational hazard in the practice of psychotherapy. *Amer. J. of Psychiatry*, 370–376.

Mathers, N.J. and Gask, L. (1995) Surviving the 'heartsink' experience. *Fam. Pract.* **12**(2), 176–183.

Matt, G.E. and Nararro, A.M. (1997) What meta-analyses have and have not taught us about psychotherapy effects: a review and future directions. *Clin. Psych. Rev.* **17**(1), 1–32.

Mayer, R., Graham, H., Schuberth, C.,Launer, J., Tomson, D. and Czauderna, J. (1996) Family systems ideas in the 10-minute consultation: using a reflecting partner or observing team in a surgery. *Brit. J. Gen. Pract.* **46**, 229–230.

McCallum, M. and Piper, W.E. (1996) Psychological mindedness. *Psychiatry* **59**, 48–64.

McCauley, J., Kern, D.E., Kolodner, K., Dill, L. et al. (1997) Clinical characteristics of women with a history of childhood abuse: unhealed wounds. *JAMA* **277**(17),

1362–1368.

McAvoy, B.R. and Donaldson, L.J. (1990) *Health Care for Asians*. Oxford: Oxford University Press.

McDaniel, S.H. (1995) Collaboration between psychologists and family physicians: implementing the biopsychosocial model. *Prof. Psychol. Res. Pract.* **26**(2), 117–122.

Mellor-Clark, J. (1997) Evaluating effectiveness: needs, problems and potential benefits. Paper presented at the BAC Counselling Research Conference, Birmingham, 14 June.

Mellor-Clark, J. and Barkham, M. (1996) Evaluating counselling. In R. Bayne, I. Horton and J. Bimrose (eds) *New Directions in Counselling*. London: Routledge, pp. 79–93.

Mellor-Clark, J. and Barkham, M. (1998) Effectiveness, evaluation and audit of counselling in primary care. In L. Rain (ed.) *A Practical Guide to Counselling in Primary Care*. London: Sage.

Messer, S.B. and Warren, C.S. (1995) *Models of Brief Psychodynamic Psychotherapy: A Comprehensive Approach*. New York: Guilford Press.

Miller, I.J. (1996a) Managed care is harmful to outpatient mental health services: a call for accountability. *Prof. Psych. Res. Pract.* **27**(4), 349–363.

Miller, I.J. (1996b) Time-limited brief therapy has gone too far: the result is invisible rationing. *Prof. Psych. Res. Pract.* **27**(6), 567–576.

Miller, I.J. (1996c) Some 'short-term therapy values' are a formula for invisible rationing. *Prof. Psych. Res. Pract.* **27**(6), 577–582.

Miller, R. (1994) Clinical psychology and counselling in primary care: opening the stable door. *Clin. Psych. Foum* **65**, 11–14.

Miller, R. (1997) *Improving our chances – perfecting our 'roll'?* Paper presented at the Sixth St. George's Counselling in Primary Care Conference, London, 25 April.

Milton, J. (1997) Why assess? Psychoanalytical assessment in the NHS. *Psychoanal. Psychother.* **11**(1), 47–58.

Milton, M. (1995) The development of counselling psychology in a clinical psychology service. *Couns. Psychol. Quart.* **8**(3), 243–247.

Mitchell, A.R.K. (1989) Participating in primary care: differing styles of psychiatric liaison. *Psychiatric Bull.* **13**, 135–137.

Mollon, P. (1998) *Remembering Trauma: A Psychotherapist's Guide to Memory and Illusion*. Chichester: Wiley.

Molnos, A. (1995) *A Question of Time: Essentials of Brief Dynamic Psychotherapy*. London: Karnac Books.

Monach, J. and Monro, S. (1995) Counselling in general practice: issues and opportunities. *Brit. J. Guid. Couns.* **23**(3), 313–325.

Morrison, J. (1997) *When Psychological Problems Mask Medical Disorders: A Guide for Psychotherapists*. New York: Guilford Press.

Mueser, K.T., Bellack, A.S. and Blanchard, J.J. (1992) Comorbidity of schizophrenia and substance abuse: implications for treatment. *J. Cons. Clin. Psych.* **60**, 845–856.

Munoz, R.F., Hollon, S.D., McGrath, E., Rehm, L.P. and VandenBos, G.R. (1994) On the AHCPR depression in primary care guidelines: further considerations for practioners. *Amer. Psych.* **49**(1), 42–61.

Mynors-Wallis, L., Davies, I., Gray, A., Barbour, F. and Gath, D. (1997) A randomized controlled trial and cost analysis of problem-solving treatment for emotional disorders given by community nurses in primary care. *Brit. J. Psychiatry* **170**, 113–119.

Naylor-Smith, A. (1994) Counselling and psychotherapy: is there a difference? *Counselling* **5**(4), 284–286.

Neal, R., Dowell, A., Heywood, P. and Morley, S. (1996) Frequent attenders: who needs treatment? *Brit. J. Gen. Pract.* **46**, 131–132.

Nelson-Gray, R.O. (1996) Treatment outcome measures: nomothetic or idiographic? *Clin. Psych. Res. Pract.* **3**(2), 164–167.

Nettleton, B. (1996) Counselling in primary care: report on a one–year pilot project in the Scottish Borders, 1995–1996. Borders Health Board. Unpublished manuscript.

Nickels, M.W. and McIntyre, J.S. (1996) A model for psychiatric services in primary care settings. *Psychiatr. Serv.* **47**(5), 522–526.

Odell, S.M., Commander, M.J., Sashidharan, S.P. and Surtees, P.G. (1996) Recognition of psychological problems in primary care: differences between ethnic groups. Paper presented at annual conference of the BPS Special Group in Health Psychology, College of Ripon and York, July 1996.

O'Dowd, T.C. (1988) Five years of heartsink patients in general practice. *BMJ* **297**, 528–530.

Ogles, B.M., Lambert, M.J. and Masters, K.S. (1996) *Assessing Outcome in Clinical Practice.* Boston: Allyn & Bacon.

Ohanian, V. (1997) Brief intervention and counselling service – the Hounslow model. *Primary Care Psychology: Special Interest Group Newsletter* **5**, 20–27.

Olfson, M., Leon, A.C., Broadhead, W.E., Weissman, M.M., Barrett, M.E., Blacklow, R.S., Gilbert, T.T. and Higgins, E.S. (1995) The SDDS-PC: a diagnostic aid for multiple mental disorders in primary care. *Psychopharm. Bull.* **31**(2), 415–420.

O'Neill-Byrne, K. and Browning, S.M. (1996) Which patients do GPs refer to which professional? *Psychiatric Bull.* **20**, 584–587.

Pace, T.M., Chaney, J.M., Mullins, L.L. and Olson, R.A. (1995) Psychological consultation with primary care physicians: obstacles and opportunities in the medical setting. *Prof. Psych. Res. Pract.* **26**(2), 123–131.

Palmer, S. and McMahon, G. (eds) (1997) *Client Assessment.* London: Sage.

Papadopoulos, L. and Bor, R. (1995) Counselling psychology in primary health care: a review. *Couns. Psychol. Quart.* **8**(4), 291–303.

Parker, T., Leyland, M. and Paxton, R. (1997) Clinical psychology and counselling in primary care: where is the boundary? *Clin. Psychol. Forum* **104**, 3–6.

Parkes, C.M. (1971) Psychosocial transitions. A field for study. *Soc. Sci. Med.* **5**, 101–115.

Parkes, C.M. (1996) Bereavement. In T. Kendrick, A. Tylee and P. Freeling (eds) *The Prevention of Mental Illness in Primary Care*. Cambridge: Cambridge University Press, pp. 74–87.

Parry, G. (1992) Improving psychotherapy services: applications of research, audit and evaluation. *Brit. J. Clin. Psych.* **31**, 3–19.

Parry, G. (1995) Bambi fights back: psychotherapy research and service improvement. *Changes* **13**, 154–167.

Parry, G. (1997) Psychotherapy services in the English National Health Service. In N.E. Miller and K. Magruder (eds) *The Cost Effectiveness of Psychotherapy: A Guide for Practitioners, Researchers and Policymakers*. New York: Wiley.

Parry, G. and Richardson, A. (1996) *NHS Psychotherapy Services in England: Review of Strategic Policy*. Wetherby: Department of Health.

Patel, S. (1996) Preventing mental illness amongst people of ethnic minorities. In T. Kendrick, A. Tylee and P. Freeling (eds), *The Prevention of Mental Illness in Primary Care*. Cambridge: Cambridge University Press, pp. 88–112.

Patience, D.A. et al. (1995) The Edinburgh primary care depression study: personality disorder and outcome. *Brit. J. Psychiatry* **167**, 324–330.

Paykel, E.S., Mangen, S.P., Griffith, J.H. and Burns, T.P. (1982) Community psychiatric nursing for neurotic patients: a controlled study. *Brit. J. Psychiatry* **140**, 573–581.

Pekarik, G. (1996) *Psychotherapy Abbreviation: A Practical Guide*. New York: Haworth Press.

Persons, J. (1989) *Cognitive Therapy in Practice: The Case Formulation Approach*. New York: Norton.

Persons, J.B. and Tompkins, M.A. (1997) Cognitive-behavioral case formulation. In T.D. Eells (ed.) *Handbook of Psychotherapy Case Formulation*. New York, Guilford Press, pp. 314–339.

Persons, J.B., Thase, M.E. and Crits-Christoph, P. (1996) The role of psychotherapy in the treatment of depression: Review of two practice guidelines. *Arch. Gen. Psychiatry* **53**, 283–290.

Perry, S., Cooper, A.M. and Michels, R. (1987) The psychodynamic formulation: its purpose, structure, and clinical application. *Amer. J. Psychiatry* **144**, 543–550.

Piccinelli, M., Tessari, E., Bortolomasi, M., Piasere, O., Semenzin, M., Garzotto, N. and Tansella, M. (1997) Efficacy of the alcohol use disorders identification test as a screening tool for hazardous alcohol intake and related disorders in primary care: a validity study. *BMJ* **314**, 420–424.

Pincus, H.A., Vettorello, N.E., McQueen, L.E., First, M., Wise, T.N., Zarin, D. and Davis, W.W. (1995) Bridging the gap between psychiatry and primary care: the DSM-IV-PC. *Psychosomatics* **36**(4), 328–335.

Pipal, J.E. (1995) Managed care: is it the corpse in the living room? An exposé. *Psychotherapy* **32**(2), 323–332.

Piper, W.E., McCallum, M. and Azim, H.F.A. (1992) *Adaptation to Loss through Short-term Group Psychotherapy*. New York: Guilford Press.

Piper, W.E., Azim, H.F.A., Joyce, A.S., McCallum, M., Nixon, G.W.H. and Segal,

P.S. (1991) Quality of object relations versus interpersonal functioning as predictors of therapeutic alliance and psychotherapy outcome. *J. Nerv. Ment. Dis.* **179**(7), 432–438.

Pollack, W.S. (1996) The survival of psychoanalytic psychotherapy in managed care: 'Reports of my death are greatly exaggerated'. In J.W. Barron and H. Sands (eds) *Impact of Managed Care on Psychodynamic Treatment.* Madison CT: International Universities Press, pp. 107–129.

Power, M.J. and Brewin, C.R. (1997) Foundations for the systematic study of meaning and therapeutic change. *BPS Psychotherapy Section Newsletter* **22**, 12–26.

Prochaska, J.O. and DiClemente, C.C. (1986) Towards a comprehensive model of change. In R. Miller and N. Heather (eds) *Treating Addictive Behaviours, Processes of Change.* New York: Plenum Press, pp. 3–27.

Quick, E.K. (1996) *Doing What Works in Brief Therapy: A Strategic Solution Focused Approach.* San Diego: Academic Press.

Qureshi, B. (1989) *Transcultural Medicine: Dealing with Patients from Different Cultures.* London: Kluwer Academic Publishers.

Raczek, S.W. (1992) Childhood abuse and personality disorders. *J. Pers. Dis.* **6**(2), 109–116.

Rain, L. (1996) *Counselling in Primary Care: A Guide to Good Practice.* Leeds: MIND.

Rain, L. et al. (1998) *A Practical Guide to Counselling in Primary Care.* London: Sage.

Robinson, P., Bush, T., vonKorff, M. and Katon, W. (1995) Primary care physician use of cognitive behavioral techniques with depressed patients. *J. Fam. Pract.* **40**(4), 352–357.

Rogers, C. (1951) *Client-centered Therapy.* Boston: Houghton Mifflin.

Roper-Hall, A. (1997) Older adults in primary care. *Primary Care Psychology: Special Interest Group Newsletter* **5**, 37.

Rosen, L.D. and Weil, M.M. (1996) Easing the transition from paper to computer-based systems. In T. Trabin (ed.) *The Computerization of Behavioral Healthcare: How to Enhance Clinical Practice, Management, and Communications.* San Francisco: Jossey-Bass.

Roth, A. and Fonagy, P., with Parry, G., Target, M. and Woods, R. (1996) *What Works for Whom: A Critical Review of Psychotherapy Research.* New York: Guilford Press.

Roth, A. and Parry, G. (1997) The implications of psychotherapy research for clinical practice and service development: lessons and limitations. *J. Ment. Health* **6**(4), 367–380.

Rowland, N. (1993) What is counselling? In R. Corney and R. Jenkins (eds) *Counselling in General Practice.* London: Tavistock/Routledge, pp. 17–30.

Rowland, N. and Tolley, K. (1995) Economic evaluation. In J. Keithley and G. Marsh (eds) *Counselling in Primary Health Care.* Oxford: Oxford University Press, pp. 57–81.

Rowland, N., Irving, J. and Maynard, A. (1989) Can general practitioners counsel? *J. Roy. Coll. Gen. Pract.* **39**, 118–120.

Roy, B. and Peter, P. (1996) Generalized anxiety and mixed anxiety-depression: association with disability and health care utilization. *J. Clin. Psychiatry* **57**(Suppl 7), 86–91.

Ryle, A. (1990) *Cognitive-Analytic Therapy: Active Participation in Change, a New Integration in Brief Psychotherapy.* Chichester: Wiley.

Ryle, A. (ed.) (1995) *Cognitive-Analytic Therapy: Developments in Theory and Practice.* Chichester: Wiley.

Ryle, A., Leighton, T. and Pollock, P. (1997) *Cognitive Analytic Therapy for Borderline Personality Disorder.* Chichester: Wiley.

Safran, J.D. and Segal, Z.V. (1990) *Interpersonal Process in Cognitive Therapy.* New York: Basic Books.

Sage, N. (1997) Searching for sickness in the worried well. *Primary Care Psychology Special Interest Group Newsletter* **4**, 28–33.

Sager, C.J., Brown, H.S., Crohn, H., Engel, T., Rodstein, E. and Walker, L. (1983) *Treating the Remarried Family.* New York: Brunner/Mazel.

Salinsky, J. (1993) *The Last Appointment: Psychotherapy in General Practice.* East Grinstead: The Book Guild.

Sanderson, W.C. and McGinn, L.K. (1997) Psychological treatment of anxiety disorder patients with comorbidity. In S. Wetzler and W.C. Sanderson (eds) *Treatment Strategies for Patients with Psychiatric Comorbidity.* New York: Wiley, pp. 75–104.

Saporta, J.A. and Gans, J.S. (1995) Taking a history of childhood trauma in psychotherapy: achieving an optimal approach. *J. Psychother. Pract. Res.* **4**(3), 194–204.

Schachter, J. (1997) Transference and countertransference dynamics in the assessment process. *Psychoanal. Psychother.* **11**(1), 59–71.

Scharff, D.E. and Scharff, J.S. (1991) *Object Relations Couple Therapy.* Northvale NJ: Jason Aronson.

Schmidt, U., Tanner, M. and Dent, J. (1996) Evidence-based psychiatry: pride and prejudice. *Psychiatric Bulletin* **20**, 705–707.

Schulberg, H.C. and Rush, A.J. (1994) Clinical practice guidelines for managing major depression in primary care practice: implications for Psychologists. *Amer. Psych.* **49**(1), 34–41.

Scott, A.I.F. and Freeman, C.P.L. (1992) Edinburgh primary care depression study: treatment outcome, patient satisfaction, and cost after 16 weeks. *BMJ* **304**, 883–887.

Seager, M. (1991) Waiting lists are not the only problem: changing a referral system. *Clin. Psychol. Forum* **36**, 20–26.

Seager, M. J. (1994) On not 'leading horses to water': promoting true engagement in psychological therapies by psychologizing the referral process. *J. Ment. Health* **3**, 213–220.

Seager, M.J., Scales, K., Jacobson, R., Orrell, M. and Baker, M. (1995) New psychology referral system: the reaction of GPs. *Clin. Psychol. Forum* **83**, 12–14.

Segal, Z.V., Swallow, S.R., Bizzini, L. and Rouget, B.W. (1995) How we assess for short-term cognitive behaviour therapy. In C. Mace (ed.) *The Art and Science of Assessment in Psychotherapy*. London: Routledge, pp. 106–120.

Seligman, M.E.P. (1995) The effectiveness of psychotherapy: the Consumer Reports Study. *Amer. Psych.* **50**, 965–974.

Shapiro, J. (1995) The downside of managed mental health care. *Clin. Soc. Work J.* **23**(4), 441–451.

Sharp, D.M., Power, K.G., Simpson, R.J., Swanson, V. and Anstee, J.A. (1997) Global measures of outcome in a controlled comparison of pharmacological and psychological treatment of panic disorder and agoraphobia in primary care. *Brit. J. Gen. Pract.* **47**, 150–155.

Shea, M.T., Widiger, T.A. and Klein, M.H. (1992) Comorbidity of personality disorders and depression: implications for treatment. *J. Cons. Clin. Psych.* **60**(6), 857–868.

Shea, M.T., Pilkonis, P.A., Beckham, E., Collins, J.F., Elkin, I., Sotsky, S.M. and Docherty, J.P. (1990) Personality disorders and treatment outcome in the NIMH treatment of depression collaborative research program. *Amer. J. Psychiatry* **147**(6), 711–718.

Sibbald, B., Addington-Hall, J., Brenneman, D. and Freeling, P. (1993) Counsellors in English and Welsh general practices: their nature and distribution. *BMJ* **306**, 29–33.

Sibbald, B., Addington-Hall, J., Brenneman, D. and Freeling, P. (1996a) The role of counsellors in general practice. Occasional Paper 74. London: Royal College of General Practitioners.

Sibbald, B., Addington-Hall, J., Brenneman, D. and Freeling, P. (1996b) Investigation of whether on site general practice counsellors have an impact on psychotropic drug prescribing rates and costs. *Brit. J. Gen. Pract.* **46**, 63–67.

Sigrell, B., Cornell, A., Gyllenskold, K., Lindgren, I. and Stenfelt, P. (1998) Psychoanalytic psychotherapy and outcome research: a qualitative study. *Psychoanal. Psychother.* **12**(1), 57–73.

Sims, A. (1993) The scar that is only skin deep: the stigma of depression. *Brit. J. Gen. Pract.* **43**, 30–31.

Skinner, A. and Baul, J. (1997) Clinical psychologists' caseloads and waiting lists: the DCP survey. *Clin. Psych. Forum* **110**, 40–46.

Sleek, S. (1997a) Designing therapy for concurrent woes: psychologists call for new treatment strategies to help patients with two or more clinical diagnoses. *APA Monitor* **28**(1), 32.

Sleek, S. (1997b) State initiatives curb abuses of managed care. *APA Monitor* **28**(11), 22.

Sleek, S. (1997c) The 'cherrypicking' of treatment research. *APA Monitor* **29**(12), 1, 21.

Small, N. and Conlon, I. (1988) The creation of an inter–occupational relationship: the introduction of a counsellor into an NHS general practice. *Brit. J. Soc. Work* **18**(2), 171–187.

Sonne, J.C. (1994) The relevance of the dread of being aborted to models of therapy and models of the mind. Part I: case examples. *Int. J. Prenatal and Perinatal Psych. Med.* **6**(1), 67–86.

Speirs, R. and Jewell, J.A. (1995) One counsellor, two practices: report of a pilot scheme in Cambridgeshire. *Brit. J. Gen. Pract.* **45**, 31–33.

Sperry, L. (1995) *Handbook of Diagnosis and Treatment of the DSM-IV Personality disorders.* New York: Brunner/Mazel.

Sperry, L., Brill, P.L., Howard, K.I. and Grissom, G.R. (1996) *Treatment Outcomes in Psychotherapy and Psychiatric Interventions.* New York: Brunner/Mazel.

Spiegel, N., Murphy, E., Kinmonth, A.L., Ross, F., Bain, J. and Coates, R. (1992) Managing change in general practice: a step by step guide. *BMJ* **304**, 231–234.

Spielberger, C.D. (1983) *Manual for the State-Trait Anxiety Inventory.* Palo Alto CA: Consulting Psychologists Press.

Spitzer, R.L., Williams, J.B.W., Kroenke, K., Linzer, M., deGruy, F.V., Hahn, S.R., Brody, D. and Johnson, J.G. (1994) Utility of a new procedure for diagnosing mental disorders in primary care: The PRIME-MD 1000 study. *JAMA* **272**(22), 1749–1756.

Stanion, P., Papadopoulos, L. and Bor, R. (1997) Genograms in counselling practice: constructing a genogram (Part 2). *Couns. Psych. Quart.* **10**(2), 139–148.

Stechler, G. (1996) The blind oppressing the recalcitrant: psychoanalysis, managed care, and family systems. In J.W. Barron and H. Sands (eds.) *Impact of Managed Care on Psychodynamic Treatment.* Madison CN: International Universities Press, pp.181–200.

Steenbarger, B.N. (1994) Duration and outcome in psychotherapy: an integrative review. *Prof. Psych. Res. Pract.* **25**(2), 111–119.

Stern, S. (1993) Managed care, brief therapy, and therapeutic integrity. *Psychotherapy* **30**(1), 162–175.

Stevenson, J., Hill, C., Hill, J., MacLeod, S. and Bridgstock, G. (1997) We're late, we're late, we're late: yet more comments about waiting lists. *Clin. Psychol. Forum* **105**, 31–35.

Stewart, H., Elder, A. and Gosling, R. (1996) *Michael Balint: Object Relations Pure and Applied.* London: Routledge.

Stone, M. H. (1993) Long-term outcome in personality disorders. *Brit. J. Psychiatry* **162**, 299–313.

Stoudemire, A. (1996) Psychiatry in medical practice. implications for the education of primary care physicians in the era of managed care: part 1. *Psychosomatics* **37**(6), 502–508.

Strathdee, G. (1987) Primary care-psychiatry interaction: a British perspective. *Gen. Hosp. Psychiatry* **9**, 102–110.

Strathdee, G. and McDonald, E. (1992) Establishing psychiatric attachments to general practice: a six stage plan. *Psychiatric Bull.* **16**, 284–286.

Strean, H. (1980) *The Extramarital Affair.* New York: Macmillan.

Strean, H. (1985) *Resolving Marital Conflicts.* New York: Wiley.

Strupp, H.H. (1997) Research, practice and managed care. *Psychotherapy* **34**, 91–94.

Strupp, H.H. and Binder, J.L. (1984) *Psychotherapy in a New Key: A Guide to Time-limited Dynamic Psychotherapy.* New York: Basic Books.

Strupp, H.H. Hadley, S.W. and Gomes-Schwartz, B.T. (1977) *When Things Get Worse: The Problem of Negative Effects in Psychotherapy.* Northvale NJ: Jason Aronson.

Stuart, M. and Lieberman, J. (1993) *The Fifteen Minute Hour.* Westport: Praeger.

Sue, S., Zane, N. and Young, K. (1994) Research on psychotherapy with culturally diverse populations. In A.E. Bergin and S.L. Garfield (eds) *Handbook of Psychotherapy and Behavior Change,* 4th edn. New York, Wiley, 783–817.

Tait, M. (1997) Dependence: a means or an impediment to growth? *Brit. J. Guid. Couns.* **25**(1),17–26.

Talmon, M. (1990) *Single Session Therapy – Maximizing the Effect of the First (and often only) Therapeutic Encounter.* San Francisco: Jossey-Bass.

Tantum, D. (1995) Why assess? In C. Mace (ed.), *The Art and Science of Assessment in Psychotherapy.* London: Routledge, pp. 8–26.

Task Force on Promotion and Dissemination of Psychological Procedures (1995) Training in and dissemination of empirically-validated psychological procedures: report and recommendations. *Clinical Psychologist* **48**, 3–23.

Tata, P., Eagle, A. and Green, J. (1996) Does providing more accessible primary care psychology services lower the clinical threshold for referrals? *Brit. J. Gen. Pract.* **46**, 469–472.

Thomas, A. (1996) Clinical audit: setting professional standards for counselling services. *Couns. Psych. Quart.* **9**(1), 25–36.

Thomas, P., Costello, M. and Davison, S. (1997) Group work in general practice. *Psychodyn. Couns.* **3**(1), 23–32.

Tillett, R. (1996) Psychotherapy assessment and treatment selection. *Brit. J. Psychiatry* **168**, 10–15.

Tolley, K. and Rowland, N. (1995) *Evaluating the Cost-effectiveness of Counselling in Health Care.* London: Routledge.

Tuckfelt, S. et al. (1997) *How to Get Along with Big Brother: Surviving Managed Mental Healthcare in the 21st Century.* Northvale NJ: Jason Aronson.

Tylee, A. and Katona, C.L.E. (1996) Detecting and managing depression in older people. *Brit. J. Gen. Pract.* **46**, 207–208.

Vanclay, L. (1997) Team-working in primary care. *J. Roy. Soc. Med.* **90**(5), 268–270.

Wallerstein, R.S. (1995) The effectiveness of psychotherapy and psychoanalysis: conceptual issues and empirical work. In T. Shapiro and R.N. Ende (eds) *Research in Psychoanalysis: Process, Development, Outcome.* Madison CT: IUP, pp. 299–312.

Ward, M. and Loewenthal, D. (1997) Differential referral patterns in the GP setting. *Counselling* **8**(2), 129–131.

Waskett, C. (1996) Multidisciplinary teamwork in primary care: The role of the counsellor. *Couns. Psych. Quart.* **9**(3), 243–260.

Watts, M. and Bor, R. (1995) Standards for training and practice in primary care counselling. *Couns. Psychol. Rev.* **10**(3), 32–37.

Webber, V., Davies, P. and Pietroni, P. (1994) Counselling in an inner city general practice: analysis of its use and uptake. *Brit. J. Gen. Pract.* **44**, 175–178.

Welch, B.L. (1994) Managed care: the 'basic fault'. *Psychoanal. and Psychother.* **11**(2), 166–176.

Wessely, S. (1996) The rise of counselling and the return of alienism. *BMJ* **313**, 158–160.

Westermeyer, J. (1991) Problems with managed psychiatric care without a psychiatrist-manager. *Hosp. Comm. Psychiatry* **42**(12), 1221–1224.

Wetzler, S. and Sanderon, W.C. (eds) (1997) *Treatment Strategies for Patients with Psychiatric Comorbidity.* New York: Wiley.

Wheeler, S. and McLeod, J. (1995) Person-centred and psychodynamic counselling: a dialogue. *Counselling* **6**(4), 283–287.

White, J. (1997) Pilot study of personalized computer-based psychological treatment for anxiety in primary care. *Primary Care Psychology: Special Interest Group Newsletter* **5**, 28–29.

Widiger, T.A. and Axelrod, S.R. (1995) Recent developments in the clinical assessment of personality disorders. *Eur. J. Psych. Assessment* **11**(3), 213–221.

Williams, P. and Balestrieri, M. (1989) Psychiatric clinics in general practice: do they reduce admissions? *Brit. J. Psychiatry* **154**, 67–71.

Williamson, C. (1995) Psychologists, counsellors and nurses working in harmony? Paper presented at the British Psychological Society London Conference, December 1995.

Wilson, M.B. (1992) When is a year not a year? The pressures operating on a trainee in time-limited therapy. *Psychoanal. Psychother.* **6**(1), 21–31.

Wing, J., Curtis, R. and Beevor, A. (1996) *HoNOS: Health of the Nation Outcome Scales: Brief Report.* London: Royal College of Psychiatrists, College Research Unit.

Winnicott, D.W. (1960) Ego distortion in terms of true and false self. In *The Maturational Processes and the Facilitating Environment*, 1965. New York: International Universities Press, pp. 140–152.

Winnicott, D.W. (1965) *The Maturational Processes and the Facilitating Environment.* New York: International Universities Press.

Wright, A. (1994) Should general practitioners be testing for depression? *Brit. J. Gen. Pract.* **44**, 132–135.

Wright, A. (1995) Editorial: continuing to defeat depression. *Brit. J. Gen. Pract.* **45**, 170–171.

Wright, A. (1996) Editorial: unrecognized psychiatric illness in general practice. *Brit. J. Gen. Pract.* **46**, 327–328.

Ziedonis, D. and Brady, K. (1997) Dual diagnosis in primary care: detecting and treating both the addiction and mental illness. *Med. Clin. N. Amer.* **81**(4), 1017–1036.

Zigmond, A.S. and Snaith, R.P. (1983) The hospital anxiety and depression scale. *Acta Psychiatr. Scand.* **67**, 361–370.

Zimmermann, C. and Tansella, M. (1996) Psychosocial factors and physical illness in primary care: promoting the biopsychosocial model in medical practice. *J. Psychosom. Res.* **40**(4), 351–358.

INDEX

action learning 184
adolescence 122
Adult Attachment Interview 119
adulthood 122–3
alcohol problems, screening instruments
    28
computerized anxiety management 76
Areas of Change Questionnaire 97
assessment 15, 95–162
  at primary care level, need for 212
  inadequate, negative effects of 95,
     110, 149
  of therapist by patient 108
  training in relevant skills 209
assessment interviews
  number required 107
  use of intuition in 107–8
At Risk Checklist 19
'At Risk Of. . .' Checklist 180, 187,
    215–6
attachment to caregivers 121
attempted abortion 114
audit cycle 185

Balint groups 3, 32, 204
barriers to love 105–6
basic fault, benign vs. malignant 70
BATHE model 4–5
Beck Depression Inventory (BDI) 97,
    178
benign vs. malignant regression 70
bereavement 21
biomedical model 9, 23, 203
biopsychosocial model 5, 23, 203
birth trauma 114, 139
borderline patients (*see also* schizotypal
    personality disorder) 125, 130–1,

    139, 151, 154, 172, 179
  and brief therapies 61
  multiple core states, in CAT 80
brief psychodynamic therapies, 63–71
  inclusion criteria 65–6
  Gustafson's model 70
  limitations of 71
  Luborsky's model 66–7
  Malan's model 63–4
  Mann's model 68–9
  Strupp and Binder's model 67–8
Brief Symptom Inventory (BSI) 97, 178
brief therapies 15–16, 53, 59, 209–10
  Budman and Gurman model 88
  intermittent throughout the life cycle
    57, 89
  psychotherapy abbreviation 88
  solution-focused 87–8
brief therapies
  externally mandated 55, 56, 210
    and counsellors in primary care 12
    in the NHS 62–3
  negative effects 60, 61, 63, 125, 132,
    159, 169
  personality disorders 150, 152
  severe problems 40
British Association for Counselling 9,
    204

Camden & Islington MAAG referral
    guidelines 11, 42–3, 44–5, 196, 208
capacity to tolerate frustration 45
childhood sexual abuse 117–8, 141, 144
  and Cluster B personality disorders 151
  and problem-focused therapy 56
  as risk factor 21
children 30–1

choice of treatment modality 157–9
chronic physical illness
    and depression 25
    as risk factor 21
chronically endured pain 69, 79
client-/person-centered therapy 80–3, 157
clinical audit 185–6
clinical guidelines 167
clinical psychologists 7–8, 91–2
    primary vs. secondary services 41
    training in assessment 154
clinical relevance of early loss 138
clinical supervision 18
    of clinical psychologists 207
    of counsellors in primary care 204–7
clinically significant change 171
clues to transference 125
cognitive-analytic therapy (CAT) 79–80,
    157
cognitive-behavioural therapy (CBT) 43,
    44, 71–9, 157
    case formulation 78
    for anxiety 73
    for depression 73–6
    for personality disorders 76–7
community mental health team (CMHT)
    6, 40, 70, 126, 133, 200, 209
community psychiatric nurses (CPNs) 7,
    92
comorbidity 17, 37, 53, 57, 66, 147–50,
    159, 209
    clues in assessment interview 109
    excluded in RCTs 163
    on DSM-IV Axis I 149
    on DSM-IV Axes I and II 149–50
COMPASS 174–5
competition for primary care market 12,
Complexity and Severity of Problems
    Index (CASP) 159
confidentiality 17, 108, 204
    breaches, in managed care 57, 58, 59
consultation and liaison with GPs
    and clinical psychologists 8
    and counsellors in primary care 11
cookbook approaches 68
    treatments for diagnoses 169
core conflictual relationship theme
    (CCRT) 67, 101
CORE measure 97, 176–8, 181, 187, 211
core schema 76
cost containment 1, 10, 55, 58, 170, 209

cost-effectiveness 179–81, 184
counselling 43, 44
    vs. psychotherapy 89–91
Counselling in Primary Care Trust 10,
    176
counsellors in primary care 9–12, 36,
    166
    inappropriate referrals 194
    increased demands on secondary care
        184, 195
    links with secondary services 200–1
    training in assessment 92, 154, 194
    vs. secondary services 194, 196–8
couples therapy 84–6, 158
    assessment interviews 123

Defeat Depression Campaign 26, 28–9,
defence mechanisms
    primitive vs. more mature 131–2
defensive arrogance 14
Defensive Functioning Scale 132–3
Department of Health Strategic Review
        of Psychotherapy 173, 182, 194
    access to care 48–9
    five standards 15
    on validated therapies 168
    referral guidelines 42
    Types A, B and C 92
diagnosis 133–4
difficult patients 32–4
doctor–patient relationships in managed
        care 58
dose–response curve 59, 170–1, 211
dreams 64, 123
DSM-IV Axes I and II 147–8
DSM-IV-PC 30
dual diagnosis 28
dual transferences 205

earliest memory 118
early intervention 6, 9
economic deprivation 140
efficacy vs. effectiveness 62, 163, 165–6,
    169, 182, 210
elderly 30, 31
emotional costs borne by patients 62,
    210
empirically validated treatments 167–8
Employee Assistance Programmes
        (EAPs) 62, 172
equivalence paradox 163, 166, 182, 185

ethnic minorities 48–50, 208
  somatization 48,50
  stigma 49
  suicide 49
evidence-based practice 167, 210
experiencing symptoms 22

false self organization 65
family therapy 86, 158
field trials 164, 165, 177
focusing 82
frequent attenders 32–5
functional analysis 72

gag clauses 57, 62
gender 47
General Health Questionnaire (GHQ) 29, 178, 182
generalized anxiety disorder (GAD) 37
genogram 113
Geriatric Depression Scale (GDS) 29
Global Assessment Scale (GAS) 47
goals of treatment 216–17
GP as counsellor 2–5
GP consultation rate 21, 22, 35, 36, 180
GP detection of psychological problems 3, 20, 23–30, 36, 207–8
  efforts to improve 28, 30
  failure to detect alcohol problems 28
  failure to detect depression 25–7
    GP variables 27
    patient variables 28
GP fundholding
  and clinical psychologists 8
  and counsellors in primary care 12
GP interruption of patients 27
GP referral patterns 10, 23, 24, 40–4
  childhood sexual abuse 41, 42
  counsellors and clinical psychologists 40, 42
  counsellors and CPNs 41
  GP variables 41
  patient variables 41
  personality disorder 41, 42
group therapy 83–4, 158

Health of the Nation Outcome Scales (HoNOS) 28, 176
health promotion 1

heartsink patients 32–5
Henderson Hospital 180
holding environment 64, 113
homework assignments 72
Hospital Anxiety and Depression Scale (HADS) 29, 97, 178
house moves 117
humanistic therapies 80–3
  assessment in 82–3
  varieties of 82

ICD-10-PHC 29
illnesses, accidents and separations 115–16
information booklets 203
integrative therapies (see also CAT) 82
interest in self-exploration 44
interpersonal issues 102–5
interpretations
  early 123–4
  transference 124–5
inter-professional rivalry 12–13, 208
Inventory of Early Loss (IEL) 17, 138–47
  and length of treatment 144
  and personality disorder 145
  raw scores 140
  severity scores 140, 143, 145–7
Inventory of Interpersonal Problems (IIP) 97, 178

Keele EAP Evaluation Scale 62, 180

lay understanding depression 26
Leeds MIND referral guidelines 44
length of treatment 170
life script 68
long-term follow-up 59, 211
long-term therapies 170, 207, 210
  negative effects 70
loss events 138–9

maladaptive coping strategies 20
managed care 54–63
  ethical questions 56, 58, 60
  excluded diagnoses 58
manualized therapies 163, 165
marital discord 140
marriage guidance counsellors 86
medical necessity 57, 60, 148, 174–5
medical utilization rates 32, 53, 163, 180, 211
Mental Health Index (MHI) 174–6

mental health promotion 50
mental health service delivery 17,
    193–200
  integrated service 195–200
metaphors 101–2
mixed anxiety-depression (MAD) 37
mortality
  and bereavement 21
  and depression 25
  and neurotic patients 36
  and psychiatric outpatients 36
most difficult time 123
motivation for change 217
  six-stage model 45
multiple referrals and negative effects 37,
    42, 61, 96, 193

National Health Service
  internal market 13, 195, 205, 208
  market anxiety 13,
  primary care led 1
negative automatic thoughts 75
'nervous trouble' in family 121
nonconsulters 24
nonspecific factors 182, 185
nonverbal communication 127–8

object relations 64–5, 67–8, 130–1, 133,
    145
only child 113, 140, 141
opting-in 9
outcome measures (see also individual
    measures) 173–81
  in psychodynamic therapy 53, 55,
    178–9
    Human Figure Drawings 178
    Malan's outcome measure 179
    Quality of Object Relations Scale
      (QORS) 179
    Rorschach Test 178
    Thematic Apperception Test 178
    therapist-rated change 179
Outcome Questionnaire (OQ) 172
outcome studies and staff support 187-8

parents' personalities 119–21
pathway to care 16, 19,
patient-centred medicine 3
patient expectations of therapy 112
patient preferences 44, 78
Patient Record Form 187, 213–18

patient satisfaction 1, 163, 180–1, 184,
    211
Patient Satisfaction Questionnaire 225–6
perinatal losses 114
performance indicators 54, 62
personal history questionnaire 98–100
personal list system 28
personality disorders (see also DSM-IV
    Axis II) 36, 37, 53, 180, 196, 208
  and brief psychodynamic therapy 71
  and brief therapies 66
  and difficult patients 32–33
  and motivation for change 45–6
  and psychodynamic therapy 43
  and regression to dependence 65
  and social support 46
  indications of in assessment interview
    109, 152–3
  Clusters A, B and C 151, 153
  definition 150
  description of DSM-IV personality dis-
    orders 154–7
  excluded by EAPs 173
  not disclosed in managed care 55, 60
personality structure 215, 222–4
placebo attention control 185
playmates 119
pre-assessment questionnaires 97–100
precipitating events 110
predictor variables 44, 172, 187
preoedipal conditions 60, 71, 130–1
presenting problem(s) 109–111, 215
  'any other problems?' 110
primary care outcome studies 181–85
primary health care team 9, 208, 203–4,
    208
  and clinical psychologists 8
  and counsellors in primary care 10
  and psychiatrists 6
PRIME-MD 30
PROQSY 29
protective factors 19–20,
psychiatric emergencies 184, 194
psychiatric referral 160
psychiatrists 6, 92
psychodynamic counselling 89
psychodynamic formulation 128–134
  developmental arrest 129
  early conflict 129
  identification with the aggressor 130
  re-enactment 128

survival kits 129
  unconscious guilt 130
psychodynamic therapies 43, 44, 157, 166
  and managed care 59, 60
  brief and long-term 65
psychological mindedness 46, 217
psychological problems in primary care 24
screening instruments 28–30
Psychological Therapies Research Centre (PTRC) 97, 176, 187
psychosexual counselling 84–6, 158
psychosocial history 112–23
  and Inventory of Early Loss 141
  need for 125, 147
  negative effects of neglect 113
psychosocial transitions 21
psychotherapists 89–91
  consultant psychotherapists 90
psychotherapy
  negative effects 170
  outcome studies 17, 163–73
psychotropic medication 72, 78, 157, 160, 180, 183, 205, 214

quality of intimate relationships 46, 47, 217–18
Quality of Life Questionnaire 178, 219
Quality of Object Relations Scale (QORS) 131–2

randomized controlled trials (RCTs)
  comorbidity excluded 149
  counselling in primary care 183–5
  limitations 164, 181
range of treatment modalities 17, 200, 208
record keeping 108–9, 112, 205
recovered memories 144
re-enactments 64, 138, 145
referral letter from GP 96–7
referral to others 159–60
reflection of feelings 81, 111, 182
relaxation techniques 73
retraumatization 56, 145
revolving door patients 95, 211
risk factors 19, 215

schema-focused CBT 76–8
schizotypal personality disorder 156–7
school years 122

SCID-II 151–2
  Personality Questionnaire (PQ) 151
script analysis 82
script signal 127
SDDS-PC 30
secondary mental health services 208
separation from mother at birth 114, 140
separation–individuation 68
sequences of feelings 100–1
sequential diagrammatic reformulation 79
service evaluation 186–7
session-by-session tracking 171, 174
severe mental illness 95, 201
  and CPNs 7
severity of psychological problems 35, 43
  mild 38
  moderate 38–9
  primary vs. secondary services 37
  severe 39
siblings 113, 117
single-session therapy 86–7
social class 213
social defences 13
social support 217
socioeconomic status 47
somatizers 34
State-Trait Anxiety Inventory (STAI) 178
stigma 1, 6, 7, 9, 10, 26
stressful life events 19–20, 34
structuring the assessment interview 106–9
suicide risk 111
superiority feeling 14
survival kits 68
Symptom Checklist-90 Revised (SCL-90R) 97, 178
symptom relief 53, 72
systematic desensitization 73

2 + 1 86
team-building 204
termination of psychotherapy
  and attachment 138
  patient's decision 56
therapeutic alliance 111
therapist-rated change 187, 218
things to listen for 100–6
treatment modality 218
treatment not offered 158–9
typical twelve 81

ultra-brief therapies 59, 172
  need for long-term follow-up 173

unconscious processes 64, 123
unempathic parental responses 140
  and object relations 139
  and self psychology 139
unmanageable problems 37, 56, 80, 95
unwanted babies 114

vulnerability factors 19–20

waiting lists 1, 4, 17, 201–3, 205
  and clinical psychologists 9, 10
  and counsellors in primary care 12
  assessment prior to treatment 202
  opting in 202–3
'worried well' 35

young adulthood 122

Related titles of interest...

Developing Self-Acceptance
A Brief, Educational, Small Group Approach
Windy Dryden

Presents an account of how to run brief, structured, educationally oriented groups which aim to develop self-acceptance as a step in helping clients who have emotional problems.

0-471-98099-4   240pp   1998   Paperback

Case Studies in Existential Psychotherapy and Counselling
Simon Du Plock

Provides a brief introduction to existential psychotherapy, and applies the concepts to a wide range of mental health problems through the life-cycle, including health and personal development processes.

0-471-96192-2   218pp   1997   Hardback
0-471-97079-4   218pp   1997   Paperback

Psychology in Counselling and Therapeutic Practice
Jill D. Wilkinson, Elizabeth A. Campbell, with contributions by Adrian Coyle and Alyson Davis

A concise text and accessible reference book dealing with the areas of psychology which particularly support and enlighten the practice of counselling and psychotherapy. By bringing psychology into the consulting room, the authors ensure that psychological theory and research are accessible and applicable to the therapist's work with clients.

0-471-95562-0   286pp   1997   Paperback

Brief Rational Emotive Behaviour Therapy
Windy Dryden

Provides concepts in the context of a brief therapy process. Practitioners will find useful insights and guidance on applying these methods throughout the process of therapy, including building the working alliance, assessment, formulation, and work in sessions and outside the sessions. The whole process is illustrated by a case study which reflects the problems of real life work with a client.

0-471-95786-0   244pp   1995   Paperback

Visit the Wiley Home Page at http://www.wiley.co.uk